M000276074

Angular 6 for Enterprise-Ready Web Applications

Deliver production-ready and cloud-scale Angular web apps

Doguhan Uluca

10/5/18

For Justin,

Great meeting you.

Best,

D. Ulu

BIRMINGHAM - MUMBAI

Angular 6 for Enterprise-Ready Web Applications

Copyright © 2018 Packt Publishing

All rights reserved. No part of this book may be reproduced, stored in a retrieval system, or transmitted in any form or by any means, without the prior written permission of the publisher, except in the case of brief quotations embedded in critical articles or reviews.

Every effort has been made in the preparation of this book to ensure the accuracy of the information presented. However, the information contained in this book is sold without warranty, either express or implied. Neither the author, nor Packt Publishing or its dealers and distributors, will be held liable for any damages caused or alleged to have been caused directly or indirectly by this book.

Packt Publishing has endeavored to provide trademark information about all of the companies and products mentioned in this book by the appropriate use of capitals. However, Packt Publishing cannot guarantee the accuracy of this information.

Commissioning Editor: Amarabha Banerjee
Acquisition Editor: Nigel Fernandes
Content Development Editor: Francis Carneiro
Technical Editor: Sachin Sunilkumar
Copy Editor: Shaila Kusanale
Project Coordinator: Devanshi Doshi
Proofreader: Safis Editing
Indexer: Tejal Daruwale Soni
Graphics: Jason Monteiro
Production Coordinator: Shantanu Zagade

First published: May 2018

Production reference: 1250518

Published by Packt Publishing Ltd.
Livery Place
35 Livery Street
Birmingham
B3 2PB, UK.

ISBN 978-1-78646-290-9

www.packtpub.com

`mapt.io`

Mapt is an online digital library that gives you full access to over 5,000 books and videos, as well as industry leading tools to help you plan your personal development and advance your career. For more information, please visit our website.

Why subscribe?

- Spend less time learning and more time coding with practical eBooks and Videos from over 4,000 industry professionals

- Improve your learning with Skill Plans built especially for you

- Get a free eBook or video every month

- Mapt is fully searchable

- Copy and paste, print, and bookmark content

PacktPub.com

Did you know that Packt offers eBook versions of every book published, with PDF and ePub files available? You can upgrade to the eBook version at `www.PacktPub.com` and as a print book customer, you are entitled to a discount on the eBook copy. Get in touch with us at `service@packtpub.com` for more details.

At `www.PacktPub.com`, you can also read a collection of free technical articles, sign up for a range of free newsletters, and receive exclusive discounts and offers on Packt books and eBooks.

Contributors

About the author

Doguhan Uluca is a software development expert for Excella Consulting in Washington, DC. He is the founder and director of the polyglot Tech Talk DC meetup and the creator of the DC Full Stack Web Summit conference. Doguhan has been published on DevPro and ACM. He is a speaker at international conferences, such as Ng-Conf, CodeStock, deliver:Agile and Agile XP. He is a full-stack JavaScript, Agile, and cloud engineering practitioner. Doguhan is an active contributor to the open source community, with libraries and tools published for JavaScript, Angular, Node, and MongoDB.

I would like to acknowledge my dear family, Chanda and Ada, for all their sacrifice and encouragement, allowing this book to happen. In addition, the amazing communities at NOVA Code Camp, NodeConf, ng-conf, Node.DC, and Tech Talk DC for opening up my mind and embracing my ideas. Finally, my colleagues at Excella, who allowed an open, inquisitive, and daring environment to effect real change.

About the reviewers

Wyn B. Van Devanter is currently a managing consultant and senior developer with Excella, an Agile tech firm. He has experience in various industries and government with architecture, design, and implementation of software, largely with web-based applications. He also works heavily with DevOps, cloud, and container-based architectures and strives to be a good software craftsman using XP practices. He enjoys being involved in the community and regularly speaks and conducts workshops at events around the region. Wyn likes playing music, skiing, and conversations of intrigue.

Brendon Caulkins is a DC-based full stack developer at Excella. His focus is Java, but he still harbors a secret love for PHP. He holds a computer engineering degree from Purdue University (Boiler Up!) and refuses to give up playing with Legos. He has nearly a decade of hardware environmental testing and software product testing experience, and is really, *really* good at breaking things. He is also an award-winning painter of tiny toy soldiers and goes by the name Plarzoid on the interwebs.

Packt is searching for authors like you

If you're interested in becoming an author for Packt, please visit `authors.packtpub.com` and apply today. We have worked with thousands of developers and tech professionals, just like you, to help them share their insight with the global tech community. You can make a general application, apply for a specific hot topic that we are recruiting an author for, or submit your own idea.

Table of Contents

Preface

Welcome! If you are looking to learn about and get good at Angular development, you're in the right place. This book will aim to instill an Agile and DevOps mindset in you so that you confidently create reliable and flexible solutions. Whether you consider yourself a freelancer developing software for small businesses, a full-stack developer, an enterprise developer, or a web developer, what you need to know to design, architect, develop, maintain, deliver, and deploy a web application and the best practices and patterns you need to apply to achieve those things don't vary all that much. If you're delivering an application to an audience of users, in a sense, you are a full-stack developer, since you must be aware of a lot of server technologies. In fact, if you master how to deliver Angular applications using TypeScript, it won't be difficult for you to write your own RESTful APIs using Node.js, Express.js, and TypeScript, but that is beyond the scope of this book.

By some definitions, a full-stack developer needs to know everything from catering to international copyright law to successfully creating and operating an application on today's web. If you're an entrepreneur, in a sense, this is true. However, in this book, your culinary skills and your law degree do not apply. This book assumes that you already know how to write a RESTful API with the tech stack of your choice, and if not, fear not! You can still benefit and understand how to work with RESTful APIs.

Who this book is for

This book is for beginners and experienced developers alike who are looking to learn Angular or web development in general. If you are an Angular developer, you will be exposed to the entire gamut of designing and deploying an Angular application to production. You will learn about Angular patterns that are easy to understand and teach others. If you are a freelancer, you will pick up effective tools and technologies to deliver your Angular app in a secure, confident and reliable way. If you an enterprise developer, you will learn patterns and practices to write Angular applications with a scalable architecture.

What this book covers

Chapter 1, *Setting Up Your Development Environment,* goes over a scriptable way to set up your environment.

Chapter 2, *Create a Local Weather Web Application,* introduces the Kanban method of software development with easy-to-use design tools used to communicate ideas. It also covers Angular fundamentals, unit testing, and leveraging CLI tools to maximize your impact.

Chapter 3, *Prepare Angular App for Production Release,* covers how to troubleshoot your Angular app, and using containerization with Docker to enable cloud deployments.

Chapter 4, *Staying Up to Date with Angular Updates,* goes over strategies and the reasons for keeping your development tools and environment up to date.

Chapter 5, *Enhance Angular App with Angular Material,* introduces you to Angular material and explains how to use it to build great-looking apps.

Chapter 6, *Reactive Forms and Component Interaction,* teaches you to become comfortable using Angular forms and reactive programming using RxJS.

Chapter 7, *Create a Router-First Line-of-Business App,* focuses on the Router-first architecture, a seven-step approach to the design and development of mid-to-large applications.

Chapter 8, *Continuous Integration and API Design,* goes over continuous integration using CircleCI and early integration with backend APIs using Swagger.

Chapter 9, *Design Authentication and Authorization,* dives into authentication- and authorization-related patterns in Angular and RESTful applications.

Chapter 10, *Angular App Design and Recipes,* contains recipes commonly needed for line-of-business applications.

Chapter 11, *Highly-Available Cloud Infrastructure on AWS,* moves beyond application features to go over provisioning a highly-available cloud infrastructure on AWS.

Chapter 12, *Google Analytics and Advanced Cloud Ops,* goes over the nuances of owning, operating, and optimizing your cloud infrastructure, and using Google Analytics to capture user behavior.

To get the most out of this book

1. You should already be familiar with full-stack web development
2. Follow the book in the published order, coding your solution alongside the content in each chapter

Download the example code files

You can download the example code files for this book from your account at `www.packtpub.com`. If you purchased this book elsewhere, you can visit `www.packtpub.com/support` and register to have the files emailed directly to you.

You can download the code files by following these steps:

1. Log in or register at `www.packtpub.com`.
2. Select the **SUPPORT** tab.
3. Click on **Code Downloads & Errata**.
4. Enter the name of the book in the **Search** box and follow the onscreen instructions.

Once the file is downloaded, please make sure that you unzip or extract the folder using the latest version of:

- WinRAR/7-Zip for Windows
- Zipeg/iZip/UnRarX for Mac
- 7-Zip/PeaZip for Linux

The code bundle for the book is hosted on GitHub at `https://github.com/PacktPublishing/Angular-6-for-Enterprise-Ready-Web-Applications`.

The code bundle for the book is also hosted on Author's GitHub repository at `https://github.com/duluca/local-weather-app` and `https://github.com/duluca/lemon-mart`.

We also have other code bundles from our rich catalog of books and videos available at `https://github.com/PacktPublishing/`. Check them out!

Conventions used

There are a number of text conventions used throughout this book.

`CodeInText`: Indicates code words in text, database table names, folder names, filenames, file extensions, pathnames, dummy URLs, user input, and Twitter handles. Here is an example: "Mount the downloaded `WebStorm-10*.dmg` disk image file as another disk in your system."

A block of code is set as follows:

```
{
    "name": "local-weather-app",
    "version": "0.0.0",
    "license": "MIT",
    . . .
```

When we wish to draw your attention to a particular part of a code block, the relevant lines or items are set in bold:

```
"scripts": {
  "ng": "ng",
  "start": "ng serve",
  "build": "ng build",
  "test": "ng test",
  "lint": "ng lint",
  "e2e": "ng e2e"
},
```

Any cross-platform or macOS specific command-line input or output is written as follows:

```
$ brew tap caskroom/cask
```

Windows specific command-line input or output is written as follows:

```
PS> Set-ExecutionPolicy AllSigned; iex ((New-Object
System.Net.WebClient).DownloadString('https://chocolatey.org/instal
l.ps1'))
```

Bold: Indicates a new term, an important word, or words that you see onscreen. For example, words in menus or dialog boxes appear in the text like this. Here is an example: "Launch the **Start** menu."

Warnings or important notes appear like this.

 Tips and tricks appear like this.

Get in touch

Feedback from our readers is always welcome.

General feedback: Email feedback@packtpub.com and mention the book title in the subject of your message. If you have questions about any aspect of this book, please email us at questions@packtpub.com.

Errata: Although we have taken every care to ensure the accuracy of our content, mistakes do happen. If you have found a mistake in this book, we would be grateful if you would report this to us. Please visit www.packtpub.com/submit-errata, selecting your book, clicking on the Errata Submission Form link, and entering the details.

Piracy: If you come across any illegal copies of our works in any form on the Internet, we would be grateful if you would provide us with the location address or website name. Please contact us at copyright@packtpub.com with a link to the material.

If you are interested in becoming an author: If there is a topic that you have expertise in and you are interested in either writing or contributing to a book, please visit authors.packtpub.com.

Reviews

Please leave a review. Once you have read and used this book, why not leave a review on the site that you purchased it from? Potential readers can then see and use your unbiased opinion to make purchase decisions, we at Packt can understand what you think about our products, and our authors can see your feedback on their book. Thank you!

For more information about Packt, please visit packtpub.com.

Setting Up Your Development Environment

1

Let's start with questioning the premise of this entire book, Angular itself. Why learn Angular, but not React, Vue, or some other framework? First, I won't be making an argument against learning any new tool. I believe that every tool has its place and purpose. Becoming somewhat proficient in React or Vue can only help further your understanding of Angular. **Single Page Application (SPA)** frameworks such as Backbone or Angular have grabbed my full attention since 2012, when I realized server-side rendered templates are impossible to maintain and cause very expensive rewrites of software systems. If you're intent on creating maintainable software, decoupling of APIs and business logic from the **user interface (UI)** is the prime directive you must abide by.

The question is, why get good at Angular? I have found that Angular neatly fits the Pareto principal. It has become a mature and evolving platform, allowing you to achieve 80% of tasks with 20% of the effort. Furthermore, starting with version 4, in **Long Term Support (LTS)** until October 2018, every major release is supported for 18 months, creating a continuum of learning, staying up-to-date and deprecating old features. From the perspective of a full-stack developer, this continuum is invaluable, since your skills and training will remain useful and fresh for many years to come.

This first chapter will help you and your team members create a consistent development environment. It can be tough for beginners to create the correct development environment, which is essential for a frustration-free development experience. For seasoned developers and teams, achieving a consistent and minimal development environment remains a challenge. Once achieved, such a development environment helps avoid many IT-related issues, including ongoing maintenance, licensing, and upgrade costs.

Instructions on installing GitHub Desktop, Node.js, Angular CLI, and Docker will be a good reference from absolute beginners all the way to seasoned teams, along with strategies to automate and ensure the correct and consistent configuration of your development environment.

Feel free to skip this chapter if you already have a robust development environment setup; however, beware that some of the environmental assumptions declared in this chapter may result in some instructions not working for you in later chapters. Come back to this chapter as a reference if you run into issues or need to help a colleague, pupil, or friend set up their development environment.

In this chapter, you will learn the following:

- Working with CLI package managers to install and update software:
  - Chocolatey on Windows 10
  - Homebrew on macOS X
- Using scripting to automate installation using:
  - Powershell on Windows 10
  - Bash on macOS X
- Achieving a consistent and cross-platform development environment

You should be familiar with these:

- JavaScript ES2015+
- Frontend development basics
- RESTful APIs

The supported operating system are as follows:

- Windows 10 Pro v1703+ with PowerShell v5.1+
- macOS Sierra v10.12.6+ with Terminal (Bash or Oh My Zsh)
- Most of the suggested software also works on Linux systems, but your experience may vary

The suggested cross-platform software is as follows:

- Node 8.10+ (except non-LTS versions)
- npm 5.7.1+
- GitHub Desktop 1.0.0+
- Visual Studio Code v1.16.0+
- Google Chrome 64+

CLI package managers

Installing software through a **Graphical User Interface (GUI)** is slow and difficult to automate. As a full-stack developer, whether you're a Windows or a Mac user, you must rely on **Command-Line Interface (CLI)** package managers to efficiently install and configure the software you will be depending on. Remember, anything that can be expressed as a CLI command can also be automated.

Install Chocolatey for Windows

Chocolatey is a CLI-based package manager for Windows, which can be used for automated software installation. To install Chocolatey on Windows, you will need to run an elevated command shell:

1. Launch the **Start** menu
2. Start typing in `PowerShell`
3. You should see **Windows PowerShell Desktop App** as a search result
4. Right-click on **Windows PowerShell** and select **Run as Administrator**
5. This will trigger a **User Account Control** (UAC) warning; select **Yes** to continue
6. Execute the following command in **PowerShell** to install the Chocolatey package manager:

```
PS> Set-ExecutionPolicy AllSigned; iex ((New-Object
System.Net.WebClient).DownloadString('https://chocolatey.org/instal
l.ps1'))
```

7. Verify your Chocolatey installation by executing `choco`
8. You should see a similar output, as shown in the following screenshot:

Successful installation of Chocolatey

All subsequent Chocolatey commands must also be executed from an elevated command shell. Alternatively, it is possible to install Chocolatey in a non-administrator setting that doesn't require an elevated command shell. However, this will result in a non-standard and less secure development environment, and certain applications installed through the tool may still require elevation.

For more information, refer to: `https://chocolatey.org/install`.

Installing Homebrew for macOS

Homebrew is a CLI-based package manager for macOS, which can be used for automated software installation. To install Homebrew on macOS, you will need to run a command shell.

1. Launch **Spotlight Search** with ⌘ + Space
2. Type in `terminal`
3. Execute the following command in the Terminal to install the Homebrew package manager:

   ```
   $ /usr/bin/ruby -e "$(curl -fsSL
   https://raw.githubusercontent.com/Homebrew/install/master/install)"
   ```

4. Verify your Homebrew installation by executing `brew`
5. You should see a similar output, as follows:

```
du — du@dougi-mbp13 — ~ — -zsh — 80×24
du@dougi-mbp13 -> brew
Example usage:
  brew search [TEXT|/REGEX/]
  brew (info|home|options) [FORMULA...]
  brew install FORMULA...
  brew update
  brew upgrade [FORMULA...]
  brew uninstall FORMULA...
  brew list [FORMULA...]
```

Successful installation of Homebrew

6. To enable access to additional software, execute the following command:

```
$ brew tap caskroom/cask
```

For more information, check out: https://brew.sh/.

Git and GitHub Desktop

This section aims to establish a best practice Git configuration that's suitable for the widest audience possible. In order to make the best use of this section and subsequent chapters of this book, it is presumed that you, the reader, have the following prerequisites fulfilled:

- An understanding of what Source Code Management and Git are
- Create a free account on GitHub.com

Why use GitHub?

If you are a Git user, chances are that you also use an online repository, such as GitHub, Bitbucket, or GitLab. Each repository has a free-tier for open source projects, coupled with robust websites with varying feature sets, including on-premise Enterprise options that you can pay for. GitHub, with 38+ million repositories hosted in 2016, is by far the most popular online repository. GitHub is widely considered a baseline utility that will never go offline by the community.

Over time, GitHub has added many rich features that have transformed it from a mere repository to an online platform. Throughout this book, I'll be referencing GitHub features and functionalities, so you can leverage its capabilities to transform the way you develop, maintain, and release software.

Why use GitHub Desktop?

It is true that the Git CLI tool is powerful, and you will be just fine if you stick to it. However, we, full-stack developers, are worried about a variety of concerns. In your rush to complete the task at hand, you can easily ruin your and sometimes your team's day, by following bad or incomplete advice.

See the following screenshot of such advice from StackOverflow (`http://stackoverflow.com/questions/1125968/force-git-to-overwrite-local-files-on-pull`):

```
        Try this:
539     git reset --hard HEAD
        git pull

        Should do what you want.
```

If you execute the preceding command, be prepared to lose uncommitted local changes. Unfortunately, novice users have a tendency to follow the simplest and most direct instructions, potentially leading to lost work. If you think your past commits are safe, think twice! When it comes to Git, if you can imagine it, it can be done through the CLI.

Thankfully, with GitHub, you can protect branches and implement the GitHub workflow, which entails branching, committing, merging, updating, and submitting pull requests. The protections and the workflow help prevent harmful Git commands from making irreversible changes and enable a level of quality control so that your team remains productive. Performing all of these actions through the CLI, especially when there are merge conflicts, can get complicated and tedious.

For a more in-depth understanding of the benefits and pitfalls of Git and GitHub, you can read my 2016 article on the topic at: `Bit.ly/InDepthGitHub`.

Installing Git and GitHub Desktop

GitHub Desktop provides an easy-to-use GUI to execute the GitHub workflow, in a manner that is consistent across Windows and macOS. Consistency is highly valuable when on-boarding new or junior team members or if you're not a frequent contributor to the code base.

1. Execute the installation command:

   For Windows:

   ```
   PS> choco install git github-desktop -y
   ```

   For macOS:

   ```
   $ brew install git && brew cask install github-desktop
   ```

2. Verify your Git installation by executing `git --version` and observe the version number returned

> You will need to restart your Terminal after the installation of a new CLI tool. However, you can avoid relaunching your Terminal and save some time by refreshing or sourcing your environment variables. On Windows, execute `refreshenv`; on macOS, execute `source ~/.bashrc` or `source ~/.zshrc`.

3. Verify your GitHub Desktop installation by launching the application
4. Sign in to `https://github.com/` on GitHub Desktop
5. Once you have created a repository, you can launch the application from your Terminal by executing this:

```
$ github path/to/repo
```

6. If you are already on the correct folder, you can type in the following command instead:

```
$ github .
```

> For Windows, on GitHub Desktop launch, if you get stuck on the Sign in screen, close the application, relaunch it as an administrator, complete the setup, and then you will be able to use it normally, without having to launch it as an administrator again. For more information, refer to: `https://desktop.github.com/`.

Node.js

This section aims to establish a best practice JavaScript development environment. To make the best use of this book, it is presumed that you have the following prerequisites fulfilled:

- Awareness of the modern JavaScript ecosystem and tools
- NodeJS's site: `https://nodejs.org`
- Npm's site: `https://www.npmjs.com`
- Angular's site: `https://angular.io`
- Legacy AngularJS's site: `https://angularjs.org/`
- Yarn's site: `https://yarnpkg.com`
- React's site: `https://facebook.github.io/react`

Node.js is JavaScript that runs anywhere. It's an open source project that aimed to run JavaScript on the server, built on Google Chrome's V8 JavaScript engine. In late 2015, Node.js stabilized and announced enterprise-friendly 18 month LTS cycles that brought predictability and stability to the platform, paired with a more frequently updated, but more experimental, Latest branch. Node also ships bundled with npm, the Node package manager, and as of 2018, npm is the largest repository of JavaScript packages in the world.

For a more detailed look into Node's history, read my two-part article on Node at: `Bit.ly/NodeJSHistory`.

You may have heard of yarn and how it's faster or better than npm. As of npm 5, which ships bundled with Node 8, npm is more feature rich, easier to use and on par with yarn in terms of performance. Yarn is published by Facebook, which also created the React JavaScript UI library. It must be noted that yarn relies on the npm repository, so whichever tool you use, you get access to the same library of packages.

Existing Node.js Installation

If you installed Node.js before, when installing a new version of Node using choco or brew, ensure that you read the command outputs carefully. Your package manager may return caveats or additional instructions to follow, so you can successfully complete the installation.

It is also highly likely that your system or folder permissions have been edited manually in the past, which may interfere with a frustration-free operation of Node. If the following commands do not resolve your issues, use the GUI installer from Node's site as a last resort.

Regardless, you must take care to uninstall all global tools that were installed using `npm -g` previously. With every major Node version, there's a chance that native bindings between your tool and Node have been invalidated. Further, global tools rapidly fall out of date and project-specific tools quick go out of sync. As a result, installing tools globally is now an anti-pattern that has been replaced with better techniques, which are covered in the next section and under the Angular CLI section in `Chapter 2`, *Create a Local Weather Web Application*.

To see a list of your globally install packages, execute `npm list -g --depth 0`. To uninstall a global package, execute `npm uninstall -g package-name`. I would recommend that you uninstall all globally installed packages and restart from scratch with the suggestions provided in the next section.

Installing Node.js

This book will presume that you're using Node 8.4 or a later version. Odd numbered versions of Node are not meant to be long lived. 6.x.x, 8.x.x, 10.x.x, and so on are okay, but avoid 7.x.x, 9.x.x, and so on, at all costs.

1. Execute the installation command:

   For Windows:

   ```
   PS> choco install nodejs-lts -y
   ```

   For macOS:

   ```
   $ brew install node@8
   ```

2. Verify installation of Node by executing `node -v`
3. Verify npm by executing `npm -v`

 Note that you should never upgrade your npm version using `npm install -g npm` on Windows, as highlighted in `Chapter 4`, *Staying Up to Date with Angular Updates*. It is highly recommended that you use the `npm-windows-upgrade` npm package.

The npm repository contains numerous useful and mature CLI commands that are often cross-platform. Listed here are the ones I rely on frequently and choose to install globally for performance reasons:

- `npx`: Executes CLI tools by downloading the latest version on demand or project-specific local `node_modules` folder. It ships with npm 5 and will allow you to run code generators that frequently update without a global install.
- `rimraf`: The Unix command `rm -rf`, but works on Windows as well. Very useful in deleting the `node_modules` folder, especially when Windows is unable to do so due to the nested folder structure.
- `npm-update`: Analyzes your project folder and reports on which package have newer versions or not, with the option to be able to update all of them, if you so wish.
- `n`: Dead easy to tool to switch between versions of Node quickly, without having to remember the specific version number. Unfortunately, it only works on macOS/Linux.

- `http-server`: Simple, zero-configuration command-line HTTP server, which is a great way to locally test static HTML/CSS pages or even the **dist** folder of your Angular or React project.
- `npm-windows-upgrade`: Necessary to upgrade npm on Windows.

Visual Studio Code

Visual Studio Code (VS Code) is one of the best code editors/IDEs out there. It's free and it's cross-platform. The remarkable thing is that VS Code has the lightning fast performance of a code editor, think NotePad++ or Sublime Text, but the feature set and conveniences of costly IDEs, think Visual Studio or WebStorm. For JavaScript development, this speed is essential and is a tremendous quality-of-life improvement for a developer, who frequently switches back and forth between different projects. VS Code brings together an integrated terminal, easy-to-use extension system, transparent settings, excellent search and replace functionalities, and, in my opinion, the best Node.js debugger that exists.

Installing Visual Studio Code

For Angular development, this book will be leveraging VS Code. It is highly recommended that you also use VS Code.

1. Execute the installation command:

   For Windows:

   ```
   PS> choco install VisualStudioCode -y
   ```

   For macOS:

   ```
   $ brew cask install visual-studio-code
   ```

One of the best features of Visual Studio Code is that you can also launch it from the CLI. If you're in a folder that you'd like to be editing, simply execute `code .` or a particular file by executing `code ~/.bashrc` or `code readme.md`.

2. Verify install by launching Visual Studio Code
3. Navigate to a folder and execute `code .`
4. This will open up a new VS Code window with the **Explorer** displaying the contents of the current folder

For more information, refer to `https://code.visualstudio.com`.

Automation for Windows and macOS

At the beginning of the chapter, I proclaimed *anything that can be expressed as a CLI command can also be automated.* Throughout the setup process, we have ensured that every tool being used was set up and their functionality verifiable through a CLI command. This means we can easily create a PowerShell or bash script to string these commands together and ease the task of setting up and verifying new environments. In fact, I have created a rudimentary implementation of these scripts, which you may download from the `Chapter 1` folder of the GitHub Repository for this book:

1. Navigate to `https://github.com/duluca/web-dev-environment-setup` to find the scripts
2. Execute `install-windows-deps.ps1` in **PowerShell** to install and verify dependencies on Windows
3. Execute `install-mac-deps.sh` in **Terminal** to install and verify dependencies on macOS

The harsh reality is that these scripts do not represent a very capable or resilient solution. Scripts can't be executed or managed remotely, and they can't easily recover from errors or survive machine boot cycles. In addition, your IT requirements may be above and beyond what is covered here.

If you deal with large teams and frequent turnover, an automation tool will pay dividends handsomely, whereas if you're on your own or part of a smaller, stable team, it will be vastly overkill. I encourage you to explore tools such as Puppet, Chef, Ansible, and Vagrant to help you decide which one may best fit your needs or if a simple script is just good enough.

Summary

In this chapter, you mastered the use of CLI-based package managers for both Windows and macOS to speed up and automate the set up of development environments for you and your colleagues. By reducing variance from one developer's environment to the next, your team can overcome any individual configuration issue more easily and remain focused on the execution of the task at hand more often. With a collective understanding of a common environment, no single individual on the team will carry the burden of having to help troubleshoot everyone else's issues. As a result, your team will be more productive. By leveraging more sophisticated and resilient tools, mid-to-large sized organizations will be able to achieve great savings in their IT budgets.

In the next chapter, you will become familiar with the new Angular platform, optimize your web development environment, leverage Kanban using Waffle and GitHub issues, learn Angular fundamentals to build a simple web app with a full-stack architecture in mind, and get introduced to reactive programming with RxJS.

Further reading

The article on Automating the Setup of the Local Developer Machine by Vishwas Parameshwarappa is a great place to start for using Vagrant. You can find the article at Red-gate.com/simple-talk/sysadmin/general/automating-setup-local-developer-machine.

Create a Local Weather Web Application

2

In this chapter, we will be designing and building a simple Local Weather app with Angular and a third-party web API, using an iterative development methodology. You will focus on delivering value first, while learning about the nuances and optimal ways of using Angular, TypeScript, Visual Studio Code, Reactive Programming, and RxJS. Before we dive into coding, we will go over the philosophy behind Angular and ensure that your development environment is optimized and can enable collaboration and effortless information radiation.

Each section of this chapter will introduce you to new concepts, best practices, and optimal ways of leveraging these technologies and cover the bases to close any knowledge gaps you may have about web and modern JavaScript development basics.

In this chapter, you will learn Angular fundamentals to build a simple web app and become familiar with the new Angular platform and full-stack architecture.

In this chapter, you will learn the following:

- Get introduced to Angular and the philosophy behind it
- Configuring a repository with an optimal folder structure for full-stack development
- Using Angular CLI to generate your Angular web application
- Optimizing Visual Code for Angular & TypeScript development
- Planning out your roadmap using Waffle as a GitHub-connected Kanban board
- Crafting a new UI element to display current weather information using components and interfaces
- Using Angular Services and HttpClient to retrieve data from OpenWeatherMap APIs
- Leveraging observable streams to transform data using RxJS

The code samples provided in this book require Angular version 5 and 6. Angular 5 code is runtime compatible with Angular 6. Angular 6 will be supported in LTS until October 2019. The most up-to-date versions of the code repositories may be found at the following:

- For Chapters 2 to 6, LocalCast Weather, at: `Github.com/duluca/local-weather-app`
- For Chapters 7 to 12, LemonMart, at: `Github.com/duluca/lemon-mart`

Introduction to Angular

Angular is an open source project maintained by Google and a community of developers. The new Angular platform is vastly different from the legacy framework you may have used in the past. A collaboration with Microsoft makes TypeScript, which is a superset of JavaScript, the default development language, enabling developers to target legacy browsers such as Internet Explorer 11, while writing modern JavaScript code that is supported in evergreen browsers such as Chrome, Firefox, and Edge. The legacy versions of Angular, versions in the 1.x.x range, are now referred to as AngularJS. Version 2.0.0 and higher versions are simply called Angular. Where AngularJS is a monolithic JavaScript **Single Page Application (SPA)** framework, Angular is a platform that is capable of targeting browsers, hybrid-mobile frameworks, desktop applications, and server-side rendered views.

Each minor version increment in AngularJS meant risky updates with costly deprecations and major new features delivered at uncertain intervals. This led to an unpredictable, ever evolving framework with seemingly no guiding hand to carry code bases forward. If you used AngularJS, you likely got stuck on a particular version, because the specific architecture of your code base made it very difficult to move to a new version. In the spring/summer of 2018, the last major update to AngularJS will be released with version 1.7. This release will mark the beginning of the end for the legacy framework, with a planned end-of-life in July 2021.

Angular improves upon AngularJS in every way imaginable. The platform follows semver, as defined at `https://semver.org/`, where minor version increments denote new feature additions and potential deprecation notices for the second next major version, but no breaking changes. Furthermore, the Angular team at Google has committed to a deterministic release schedule for major version increments to be released every 6 months. After this 6-month development window, starting with Angular 4, all major releases receive **long-term support (LTS)** with bug fixes and security patches for an additional 12 months. From release to end-of-life, each major version is supported for 18 months. Refer to the following chart for the tentative release and support schedule for AngularJS and Angular:

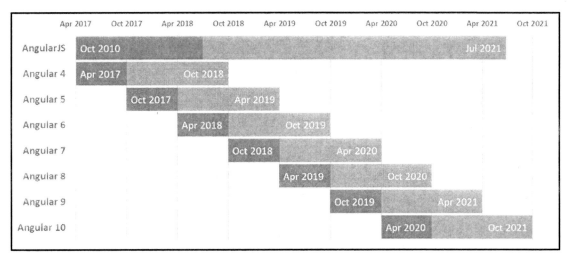

Tentative Angular Release and Support Schedule

So, what does this mean for you? You can be confident that the code you write in Angular will be supported and backwards compatible for an approximate time frame of 24 months, even if you make no changes to it. So, if you wrote an Angular app in version 4 in April 2017, your code is now runtime compatible with Angular 5, which itself is supported until April 2019. In order to upgrade your Angular 4 code to Angular 6, you will need to ensure that you're not using any of the deprecated APIs that were announced as deprecated in Angular 5. In reality, the deprecations are minor and unless you are working with low-level APIs for a highly specialized user experience, the time and effort it takes to update your code base should be minimal. However, this is a promise made by Google and not a contract. The Angular team has a major incentive to ensure backwards compatibility, because Google runs around 600+ Angular apps with a single version of Angular active at any one time throughout the organization. This means, by the time you read this, all of those 600+ apps will be running in Angular 6. You may think Google has infinite resources to make this happen, but like any other organization, they too have limited resources and not every app is actively maintained with a dedicated team. This means the Angular team must ensure compatibility through automated tests and make it as painless as possible to move through major releases going forward. In Angular 6, the update process was made much easier with the introduction of `ng update`. In the future, the team will release automated CLI tools to make upgrades of deprecated functionality a reasonable endeavor.

This is great news for developers and organizations alike. Now, instead of being perpetually stuck on a legacy version of Angular, you can actually plan and allocate the necessary resources to keep moving your application to the future without costly rewrites. As I wrote in a 2017 blog post, *The Best New Feature of Angular 4*, at `bit.ly/NgBestFeature`, the message is clear:

> *For Developers & Managers: Angular is here to stay, so you should be investing your time, attention, and money in learning it – even if you're currently in love with some other framework.*

> *For Decision Makers (CIOs, CTOs, etc.): Plan to begin your transition to Angular in the next 6 months. It'll be an investment you'll be able to explain to business minded people, and your investment will pay dividends for many years to come, long after the initial LTS window expires, with graceful upgrade paths to Angular vNext and beyond.*

So, why does Google (Angular) and Microsoft (TypeScript, Visual Studio Code) give away such technologies for free? There are multiple reasons, some including demonstration of technical proves to retain and attract talent, proving and debugging new ideas and tools with millions of developers at scale, and ultimately allowing developers to more easily create great web experiences that ultimately drive more business for Google and Microsoft. I personally don't see any nefarious intent here and welcome open, mature, and high-quality tools that I can tinker with and bend to my own will, if necessary, and not have to pay for a support contract for a proprietary piece of tech.

Beware, looking for Angular help on the web may be tricky. You'll note that most of the time, Angular is referred to as Angular 2 or Angular 4. At times, both Angular and AngularJS are simply referred to as AngularJS. This, of course, is incorrect. The documentation for Angular is at `angular.io`. If you land on `angularjs.org`, you'll be reading about the legacy AngularJS framework.

For the latest updates on the upcoming Angular releases, view the official Release Schedule
at: `Github.com/angular/angular/blob/master/docs/RELEASE_SCHEDULE.md`.

Angular's philosophy

The philosophy behind Angular is to err on the side of configuration over convention. Convention-based frameworks, although may seem elegant from the outside, make it really difficult for newcomers to pick up the framework. Configuration-based frameworks, however, aim to expose their inner workings through explicit configuration elements and hooks, where you can attach your custom behavior to the framework. In essence, Angular tries to be non-magical, where AngularJS was a lot of magic.

This results in a lot of verbose coding. This is a good thing. Terse code is the enemy of maintainability, only benefiting the original author. However, as Andy Hunt and David Thomas put it in the Pragmatic Programmer,

> *Remember that you (and others after you) will be reading the code many hundreds of times, but only writing it a few times.*

Verbose, decoupled, cohesive, and encapsulated code is the key to future proofing your code. Angular, through its various mechanisms, enables the proper execution of these concepts. It gets rid of many custom conventions invented in AngularJS, such as `ng-click`, and introduces a more intuitive language that builds on the existing HTML elements and properties. As a result, `ng-click` becomes `(click)`, extending HTML rather than replacing it.

What's new in Angular 6?

Most, if not all, of the content, patterns, and practices in this book are compatible with Angular 4 and up. Angular 6 is the latest version of Angular, which brings a lot of under-the-cover improvements to the platform and overall stability and cohesion across the ecosystem. The development experience is being vastly improved with additional CLI tools that make it easier to update versions of packages and faster build times to improve your code-build-view feedback cycle. With Angular 6, all platform tools are version synced to 6.0, making it easier to reason about the ecosystem. In the following chart, you can see how this makes it easier to communicate tooling compatibility:

	Previously	With v6
CLI	1.7	6.0
Angular	5.2.10	6.0
Material	5.2.4	6.0

Angular CLI 6.0 comes with major new capabilities, such as ng update and ng add commands; ng update makes it much easier to update your version of Angular, npm dependencies, RxJS, and Angular Material, including some deterministic code rewriting capabilities to apply name changes to APIs or functions. The topic of updating your version of Angular is covered in depth in Chapter 4, *Staying Up to Date with Angular Updates.* ng add brings schematics support to the Angular CLI. With schematics, you can write custom code to add new capabilities to an Angular app, adding any dependencies, boilerplate configuration code, or scaffolding. A great example is to be able to add Angular Material to your project by executing ng add @angular/material. The topic of adding Angular Material to your project is covered in depth in Chapter 5, *Enhance Angular App with Angular Material.* A standalone Material Update tool aims to make Angular Material updates less painful, found at Github.com/angular/material-update-tool, but expect this functionality to be merged into ng update. Further schematics can bring their own generate commands to CLI, making your life easier and code base more consistent over time. In addition, version 4 of Webpack is configured to build your Angular application into smaller modules with scope hosting, shortening the first-paint time of your app.

The major theme of Angular 6 is under-the-hood performance improvements and Custom Elements support. Version 6 improves upon v5 in terms of the base bundle size by 12% at 65 KB, which improves load times a whopping 21-40% from Fast 3G to Fiber connections. As your applications grows, Angular takes advantage of a better tree-shaking technique to further prune unused code out of your final deliverable. Speed is a UX feature in Angular 6. This is accomplished with better support for Angular **Component Development Kit (CDK)**, Angular Material, Animations, and i18n. Angular Universal allows for server-side assisted fast startup times, and Angular **Progressive Web App (PWA)** support takes advantage of native platform features such as caching and offline, so in subsequent visits, your app remains fast. RxJS 6 support allows for the tree-shakeable pipe command, reducing bundle sizes more often, and fix the behavior of throttle as I caution you in Chapter 6, *Reactive Forms and Component Interaction,* among numerous bug fixes and performance improvements. TypeScript 2.7 brings in better support for importing different types of JavaScript packages and more advanced features to catch coding errors during build time.

Custom Elements support, part of the Web Components spec, is huge. With Angular Elements, you can code an Angular component and reuse that component in *any* other web application using *any* web technology, in essence declaring your very own custom HTML element. These custom elements would be cross-compatible with any HTML-based tool chain, including other web application libraries or frameworks. For this to work, the entire Angular framework needs to be packaged alongside your new custom element. This is not feasible in Angular 6, because that will mean tacking on at least 65 KB, each and every time you create a new user control. Furthermore, in early 2018, only Chrome supports Custom Elements without polyfills adding more payload to make these custom elements work. Due to its experimental nature, I do not cover custom elements in this book. Future updates of Angular, in late 2018 or early 2019, should bring in the Ivy rendering engine, enabling base bundle sizes as small as 2.7 KB, resulting in lightning fast load times and making it feasible to ship Angular-based Custom Elements. In this time frame, tooling to build such components easily and native browser support for Custom Elements will also improve, including Firefox and Safari support, leaving Microsoft Edge the last browser to implement the standard.

 Always check `https://caniuse.com` before getting too excited about a new web technology to ensure that you are indeed able to use that feature in browsers that you must support.

Regardless of `Angular.io` being updated with custom elements to demonstrate the feasibility of the technology, the documentation website attracts 1 million+ unique visitors per month, so it should help work out some of the kinks as it matures. Custom elements are great use cases to host interactive code samples alongside static content. In early 2018, `Angular.io` started using `StackBlitz.io` for interactive code samples. This is an amazing website, in essence a Visual Studio Code IDE in the cloud, where you can experiment with different ideas or run GitHub repositories without needing to locally pull or execute any code.

The Angular ecosystem also welcomes the NgRx library, bringing Redux-like state management to Angular based on RxJS. Such state management is necessary for building offline-first applications in PWA and Mobile contexts. However, PWAs are not well supported in iOS's Safari browser and will not find widespread adoption until the new IE6 of browsers decides to join the party. Furthermore, NgRx, is an abstraction over already confusing and sophisticated tooling like RxJS. Given my positive attitude toward minimal tooling and a lack of clear necessity for RxJS beyond niche audience, I will not be covering this tool. RxJS is powerful and capable enough to unlock sophisticated and scalable patterns to help you build a great Angular application, as demonstrated in the lead up to `Chapter 10`, *Angular App Design and Recipes*.

Angular Material 6 adds new user controls such as tree and badge, while making the library a lot more stable with a slew of bug fixes, completeness of functionality, and theming in existing components. Angular Flex Layout 6 brings in polyfills, enabling Internet Explorer 11 support CSS Flexbox. This makes Angular apps using Material and Flex Layout fully compatible with the last major legacy browser technology that still persists in enterprises and governments despite leaving mainstream support in January 2018 alongside Windows 8.1 and being superseded 16 times by Microsoft Edge. Angular 6 itself can be configured to be compatible down to IE9 using polyfills. This is great news for developers, who must support such legacy browsers and still be able to use modern technologies to build their solutions.

Some exciting, new ancillary tooling is also released that can enable high frequency, high performance, or large enterprise use cases. The Nx CLI tool, built by former Angular team members, brings an opinionated development environment setup to Angular, suitable for consultants and large organizations that must ensure a consistent environment. This book follows a similar pattern and aims to educate you in establishing a consistent architecture and design pattern to apply across your applications. Google's Bazel build tool enables incremental builds, so portions of your application that haven't changed don't need to be rebuilt, vastly improving build times for larges projects and allowing for packaging of libraries to be shared between Angular applications.

I hope you are as excited as I am about Angular 6 and the future possibilities it unlocks. Now, let's put all that aside and dive deep into getting things done by building a simple Angular application that can display the current weather.

Angular in Full-Stack Architecture

In this chapter, we will design, architect, create a backlog, and establish the folder structure for your Angular project that will be able communicate with a REST API. This app will be designed to demonstrate the uses of the following:

- Angular CLI tool (ng)
- Angular Reuse of UI through components
- Angular HttpClient
- Angular Router
- Angular Reactive Forms

- Material Autocomplete
- Material Toolbar
- Material Sidenav

Regardless of your backend technology, I recommend that your frontend always resides in its own repository and is served using its own web server that is not depended on your API server.

First things first, you need a vision and a road map to act upon.

Wireframe design

There are some great tools out there to do rough looking mock-ups to demonstrate your idea with surprising amounts of rich functionality. If you have a dedicated UX designer, such tools are great for creating quasi prototypes. However, as a full-stack developer, I find the best tool out there to be pen and paper. This way, you don't have to learn yet another tool (YAL), and it is a far better alternative having no design at all. Putting things on paper will save you from costly coding detours down the line and if you can validate your wireframe design with users ahead of time, even better. I will call my app **LocalCast Weather**, but get creative and pick your own name. Behold, the wireframe design for your weather app:

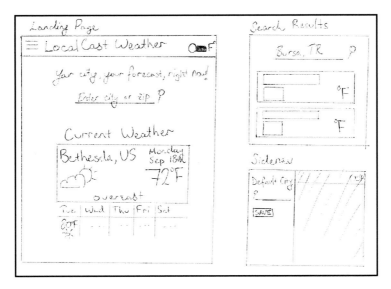

Wireframe for LocalCast. Intentionally hand-drawn.

The wireframe shouldn't be anything fancy. I recommend starting with a hand-drawn design, which is very quick to do and carries over the rough outlines effectively. There are great wireframing tools out there and I will be suggesting and using a couple of them throughout this book, however in the first days of your project, every hour matters. Granted, this kind of rough design may never leave the boundaries of your team, but please know that nothing beats getting that instantaneous feedback and collaboration by putting your ideas down on paper or a whiteboard.

High level architecture

No matter how small or large your project is, and frankly most of the times you will not be able to accurately predict this ahead of time, it is critical to start with a sound architecture that can scale if duty calls, but is not so burdensome that it will add days of effort to the execution of a simple app idea. The key is to ensure proper decoupling from the get go. In my view, there are two types of decoupling, one is a soft-decoupling, where essentially a *Gentlemen's Agreement* is made to not mix concerns and try and not mess up the code base. This can apply to the code you write, all the way to infrastructure-level interactions. If you maintain your frontend code under the same code structure as your backend code and if you let your REST server serve up your frontend application, then you are only practicing soft-decoupling.

You should instead practice hard-decoupling, which means frontend code lives in a separate repository, never calls the database directly, and is hosted on its own web server altogether. This way, you can be certain that at all times, your REST APIs or your frontend code is entirely replaceable independent of each other. Practicing hard-decoupling has monetary and security benefits as well. The serving and scaling needs of your frontend application are guaranteed to be different from your backend, so you will be able to optimize your host environment appropriately and save money. If you white list access to your REST APIs to only the calls originating from your frontend servers, you will vastly improve your security. Consider the high-level architecture diagram for our LocalCast Weather app below:

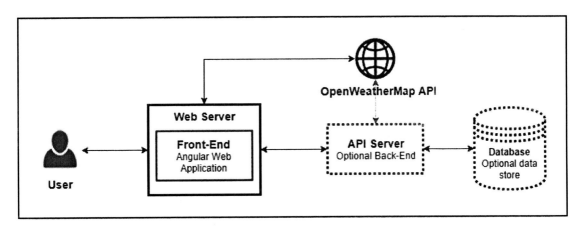

LocalCast High-Level Architecture

The high-level architecture shows that our Angular web application is completely decoupled from any backend. It is hosted on its own web server, can communicate to a web API such as **OpenWeatherMap**, or optionally be paired with a backend infrastructure to unlock rich and customized features that a web API alone can't provide, such as storing per user preferences or complimenting OpenWeatherMap's dataset with our own.

Folder structure

I advise against keeping your frontend and backend code in the same code repository. Using the same repository leads to bizarre dependencies when you need to enable Continuous Integration or deploy your code to production. In order to get an integrated development experience with the ability to quickly switch between repositories, you can use IDE features, such as VS Code Workspace, to open multiple repositories under the same tree-structure at once.

If you must use a single repository, create separate folders for backend code and frontend code, named `server` and `web-app`, respectively. The benefit of doing this at a minimum is great, because team members can start working on either the frontend or the backend without stepping over each other's toes.

Follow the instructions in the next two sections to set up your application correctly. If you already have a robust development directory setup and you're a Git pro, then skip over to the *Generate Your Angular Application* section.

Set up your development directory

Setting up a dedicated `dev` directory is a life saver. Since all the data under this directory will be backed up using GitHub, you can safely configure your antivirus, cloud sync, or backup software to ignore it. This will help greatly reduce CPU, disk, and network utilization. As a full-stack developer, you're likely to be multitasking a lot, so avoiding unnecessary activity will have a net positive impact on performance, power, and data consumption on a daily basis, especially if your development environment is a laptop that is either resource starved or you wish to squeeze as much battery life as possible when you're on the move.

Creating a `dev` folder directly under the `c:\` drive is very important, because Windows, or rather NTFS, isn't able handle file paths longer than 260 characters. This may seem adequate at first, but when you install npm packages in a folder structure that is already deep in the hierarchy, the `node_modules` folder structure can get deep enough to hit this limit very easily. With npm 3+, a new, flatter package installation strategy was introduced, which helps with npm-related issues, but being as close to the `root` folder as possible will help tremendously with any tool. In late 2016, there were reports that Microsoft may introduce an **Enable NTFS long paths** group policy to remedy this situation, but as of late 2017, this has not landed on Windows 10.

1. Create your `dev` folder using the following commands:

   For Windows:

   ```
   PS> mkdir c:\dev
   PS> cd c:\dev
   ```

In Unix-based operating systems, ~ (pronounced tilde) is a shortcut to the current users `home` directory, which resides under `/Users/your-user-name`.

   For macOS:

   ```
   $ mkdir ~/dev
   $ cd ~/dev
   ```

Now that your development directory is ready, let's start with generating your Angular application.

Generate your Angular application

The Angular CLI (Angular CLI) is an official Angular project to ensure that newly created Angular applications have a uniform architecture, following the best practices perfected by the community over time. This means that any Angular application you encounter going forward should have the same general shape. Angular CLI goes beyond initial code generation. You will be using it frequently to create new components, directives, pipes, services, modules, and more. Angular CLI will also help you during development with live-reloading features so that you can quickly see the results of your changes. Angular CLI can also test, lint, and build optimized versions of your code for a production release. Furthermore, as new Angular versions are released, Angular CLI will help you upgrade your code, by automatically rewriting portions of it so that it remains compatible with potential breaking changes.

Installing Angular CLI

The documentation at `https://angular.io/guide/quickstart` will guide you to install `@angular/cli` as a global npm package. Do *not* do this. Overtime, as Angular CLI is upgraded, it is a constant irritant to have to keep the global and the in-project version in sync. If you don't, the tool complains endlessly. Additionally, if you are working on multiple projects, you will have varying versions of Angular CLI overtime. As a result, your commands may not return the results you expect or your team members get.

The strategy detailed in the next section will make your initial configuration of your Angular project a bit more complicated than it needs to be; however, you'll be more than making up for this pain if you return to a project a few months or a year later. In that case, you will be able to use the version of the tool that you last used on that project, instead of some future version that may require upgrades that you're not willing to perform. In the next section, you will apply this best practice to initialize your Angular app.

Initializing Angular app

Now, we will initialize the application for development using `npx`, which is already installed on your system when you installed the latest version of Node LTS:

1. Under your `dev` folder, execute `npx @angular/cli new local-weather-app`

2. On your terminal, you should see a success message similar to this:

```
. . .
    create local-weather-app/src/tsconfig.app.json (211 bytes)
    create local-weather-app/src/tsconfig.spec.json (283 bytes)
    create local-weather-app/src/typings.d.ts (104 bytes)
    create local-weather-app/src/app/app.module.ts (316 bytes)
    create local-weather-app/src/app/app.component.html (1141 bytes)
    create local-weather-app/src/app/app.component.spec.ts (986
bytes)
    create local-weather-app/src/app/app.component.ts (207 bytes)
    create local-weather-app/src/app/app.component.css (0 bytes)
added 1273 packages from 1238 contributors in 60.594s
Project 'local-weather-app' successfully created.
```

Your project folder—`local-weather-app`—has been initialized as a Git repository and scaffolded with the initial file and folder structure, which should look like this:

```
local-weather-app
├───── angular.json
├───── .editorconfig
├───── .gitignore
├───── .gitkeep
├───── e2e
├───── karma.conf.js
├───── node_modules
├───── package-lock.json
├───── package.json
├───── protractor.conf.js
├───── README.md
├───── src
├───── tsconfig.json
└───── tslint.json
```

The alias for `@angular/cli` is ng. If you were to install Angular CLI globally, you would have simply executed `ng new local-weather-app`, but we didn't do this. So it is important to remember that going forward, you will be executing the `ng` command, but this time under the `local-weather-app` directory. The latest version of Angular CLI has been installed under the `node_modules/.bin` directory, so you can run `ng` commands such as `npx ng generate component my-new-component` and continue working in an effective manner.

If you are on macOS, you can further improve your development experience by implementing shell auto fallback, which removes the necessity of having to use the `npx` command. If an unknown command is found, npx will take over the request. If the package already locally exists under `node_modules/.bin`, the npx will pass along your request to the correct binary. So, you will just be able to run commands like `ng g c my-new-component` as if they're globally installed. Refer to npx's readme on how to set this up at `npmjs.com/package/npx#shell-auto-fallback`.

Publishing Git Repository using GitHub Desktop

GitHub Desktop allows you to create a new repository directly within the application:

1. Open GitHub for Desktop
2. **File | Add local repository...**
3. Locate the `local-weather-app` folder by clicking on **Choose...**
4. Click on **Add repository**
5. Note that Angular CLI already created the first commit for you in the **History** tab

6. Finally, click on **Publish repository**, as shown:

GitHub Desktop

Inspecting and updating package.json

Package.json is the single most important configuration file that you should be keenly aware of at all times. Your project's scripts, runtime, and development dependencies are stored in this file.

1. Open package.json and locate the name and version properties:

package.json
```
{
  "name": "local-weather-app",
  "version": "0.0.0",
  "license": "MIT",
  ...
```

2. Rename your app to whatever you wish; I will be using `localcast-weather`

3. Set your version number to `1.0.0`

> `npm` uses semantic versioning (semver), where version number digits represent Major.Minor.Patch increments. Semver starts version numbers at `1.0.0` for any published API, though it doesn't prevent 0.x.x versioning. As the author of a web application, the versioning of your app has no real impact on you, outside of internal tooling, team, or company communication purposes. However, the versioning of your dependencies is highly critical to the reliability of your application. In summary, Patch versions should just be bug fixes. Minor versions add functionality without breaking the existing features, and major version increments are free to make incompatible API changes. However, in reality, any update is risky to the tested behavior of your application. This is why the `package-lock.json` file stores the entire dependency tree of your application, so the exact state of your application can be replicated by other developers or Continuous Integration servers. For more information, visit: `https://semver.org/`.

In the following code block, observe that the `scripts` property contains a collection of helpful starter scripts that you can expand on. The `start` and `test` commands are npm defaults, so they can just be executed by `npm start` or `npm test`. However, the other commands are custom commands that must be prepended with the `run` keyword. For example, in order to build your application, you must use `npm run build`:

package.json

```
...
"scripts": {
  "ng": "ng",
  "start": "ng serve",
  "build": "ng build",
  "test": "ng test",
  "lint": "ng lint",
  "e2e": "ng e2e"
},
...
```

Before the introduction of npx, if you wanted to use Angular CLI without a global install, you would have to run it with `npm run ng -- g c my-new-component`. The double-dashes are needed to let npm know where the command-line tool name ends and options begin. For example, in order to start your Angular application on a port other than the default 4200, you will need to run `npm start -- --port 5000`.

4. Update your `package.json` file to run your development version of the app from a little used port like `5000` as the new default behavior:

package.json

```
. . .
    "start": "ng serve --port 5000",
. . .
```

Under the `dependencies` property, you can observe your runtime dependencies. These are libraries that will get packaged up alongside your code and shipped to the client browser. It's important to keep this list to a minimum:

package.json

```
. . .
    "dependencies": {
      "@angular/animations": "^6.0.0",
      "@angular/common": "^6.0.0",
      "@angular/compiler": "^6.0.0",
      "@angular/core": "^6.0.0",
      "@angular/forms": "^6.0.0",
      "@angular/http": "^6.0.0",
      "@angular/platform-browser": "^6.0.0",
      "@angular/platform-browser-dynamic": "^6.0.0",
      "@angular/router": "^6.0.0",
      "core-js": "^2.5.4",
      "rxjs": "^6.0.0",
      "zone.js": "^0.8.26"
    },
. . .
```

In the preceding example, all Angular components are on the same version. As you install additional Angular components or upgrade individual ones, it is advisable to keep all Angular packages on the same version. This is especially easy to do since npm 5 doesn't require the `--save` option anymore to permanently update the package version. For example, just executing `npm install @angular/router` is sufficient to update the version in `package.json`. This is a positive change overall, since what you see in `package.json` will match what is actually installed. However, you must be careful, because npm 5 will also automatically update `package-lock.json`, which will propagate your, potentially unintended, changes to your team members.

Your development dependencies are stored under the `devDependencies` property. When installing new tools to your project, you must take care to append the command with `--save-dev` so that your dependency will be correctly categorized. Dev dependencies are only used during development and are not shipped to the client browser. You should familiarize yourself with every single one of these packages and their specific purpose. If you are unfamiliar with a package shown as we move on, your best resource to learn more about them is `https://www.npmjs.com/`:

package.json
```
  . . .
  "devDependencies": {
    "@angular/compiler-cli": "^6.0.0",
    "@angular-devkit/build-angular": "~0.6.1",
    "typescript": "~2.7.2",
    "@angular/cli": "~6.0.1",
    "@angular/language-service": "^6.0.0",
    "@types/jasmine": "~2.8.6",
    "@types/jasminewd2": "~2.0.3",
    "@types/node": "~8.9.4",
    "codelyzer": "~4.2.1",
    "jasmine-core": "~2.99.1",
    "jasmine-spec-reporter": "~4.2.1",
    "karma": "~1.7.1",
    "karma-chrome-launcher": "~2.2.0",
    "karma-coverage-istanbul-reporter": "~1.4.2",
```

```
      "karma-jasmine": "~1.1.1",
      "karma-jasmine-html-reporter": "^0.2.2",
      "protractor": "~5.3.0",
      "ts-node": "~5.0.1",
      "tslint": "~5.9.1"
    }
    ...
```

The characters in front of the version numbers have specific meanings in semver.

- Tilde ~ enables tilde ranges when all three digits of the version number are defined, allowing for patch version upgrades to be automatically applied
- Up-caret character ^ enables caret ranges, allowing for minor version upgrades to be automatically applied
- Lack of any character signals npm to install that exact version of the library on your machine

You may notice that major version upgrades aren't allowed to happen automatically. In general, updating packages can be risky. In order to ensure, no package is updating without your explicit knowledge, you may install exact versions packages by using npm's `--save-exact` option. Let's experiment with this behavior by installing an npm package that I published called, `dev-norms`, a CLI tool that generates a markdown file with sensible default norms for your team to have a conversation around, as shown here:

5. Under the `local-weather-app` directory, execute `npm install dev-norms --save-dev --save-exact`. Note that `"dev-norms": "1.3.6"` or similar has been added to `package.json` with `package-lock.json` automatically updated to reflect the changes accordingly.

6. After the tool is installed, execute `npx dev-norms create`. A file named `dev-norms.md` has been created containing the aforementioned developer norms.

7. Save your changes to `package.json`.

Working with stale packages comes with its own risks. With npm 6, the `npm audit` command has been introduced to make you aware of any vulnerabilities discovered in packages you're using. During `npm install` if you receive any vulnerability notices, you may execute `npm audit` to find out details about any potential risk.

In the next section, you will commit the changes you have made to Git.

Commiting code using VS Code

In order to commit your changes to Git and then synchronize your commits to GitHub, you can use VS Code.

1. Switch over to the **Source Control** pane, marked as **1** here:

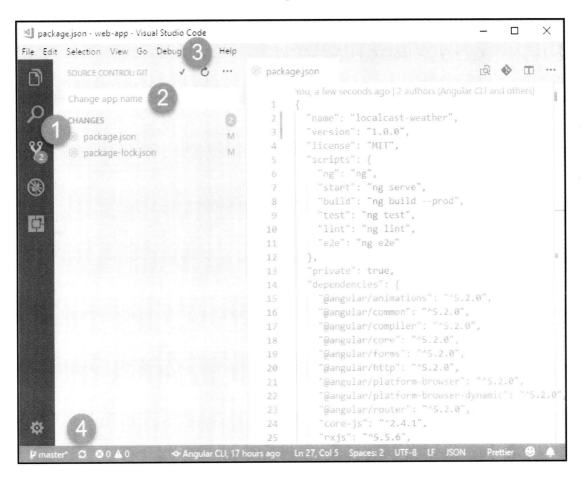

Visual Studio Code Source Control pane

2. Enter a commit message in **2**
3. Click on the check-mark icon to commit your changes in **3**
4. Finally, synchronize your changes with your GitHub repository by clicking on the refresh icon in **4**.

Going forward, you can do most Git operations from within VS Code.

Running your Angular app

Run your Angular app to check whether it works. During development, you can execute `npm start`, through the `ng serve` command; this action will transpile, package, and serve the code on localhost with live-reloading enabled:

1. Execute `npm start`
2. Navigate to `http://localhost:5000`
3. You should see a rendered page similar to this:

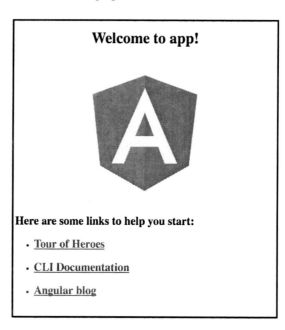

Default Angular CLI landing page

4. Stop your application by pressing *Ctrl + C* in the integrated terminal.

Optimizing VS Code for Angular

Saving files all the time can get tedious. You can enable automatic saving by doing the following:

1. Open VS Code
2. Toggle the setting under **File** | **Auto Save**

You can further customize many aspects of VS Code's behavior by launching **Preferences**. The keyboard shortcut to launch **Preferences** is *Ctrl +* , on Windows and ⌘ *+* , on macOS.

IDE settings

You can share such settings with your coworkers by creating a `.vscode` folder in the root of your project directory and placing a `settings.json` file in it. If you commit this file to the repository, everyone will share the same IDE experience. Unfortunately, individuals aren't able to override these settings with their own local preferences, so ensure that shared settings are minimal and are agreed upon as a team norm.

Here are the customizations that I use for an optimal, battery-life conscious Angular development experience:

`.vscode/settings.json`

```
{
  "editor.tabSize": 2,
  "editor.rulers": [90, 140],
  "files.trimTrailingWhitespace": true,
  "files.autoSave": "onFocusChange",
  "editor.cursorBlinking": "solid",
  "workbench.iconTheme": "material-icon-theme", // Following setting
                                                   requires Material Icon
                                                        Theme Extension

  "git.enableSmartCommit": true,
  "editor.autoIndent": true,
  "debug.openExplorerOnEnd": true,
  "auto-close-tag.SublimeText3Mode": true,      // Following setting
                                                requires Auto Close Tag
                                                        Extension

  "explorer.openEditors.visible": 0,
  "editor.minimap.enabled": false,
  "html.autoClosingTags": false,
  "git.confirmSync": false,
```

```
      "editor.formatOnType": true,
      "editor.formatOnPaste": true,
      "editor.formatOnSave": true,
      "prettier.printWidth": 90,                // Following setting requires
                                                          Prettier Extension

      "prettier.semi": false,
      "prettier.singleQuote": true,
      "prettier.trailingComma": "es5",
      "typescriptHero.imports.insertSemicolons": false, // Following setting
                                                   requires TypeScriptHero
                                                                Extension
      "typescriptHero.imports.multiLineWrapThreshold": 90,
    }
```

Additionally, you may enable the following settings in VS Code for a richer development experience:

```
    "editor.codeActionsOnSave": {
      "source.organizeImports": true
    },
    "npm.enableScriptExplorer": true
```

IDE extensions

For a *magical* development experience with VS Code and Angular, you should install the Angular Essentials extension pack created and curated by John Papa. John Papa is one of the leading champions and thought leaders in the Angular community. He continuously and relentlessly seeks the best possible development experience you can attain so that you are more productive and happier as a developer. He is a resource to trust and take very seriously. I highly recommend you follow him on twitter at @john_papa.

Similar to settings, you can also share recommended extensions via a JSON file. These are the extensions that I use for Angular development:

.vscode/extensions.json
```
{
  "recommendations": [
    "johnpapa.angular-essentials",
    "PKief.material-icon-theme",
    "formulahendry.auto-close-tag",
    "PeterJausovec.vscode-docker",
    "eamodio.gitlens",
    "WallabyJs.quokka-vscode",
    "rbbit.typescript-hero",
```

```
    "DSKWRK.vscode-generate-getter-setter",
    "esbenp.prettier-vscode"
  ]
}
```

VS Code will also recommend some extensions for you to install. I would caution against installing too many extensions, as these will noticeably start slowing down the launch performance and optimal operation of VS Code.

Coding style

You can customize the coding style enforcement and code generation behavior in VS Code and Angular CLI. When it comes to JavaScript, I prefer StandardJS settings, which codifies a minimal approach to writing code, while maintaining great readability. This means 2-spaces for tabs and no semicolons. In addition to the reduced keystrokes, StandardJS also takes less space horizontally, which is especially valuable when your IDE can only utilize half of the screen with the other half taken up by the browser. You can read more about StandardJS at: https://standardjs.com/.

With the default settings, your code will look like this:

```
import { AppComponent } from "./app.component";
```

With StandardJS settings, your code will look like this:

```
import { AppComponent } from './app.component'
```

Ultimately, this is an optional step for you. However, my code samples will follow the StandardJS style. You can start making the configuration changes by following these steps:

1. Install the **Prettier - Code formatter** extension
2. Update .vscode/extensions.json file with the new extension
3. Execute npm i -D prettier

You can use i for install and -D instead of the more verbose --save-dev option. However, if you mistype -D as -d, you will end up saving the package as a production dependency.

4. Edit `package.json` with a new script, update the existing ones, and create new formatting rules:

package.json

```
. . .
"scripts": {
  . . .
  "standardize": "prettier **/*.ts --write",
  "start": "npm run standardize && ng serve --port 5000",
  "build": "npm run standardize && ng build",
  . . .
},
. . .
"prettier": {
  "printWidth": 90,
  "semi": false,
  "singleQuote": true,
  "trailingComma": "es5",
  "parser": "typescript"
}
. . .
```

 macOS and Linux users must modify the `standardize` script to add single-quotes around `**/*.ts` for the script to correctly traverse the directory. In macOS and Linux, the correct script looks like `"standardize": "prettier '**/*.ts' --write"`.

5. Similarly, update `tslint.json` with new formatting rules:

tslint.json

```
. . .
"quotemark": [
  true,
  "single"
],
. . .
"semicolon": [
  true,
  "never"
],
. . .
"max-line-length": [
  true,
  120
],
. . .
```

6. Execute `npm run standardize` to update all your files to the new style
7. Observe all the file changes in GitHub Desktop
8. Going forward, every time you execute `npm start` or `npm run build`, the new `standardize` script will automatically run and keep the formatting of your files in shape
9. Commit and push your changes to your repository

As you type in new code or generate new components using Angular CLI, you will encounter double-quotes or semicolons being underlined with a red-squiggly line to indicate an issue. In most of those cases, a yellow bulb icon will appear next to the issue. If you click on the bulb, you will see an action to **Fix: Unnecessary semicolon** or a similar message. You can either take advantage of these auto-fixers or press *Shift + Alt + F* to run the Prettier Format Document command on the entire file. In the following screenshot, you can see the auto-fixer in action with the yellow bulb and the corresponding contextual menu:

VS Code Auto-Fixer

Planning a feature road map using Waffle

Building a rough plan of action before you start coding is a very important so that you and your colleagues or clients are aware of the road map you're planning to execute. Whether you're building an app for yourself or for someone else, a living backlog of features will always serve as a great reminder when you get back to a project after a break or serve as an information radiator that prevent constant requests for status updates.

In Agile development, you may have used various ticketing systems or tools that surface or Kanban boards. My favorite tool is Waffle.io, `https://waffle.io/`, because it directly integrates with your GitHub repository's issues and keeps track of status of issues via labels. This way, you can keep using the tool of your choice to interact with your repository and still, effortlessly, radiate information. In the next section, you will set up a Waffle project to achieve this goal.

Setting up a Waffle project

We will now set up our Waffle project:

1. Go to Waffle.io `https://waffle.io/.`
2. Click on **Login** or **Get Started for Free**.
3. Select **Public & Private Repos** to allow access to all of your repositories.
4. Click on **Create Project**.
5. Search for the **local-weather-app** repository and select it.
6. Hit **Continue.**

You will get two starter layout templates, as shown in the following image:

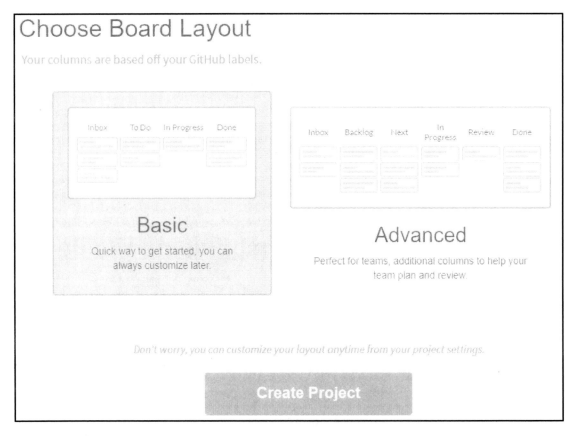

Waffle.io Default Board Layouts

For this simple project, you will be selecting **Basic**. However, the **Advanced** layout demonstrates how you can modify the default setup of Waffle, by adding additional columns such as **Review**, to account for testers or product owners participating in the process. You can further customize any board to fit your existing process.

7. Select the **Basic** layout and click on **Create Project**.
8. You will see a new board created for you.

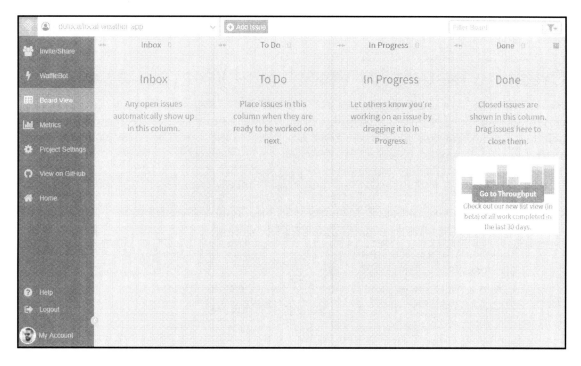

Empty Waffle Board

By default, Waffle will serve as a Kanban board. Allowing you to move a task from one state to another. However, the default view will show all the issues that are present on the repository. To use Waffle as a Scrum board, you need to assign issues to GitHub milestones that will represent sprints. You can then use the filtering functionality to only display issues from that milestone, or put another way from the current sprint.

On Waffle, you can attach story points to issues by clicking on the ⚖ scale icon. The columns will automatically show totals and card orders, which represent priority, and they will be retained from session to session. Furthermore, you can switch to the **Metrics** view to get **Milestone Burndown** and **Throughput** graphs and statistics.

Creating issues for your Local Weather app

We will now create a backlog of issues that you will use to keep track of your progress as you implement the design of your application. When creating issues, you should focus on delivering functional iterations that bring some value to the user. The technical hurdles you must clear to achieve those results are of no interest to your users or clients.

Here are the features we plan to be building in our first release:

- Display Current Location weather information for the current day
- Display forecast information for current location
- Add city search capability so that users can see weather information from other cities
- Add a preferences pane to store the default city for the user
- Improve the UX of the app with Angular Material

Go ahead with creating your issues on Waffle or on GitHub; whichever you prefer is fine. While creating the scope for **Sprint 1**, I had some other ideas for features, so I just added those issues, but I did not assign them to a person or a milestone. I also went ahead and added story points to the issues I intended to work on. The following is what the board looks like, as I'm to begin working on the first story:

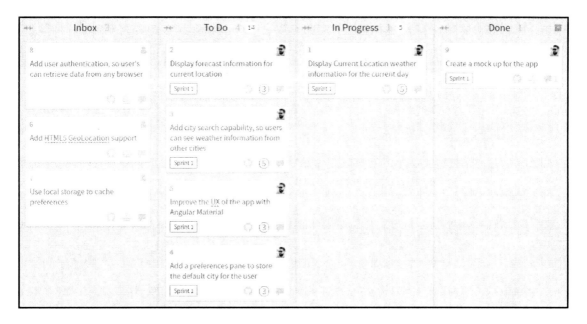

A snapshot of the initial state of the board at `https://waffle.io/duluca/local-weather-app`

Ultimately, Waffle provides an easy-to-use GUI so that non-technical people can easily interact with GitHub issues. By allowing non-technical people to participate in the development process on GitHub, you unlock the benefit of GitHub becoming the single source of information for your entire project. Questions, answers, and discussions around features and issues are all tracked as part of GitHub issues, instead of being lost in emails. You can also store wiki type documentation on GitHub, so by centralizing all project-related information, data, conversations, and artifacts on GitHub, you are greatly simplifying a potentially complicated interaction of multiple systems that require continued maintenance, at a high cost. For private repositories and on-premise Enterprise installations, GitHub has a very reasonable cost. If you're sticking with open source, as we are in this chapter, all these tools are free.

As a bonus, I created a rudimentary wiki page on my repository at `https://github.com/duluca/local-weather-app/wiki`. Note that you can't upload images to `README.md` or wiki pages. To get around this limitation, you can create a new issue, upload an image in a comment, and copy and paste the URL for it to embed images to `README.md` or wiki pages. In the sample wiki, I followed this technique to embed the wireframe design into the page.

With a concrete road map in place, you're now ready to start implementing your application.

Crafting UI elements using components and interfaces

You will be leveraging Angular components, interfaces, and services to build the current weather feature in a decoupled, cohesive, and encapsulated manner.

The landing page of an Angular app, by default, resides in `app.component.html`. So, start by editing the template of `AppComponent` with rudimentary HTML, laying out the initial landing experience for the application.

 We are now beginning the development of Feature 1: **Display Current Location weather information for the current day**, so, you can move the card in Waffle to the **In Progress** column.

We will add a header as an `h1` tag, followed by the tagline of our app as a `div` and placeholders for where we may want to display the current weather, as demonstrated as shown in the following code block:

src/app/app.component.html
```html
<div style="text-align:center">
  <h1>
  LocalCast Weather
  </h1>
  <div>Your city, your forecast, right now!</div>
  <h2>Current Weather</h2>
  <div>current weather</div>
</div>
```

 At this point, you should run `npm start` and navigate to `http://localhost:5000` on your browser so that you can observe the changes you're making in real time.

Adding an Angular component

We need to display the current weather information, where `<div>current weather</div>` is located. In order to achieve this, you need to build a component that will be responsible for displaying the weather data.

The reason behind creating a separate component is an architectural best practice that is codified in the **Model-View-ViewModel** (**MVVM**) design pattern. You may have heard of the **Model-View-Controller** (**MVC**) pattern before. Vast majority of web-based code written circa 2005-2015 has been written following the MVC pattern. MVVM differs, in important ways, from the MVC pattern. As I have explained in my 2013 article on DevPro:

> *[An effective implementation of MVVM] inherently enforces proper separation of concerns. Business logic is clearly separated from presentation logic. So when a View is developed, it stays developed, because fixing a bug in one View's functionality doesn't impact other views. On the flip side, if [you use] visual inheritance effectively and [create] reusable user controls, fixing a bug in one place can fix issues throughout the application.*

Angular provides an effective implementation of MVVM.

> *ViewModels neatly encapsulate any presentation logic and allow for simpler View code by acting as a specialized version of the model. The relationship between a View and ViewModel is straightforward, allowing for more natural ways to wrap UI behavior in reusable user controls.*

You can read further about the architectural nuance, with illustrations, at `http://bit.ly/MVVMvsMVC`.

Next, you will create your very first Angular component, which will include the View and the ViewModel, using Angular CLI's `ng generate` command:

1. In the terminal, execute `npx ng generate component current-weather`

Ensure that you are executing `ng` commands under the `local-weather-app` folder, and not under the `root` project folder. In addition, note that `npx ng generate component current-weather` can be rewritten as `ng g c current-weather`. Going forward, this book will utilize the shorthand format and expect you to prepend `npx`, if necessary.

2. Observe the new files created in your `app` folder:

```
src/app
├──── app.component.css
├──── app.component.html
├──── app.component.spec.ts
├──── app.component.ts
├──── app.module.ts
├──── current-weather
      ├──── current-weather.component.css
      ├──── current-weather.component.html
      ├──── current-weather.component.spec.ts
      └──── current-weather.component.ts
```

A generated component has four parts:

- `current-weather.component.css` contains any CSS that is specific to the component and is an optional file
- `current-weather.component.html` contains the HTML template that defines the look of the component and rendering of the bindings, and can be considered the View, in combination with any CSS styles used
- `current-weather.component.spec.ts` contains Jasmine-based unit tests that you can extend to test your component functionality
- `current-weather.component.ts` contains the `@Component` decorator above the class definition and is the glue that ties together the CSS, HTML, and JavaScript code together. The class itself can be considered the ViewModel, pulling data from services and performing any necessary transformations to expose sensible bindings for the View, as shown as follows:

```
src/app/current-weather/current-weather.component.ts
import { Component, OnInit } from '@angular/core'
@Component({
  selector: 'app-current-weather',
  templateUrl: './current-weather.component.html',
  styleUrls: ['./current-weather.component.css'],
})
export class CurrentWeatherComponent implements OnInit {
  constructor() {}

  ngOnInit() {}
}
```

If the component you're planning to write is a simple one, you can rewrite it using inline styles and an inline template, to simplify the structure of your code.

3. Update `CurrentWeatherComponent` with an inline template and styles:

src/app/current-weather/current-weather.component.ts
```
import { Component, OnInit } from '@angular/core'

@Component({
  selector: 'app-current-weather',
  template: `
  <p>
    current-weather works!
  </p>
  `,
  styles: ['']
})
export class CurrentWeatherComponent implements OnInit {
constructor() {}

ngOnInit() {}
}
```

When you executed the generate command, in addition to creating the component, the command also added the new module you created to `app.module.ts`, avoiding an otherwise tedious task of wiring up components together:

src/app/app.module.ts
```
...
import { CurrentWeatherComponent } from './current-weather/current-weather.component'
...
@NgModule({
declarations: [AppComponent, CurrentWeatherComponent],
...
```

The bootstrap process of Angular is, admittedly, a bit convoluted. This is the chief reason Angular CLI exists. index.html contains an element named <app-root>. When Angular begins execution, it first loads main.ts, which configures the framework for browser use and loads the app module. App module then loads all its dependencies and renders within the aforementioned <app-root> element. In Chapter 7, *Create a Router-First Line-of-Business App*, when we build a line-of-business app, we will create our own feature modules to take advantage of the scalability features of Angular.

Now, we need to display our new component on the initial AppComponent template, so it is visible to the end user:

4. Add the CurrentWeatherComponent to AppComponent by replacing <div>current weather</div> with <app-current-weather></app-current-weather>:

src/app/app.component.html
```
<div style="text-align:center">
<h1>
 LocalCast Weather
 </h1>
 <div>Your city, your forecast, right now!</div>
 <h2>Current Weather</h2>
 <app-current-weather></app-current-weather>
</div>
```

5. If everything worked correctly, you should see this:

Initial render of your local weather app

 Note the icon and name in the tab of the browser window. As a web development norm, in the `index.html` file, update the `<title>` tag and the `favicon.ico` file with the name and icon of your application to customize the browser tab information. If your favicon doesn't update, append the `href` attribute with a unique version number, such as `href="favicon.ico?v=2"`. As a result, your app will start looking like a real web app, instead of a CLI-generated starter project.

Define your model using interfaces

Now that your `View` and `ViewModel` are in place, you need to define your `Model`. If you look back on the design, you will see that the component needs to display:

- City
- Country
- Current date
- Current image
- Current temperature
- Current weather description

You will first create an interface that represents this data structure:

1. In the terminal, execute `npx ng generate interface ICurrentWeather`
2. Observe a newly generated file named `icurrent-weather.ts` with an empty interface definition that looks like this:

   src/app/icurrent-weather.ts
   ```
   export interface ICurrentWeather {
   }
   ```

   This is not an ideal setup, since we may add numerous interfaces to our app and it can get tedious to track down various interfaces. Over time, as you add concrete implementations of these interfaces as classes, then it will make sense to put classes and their interfaces in their own files.

    Why not just call the interface `CurrentWeather`? This is because later on we may create a class to implement some interesting behavior for `CurrentWeather`. Interfaces establish a contract, establishing the list of available properties on any class or interface that implements or extends the interface. It is always important to be aware of when you're using a class versus an interface. If you follow the best practice to always start your interface names with a capital `I`, you will always be conscious of what type of an object you are passing around. Hence, the interface is named `ICurrentWeather`.

3. Rename `icurrent-weather.ts` to `interfaces.ts`
4. Correct the capitalization of the interface name to `ICurrentWeather`

5. Also, implement the interface as follows:

src/app/interfaces.ts
```
export interface ICurrentWeather {
  city: string
  country: string
  date: Date
  image: string
  temperature: number
  description: string
}
```

This interface and its eventual concrete representation as a class is the Model in MVVM. So far, I have highlighted how various parts of Angular fit the MVVM pattern; going forward, I will be referring to these parts with their actual names.

Now, we can import the interface into the component and start wiring up the bindings in the template of CurrentWeatherComponent.

6. Import ICurrentWeather

7. Switch back to the templateUrl and styleUrls

8. Define a local variable called current with type ICurrentWeather

src/app/current-weather/current-weather.component.ts
```
import { Component, OnInit } from '@angular/core'
import { ICurrentWeather } from '../interfaces'

@Component({
  selector: 'app-current-weather',
  templateUrl: './current-weather.component.html',
  styleUrls: ['./current-weather.component.css'],
})
export class CurrentWeatherComponent implements OnInit {
  current: ICurrentWeather
  constructor() {}
  ngOnInit() {}
}
```

If you just type current: ICurrentWeather, you can use the auto-fixer to automatically insert the import statement.

In the constructor, you will temporarily populate the current property with dummy data to test your bindings.

9. Implement dummy data as a JSON object and declare its adherence to `ICurrentWeather` using the as operator:

src/app/current-weather/current-weather.component.ts
```
...
constructor() {
  this.current = {
    city: 'Bethesda',
    country: 'US',
    date: new Date(),
    image: 'assets/img/sunny.svg',
    temperature: 72,
    description: 'sunny',
  } as ICurrentWeather
}
...
```

In the `src/assets` folder, create a subfolder named `img` and place an image of your choice to reference in your dummy data.

You may forget the exact properties in the interface you created. You can get a quick peek at them by holding *Ctrl* + hover-over the interface name with your mouse, as shown:

```
current: ICurrentWeather

                 export interface ICurrentWeather {
construct          city: string
  this.cu          country: string
    city:          date: Date
    count          image: string
                   temperature: string
                   description: string
    }            }

ngOnInit(  import ICurrentWeather
```

Ctrl + hover-over the interface

Now you update the template to wire up your bindings with a rudimentary HTML-based layout.

10. Implement the template:

src/app/current-weather/current-weather.component.html

```
<div>
  <div>
    <span>{{current.city}}, {{current.country}}</span>
    <span>{{current.date | date:'fullDate'}}</span>
  </div>
  <div>
    <img [src]='current.image'>
    <span>{{current.temperature | number:'1.0-0'}}°F</span>
  </div>
  <div>
    {{current.description}}
  </div>
</div>
```

To change the display formatting of `current.date`, we used the `DatePipe` above, passing in `'fullDate'` as the format option. In Angular, various out-of-the-box and custom pipe `|` operators can be used to change the appearance of data without actually changing the underlying data. This is a very powerful, convenient, and flexible system to share such user interface logic without writing repetitive boilerplate code. In the preceding example, we could pass in `'shortDate'` if we wanted to represent the current date in a more compact form. For more information on various `DatePipe` options, refer to the documentation at `https://angular.io/api/common/DatePipe`. To format `current.temperature` so that no fractional values are shown, you can use `DecimalPipe`. The documentation is at `https://angular.io/api/common/DecimalPipe`.

Note that you can render °C and °F using their respective HTML codes: `&#8451;` for °C and `&#8457;` for °F.

11. If everything worked correctly, you app should be looking similar to this screenshot:

App after wiring up bindings with dummy data

Congratulations, you have successfully wired up your first component.

Using Angular Services and HttpClient to retrieve data

Now you need to connect your CurrentWeather component to the OpenWeatherMap APIs. In the upcoming sections, we will go over the following steps to accomplish this goal:

1. Create a new Angular Service
2. Import HttpClientModule and inject it into the service
3. Discover the OpenWeatherMap API

4. Create a new interface that conforms to the shape of the API
5. Write a `get` request
6. Inject the new service into the `CurrentWeather` component
7. Call the service from the `init` function of the `CurrentWeather` component
8. Finally, map the API data to the local `ICurrentWeather` type using RxJS functions so that it can be consumed by your component

Creating a new Angular Service

Any code that touches outside of the boundaries of a component should exist in a service; this includes inter-component communication, unless there's a parent-child relationship, and API calls of any kind and any code that cache or retrieve data from a cookie or the browser's localStorage. This is a critical architectural pattern that keeps your application maintainable in the long term. I expand upon this idea in my DevPro MVVM article at `http://bit.ly/MVVMvsMVC`.

To create an Angular service, do this:

1. In the terminal, execute `npx ng g s weather --flat false`
2. Observe the new `weather` folder created:

```
src/app
...
└── weather
    ├── weather.service.spec.ts
    └── weather.service.ts
```

A generated service has two parts:

- `weather.service.spec.ts` contains Jasmine-based unit tests that you can extend to test your service functionality.
- `weather.service.ts` contains the `@Injectable` decorator above the class definition, which makes it possible to inject this service into other components, leveraging Angular's provider system. This will ensure that our service will be a singleton, meaning only instantiated once, no matter how many times it is injected elsewhere.

The service is generated, but it's not automatically provided. To do this, follow these steps:

1. Open `app.module.ts`
2. Type in `WeatherService` inside the providers array
3. Use the auto-fixer to import the class for you:

src/app/app.module.ts

```
...
import { WeatherService } from './weather/weather.service'
...
@NgModule({
  ...
  providers: [WeatherService],
  ...
```

 If you installed the recommended extension **TypeScript Hero**, the import statement will be automatically added for you. You won't have to use the auto-fixer to do it. Going forward, I will not call out the need to import modules.

Inject dependencies

In order to make API calls, you will be leveraging the `HttpClient` module in Angular. The official documentation (`https://angular.io/guide/http`) explains the benefits of this module succinctly:

"With HttpClient, @angular/common/http provides a simplified API for HTTP functionality for use with Angular applications, building on top of the XMLHttpRequest interface exposed by browsers. Additional benefits of HttpClient include testability support, strong typing of request and response objects, request and response interceptor support, and better error handling via APIs based on Observables."

Let's start with importing the `HttpClientModule` in to our app, so we can inject the `HttpClient` within the module into the `WeatherService`:

1. Add `HttpClientModule` to `app.module.ts`, as follows:

   src/app/app.module.ts
   ```
   . . :
   import { HttpClientModule } from '@angular/common/http'
   . . .
   @NgModule({
     . . .
     imports: [
       . . .
       HttpClientModule,
       . . .
   ```

2. Inject `HttpClient` provided by the `HttpClientModule` in the `WeatherService`, as follows:

   src/app/weather/weather.service.ts
   ```
   import { HttpClient } from '@angular/common/http'
   import { Injectable } from '@angular/core'

   @Injectable()
   export class WeatherService {
     constructor(private httpClient: HttpClient) {}
   }
   ```

Now, `httpClient` is ready for use in your service.

Discover OpenWeatherMap APIs

Since `httpClient` is strongly typed, we need to create a new interface that conforms to the shape of the API we'll call. To be able to do this, you need to familiarize yourself with the Current Weather Data API.

1. Read documentation by navigating to `http://openweathermap.org/current`:

OpenWeatherMap Current Weather Data API Documentation

You will be using the API named **By city name**, which allows you to get current weather data by providing the city name as a parameter. So, your web request will look like this:

```
api.openweathermap.org/data/2.5/weather?q={city name},{country
code}
```

2. On the documentation page, click on the link under **Example of API calls**, and you will see a sample response like the following:

```
http://samples.openweathermap.org/data/2.5/weather?q=London,uk&appi
d=b1b15e88fa797225412429c1c50c122a1
{
  "coord": {
    "lon": -0.13,
    "lat": 51.51
  },
  "weather": [
    {
      "id": 300,
      "main": "Drizzle",
      "description": "light intensity drizzle",
      "icon": "09d"
    }
  ],
  "base": "stations",
  "main": {
    "temp": 280.32,
    "pressure": 1012,
    "humidity": 81,
    "temp_min": 279.15,
    "temp_max": 281.15
  },
  "visibility": 10000,
  "wind": {
    "speed": 4.1,
    "deg": 80
  },
  "clouds": {
    "all": 90
  },
  "dt": 1485789600,
  "sys": {
    "type": 1,
    "id": 5091,
    "message": 0.0103,
    "country": "GB",
```

```
    "sunrise": 1485762037,
    "sunset": 1485794875
  },
  "id": 2643743,
  "name": "London",
  "cod": 200
}
```

Given the existing `ICurrentWeather` interface that you have already created, this response contains more information than you need. So you will write a new interface that conforms to the shape of this response, but only specify the pieces of data you will use. This interface will only exist in the `WeatherService` and we won't export it, since the other parts of the application don't need to know about this type.

3. Create a new interface named `ICurrentWeatherData` in `weather.service.ts` between the `import` and `@Injectable` statements

4. The new interface should like this:

src/app/weather/weather.service.ts
```
interface ICurrentWeatherData {
  weather: [{
    description: string,
    icon: string
  }],
  main: {
    temp: number
  },
  sys: {
    country: string
  },
  dt: number,
  name: string
}
```

With the `ICurrentWeatherData` interface, we are defining new anonymous types by adding children objects to the interface with varying structures. Each of these objects can be individually extracted out and defined as their own named interface. Especially, note that `weather` will be an array of the anonymous type that has the `description` and `icon` properties.

Storing environment variables

It's easy to miss, but the sample URL from previous sections contains a required `appid` parameter. You must store this key in your Angular app. You can store it in the weather service, but in reality, applications need to be able to target different sets of resources as they move from development to testing, staging, and production environments. Out of the box, Angular provides two environments: one `prod` and the other one as the default.

Before you can continue, you need to sign up for a free `OpenWeatherMap` account and retrieve your own `appid`. You can read the documentation for `appid` at `http://openweathermap.org/appid` for more detailed information.

1. Copy your `appid`, which will have a long string of characters and numbers
2. Store your `appid` in `environment.ts`
3. Configure `baseUrl` for later use:

```
src/environments/environment.ts
export const environment = {
  production: false,
  appId: 'xxxxxxxxxxxxxxxxxxxxxxxxxxxxxxxx',
  baseUrl: 'http://',
}
```

In code, we use a camel-case `appId` to keep our coding style consistent. Since URL parameters are case-insensitive, `appId` will work as well as `appid`.

Implementing an HTTP GET operation

Now, we can implement the GET call in the Weather service:

1. Add a new function to the `WeatherService` class named `getCurrentWeather`
2. Import the `environment` object
3. Implement the `httpClient.get` function

4. Return the results of the HTTP call:

src/app/weather/weather.service.ts
```
import { environment } from '../../environments/environment'
...
export class WeatherService {
  constructor(private httpClient: HttpClient) { }

  getCurrentWeather(city: string, country: string) {
    return this.httpClient.get<ICurrentWeatherData>(
`${environment.baseUrl}api.openweathermap.org/data/2.5/weather?` +
        `q=${city},${country}&appid=${environment.appId}`
    )
  }
}
```

Note the use of ES2015's String Interpolation feature. Instead of building your string by appending variables to one another like `environment.baseUrl +` `'api.openweathermap.org/data/2.5/weather?q=' + city + ','` `+ country + '&appid=' + environment.appId,` you can use the backtick syntax to wrap `your string`. Inside the backticks, you can have newlines and also directly embed variables into the flow of your string by wrapping them with the `${dollarbracket}` syntax. However, when you introduce a newline in your code, it will be interpreted as a literal newline—\n. In order to break up the string in your code, you may add a backslash \, but then the next line of your code can have no indentation. It is easier to just concatenate multiple templates, as shown in the preceding code sample.

Note the use TypeScript Generics with the get function using the caret syntax like `<TypeName>`. Using generics is development-time quality of life feature. By providing the type information to the function, input and/or return variables types of that function will be displayed as your write your code and validated during development and also at compile time.

Retrieving service data from a component

To be able to use the `getCurrentWeather` function in the `CurrentWeather` component, you need to inject the service into the component:

1. Inject the `WeatherService` into the constructor of the `CurrentWeatherComponent` class

2. Remove the existing code that created the dummy data in the constructor:

src/app/current-weather/current-weather.component.ts
```
constructor(private weatherService: WeatherService) { }
```

3. Call the `getCurrentWeather` function inside the `ngOnInit` function:

src/app/current-weather/current-weather.component.ts
```
ngOnInit() {
  this.weatherService.getCurrentWeather('Bethesda', 'US')
    .subscribe((data) => this.current = data)
}
```

Fair warning, do not expect this code to be working just yet. You should see an error, so let's understand what's going in the next segment.

 Angular components have a rich collection of life cycle hooks that allow you to inject your custom behavior, when a component is being rendered, refreshed, or destroyed. `ngOnInit()` is the most common life cycle hook you will be using. It is only called once, when a component is first instantiated or visited. This is where you will want to perform your service calls. For a deeper understanding of component life cycle hooks, check out the documentation at `https://angular.io/guide/lifecycle-hooks`.

Note that the anonymous function you have passed to `subscribe` is an ES2015 arrow function. If you're not familiar with arrow functions, it may be confusing at first. Arrow functions are actually quite elegant and simple.

Consider the following arrow function:
```
(data) => { this.current = data }
```
You can rewrite it simply as:
```
function(data) { this.current = data }
```

There's a special condition—when you write an arrow function that simply transforms a piece of data, such as this:
```
(data) => { data.main.temp }
```
This function effectively takes `ICurrentWeatherData` as an input and returns the temp property. The return statement is implicit. If you rewrite it as a regular function, it will look like this:
```
function(data) { return data.main.temp }
```

When the `CurrentWeather` component loads, `ngOnInit` will fire once, which will call the `getCurrentWeather` function that returns an object with a type of `Observable<ICurrentWeatherData>`. An Observable, as described in the official documentation, *is the most basic building block of RxJS* that represents an event emitter, which will emit any data received over time with the type of `ICurrentWeatherData`. The `Observable` object by itself is benign and will not cause a network event to be fired unless it is being listened to. You can read more about Observables at `reactivex.io/rxjs/class/es6/Observable.js~Observable.html`.

By calling `.subscribe` on the Observable, you're essentially attaching a listener to the emitter. You've implemented an anonymous function within the `subscribe` method, which will get executed whenever a new piece of data is received and an event is emitted. The anonymous function takes a data object as a parameter, and, the specific implementation in this case, assigns the piece of data to the local variable named current. Whenever current is updated, the template bindings you implemented earlier will pull in the new data and render it on the view. Even though `ngOnInit` executes only once, the subscription to the Observable persists. So whenever there's new data, the current variable will be updated and the view will rerender to display the latest data.

The root cause of the error at hand is that the data that is being emitted is of type `ICurrentWeatherData`; however, our component only understands data that is shaped as described by the `ICurrentWeather` interface. In the next section, you will need to dig deeper into RxJS to understand how best to accomplish that task.

Beware, VS Code and CLI sometimes stop working. As previously noted, as you code, the `npm start` command is running in the integrated terminal of VS Code. Angular CLI, in combination with the Angular Language Service plug-in, continuously watches for code changes and transpiles your TypeScript code to JavaScript, so you can observe your changes with live-reloading in the browser. The great thing is that when you make coding errors, in addition to the red underlining in VS Code, you will also see some red text in the terminal or even the browser, because the transpilation has failed. In most cases, when correcting the error, the red underlining will go away and Angular CLI will automatically retranspile your code and everything will work. However, under certain scenarios, you will note that VS Code will fail to pick typing changes in the IDE, so you won't get autocompletion help or the CLI tool will get stuck with message saying webpack: **Failed to compile.**
You have two main strategies to recover from such conditions:

1. Click on the terminal and hit *Ctrl + C* to stop running the CLI task and restart by executing `npm start`
2. If **#1** doesn't work, quit VS Code with *Alt + F4* for Windows or ⌘ + *Q* for macOS and restart it

Given Angular and VS Code's monthly releases cycles, I'm confident that in time the tooling can only improve.

Transform data using RxJS

RxJS stands for Reactive Extensions, which is a modular library that enables reactive programming, which itself is an asynchronous programming paradigm and allows for manipulation of data streams through transformation, filtering, and control functions. You can think of reactive programming as an evolution of event-based programming.

Understanding Reactive programming

In Event-Driven programming, you would define an event handler and attach it to an event source. In more concrete terms, if you had a **save** button, which exposes an `onClick` event, you would implement a `confirmSave` function, which when triggered, would show a popup to ask the user **Are you sure?**. Look at the following figure for a visualization of this process.

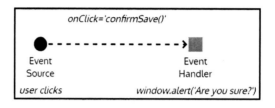

Event-Driven Implementation

In short, you would have an event firing once per user action. If the user clicks on the **save** button many times, this pattern would gladly render as many popups as there are clicks, which doesn't make much sense.

The publish-subscribe (pub/sub) pattern is a different type of event-driven programming. In this case, we can write multiple handlers to act on the result of a given event all simultaneously. Let's say that your app just received some updated data. The publisher will go through its list of subscribers and pass on the updated data to each of them. Refer to the following diagram, how can updated data event trigger an `updateCache` function that can update your local cache with new data, a `fetchDetails` function that can retrieve further details about the data from the server, and also a `showToastMessage` function that can inform the user that the app just received new data. All these events can happen asynchronously; however, the `fetchDetails` and `showToastMessage` functions will be receiving more data than they really need, and it can get really convoluted to try to compose these events in different ways to modify application behavior.

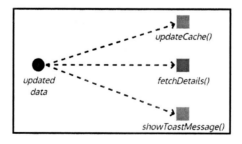

Pub/Sub Pattern Implementation

In reactive programming, everything is treated as a stream. A stream will contain events that happen over time and these events can contain some data or no data. The following diagram visualizes a scenario where your app is listening for mouse clicks from the user. Uncontrolled streams of user clicks are meaningless. You exert some control over this stream by applying the `throttle` function to it, so you only get updates every 250 **milliseconds (ms)**. If you subscribe to this new event, every 250 ms, you will receive a list of click events. You may try to extract some data from each click event, but in this case, you're only interested in the number of click events that happened. We can shape the raw event data into number of clicks using the `map` function.

Further down the stream, we may only be interested in listening for events with two or more clicks in it, so we can use the `filter` function to only act on what is essentially a double-click event. Every time our filter event fires, it means that the user intended to double-click, and you can act on that information by popping up an alert. The true power for streams comes from the fact that you can choose to act on the event at any time as it passes through various control, transformation, and filter functions. You can choose to display click data on an HTML list using `*ngFor` and Angular's `async` pipe, so the user can monitor the types of click data being captured every 250ms.

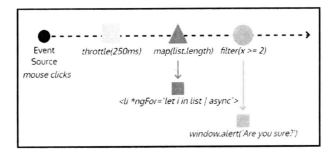

A Reactive Data Stream Implementation

Implementing Reactive transformations

To avoid future mistakes in returning the unintended type of data from your service, you need to update the `getCurrentWeather` function to define the return type to be `Observable<ICurrentWeather>` and import the `Observable` type, as shown:

src/app/weather/weather.service.ts
```
import { Observable } from 'rxjs'
import { ICurrentWeather } from '../interfaces'
...
```

```
export class WeatherService {
  ...
  getCurrentWeather(city: string, country: string):
Observable<ICurrentWeather> {
  }
  ...
}
```

Now, VS Code will let you know that Type `Observable<ICurrentWeatherData>` is not assignable to type `Observable<ICurrentWeather>`:

1. Write a transformation function named `transformToICurrentWeather` that can convert `ICurrentWeatherData` to `ICurrentWeather`

2. Also, write a helper function named `convertKelvinToFahrenheit` that converts the API provided Kelvin temperature to Fahrenheit:

   src/app/weather/weather.service.ts

```
export class WeatherService {
  ...
  private transformToICurrentWeather(data: ICurrentWeatherData):
ICurrentWeather {
    return {
      city: data.name,
      country: data.sys.country,
      date: data.dt * 1000,
      image:
`http://openweathermap.org/img/w/${data.weather[0].icon}.png`,
      temperature: this.convertKelvinToFahrenheit(data.main.temp),
      description: data.weather[0].description
    }
  }

  private convertKelvinToFahrenheit(kelvin: number): number {
    return kelvin * 9 / 5 - 459.67
  }
}
```

Note that you need to be converting the icon property to an image URL at this stage. Doing this in the service helps preserve encapsulation, binding the icon value to the URL in the view template will break the **Separation of concerns** (**SoC**) principle. If you wish to create truly modular, reusable, and maintainable components, you must remain vigilant and strict in terms of enforcing SoC. The documentation for Weather Icons and details of how the URL should be formed, including all the available icons can be found at `http://openweathermap.org/weather-conditions`.

On a separate note, the argument can be made that Kelvin to Fahrenheit conversion is actually a view concern, but we have implemented it in the service. This argument holds water, especially considering that we have a planned feature to be able to toggle between Celsius and Fahrenheit. A counter argument would be that at this time, we only need to display in Fahrenheit and it is part of the job of the weather service to be able to convert the units. This argument makes sense as well. The ultimate implementation will be to write a custom Angular Pipe and apply it in the template. A pipe can easily bind with the planned toggle button as well. However, at this time, we only need to display in Fahrenheit and I would err on the side of *not* over-engineering a solution.

3. Update `ICurrentWeather.date` to the `number` type

While writing the transformation function, you will note that the API returns the date as a number. This number represents time in seconds since the UNIX epoch (timestamp), which is January 1st, 1970 00:00:00 UTC. However, `ICurrentWeather` expects a `Date` object. It is easy enough to convert the timestamp by passing it into the constructor of the `Date` object like `new Date(data.dt)`. This is fine, but also unnecessary, since Angular's `DatePipe` can directly work with the timestamp. In the name of relentless simplicity and maximally leveraging the functionality of the frameworks we use, we will update `ICurrentWeather` to use `number`. There's also a performance and memory benefit to this approach if you're transforming massive amounts of data, but that concern is not applicable here. There's one caveat—JavaScript's timestamp is in milliseconds, but the server value is in seconds, so a simple multiplication during the transformation is still required.

4. Import the RxJS map operator right below the other import statements:

src/app/weather/weather.service.ts
```
import { map } from 'rxjs/operators'
```

 It may seem odd to have to manually import the map operator. RxJS is a very capable framework with a wide API surface. Observable alone has over 200 methods attached to it. Including all of these methods by default creates development time issues with too many functions to choose from and also, it negatively impacts the size of the final deliverable, including app performance and memory use. So you must add each operator you intend to use individually.

5. Apply the map function to data stream returned by httpClient.get method through a pipe

6. Pass the data object into the transformToICurrentWeather function:

src/app/weather/weather.service.ts
```
...
return this.httpClient
  .get<ICurrentWeatherData>(
`http://api.openweathermap.org/data/2.5/weather?q=${city},${country
}&appid=${environment.appId}`
  ).pipe(
    map(data =>
      this.transformToICurrentWeather(data)
    )
  )
...
```

Now incoming data can be transformed as it flows through the stream, ensuring that the OpenWeatherMap Current Weather API data is in the correct shape, so it can be consumed by the CurrentWeather component.

7. Ensure that your app compiles successfully
8. Inspect the results in the browser:

LocalCast Weather

Your city, your forecast, right now!

Current Weather

Bethesda, US Friday, September 22, 2017

67°F

mist

Displaying Live Data from OpenWeatherMap

Finally, you should see that your app is able to pull live data from `OpenWeatherMap` and correctly transform server data into the format you expect.

You have completed the development of Feature 1: **Display Current Location weather information for the current day.** Commit your code and move the card in Waffle to the **Done** column.

9. Finally, we can move this task to the **Done** column:

Waffle.io Kanban Board Status

Summary

Congratulations, in this chapter, you created your first Angular application with a flexible architecture while avoiding over-engineering. This was possible because we first built a road map and codified it in a Kanban board that is visible to your peers and colleagues. We stayed focused on implementing the first feature we put in progress and didn't deviate from the plan.

You can now use Angular CLI and an optimized VS Code development environment to help you reduce the amount of coding you need to do. You can leverage TypeScript anonymous types and observable streams to accurately reshape complicated API data into a simple format without having to create one-use interfaces.

You learned to avoid coding mistakes by proactively declaring input and return types of functions and working with generic functions. You used the date and decimal pipes to ensure that the data is formatted as desired, while keeping formatting-related concerns mostly in the template, where this kind of logic belongs.

Finally, you used interfaces to communicate between components and services without leaking the external data structure to internal components. By applying all these techniques in combination, which Angular, RxJS, and TypeScript have allowed us to do, you have ensured proper separation of concerns and encapsulation. As a result, the `CurrentWeather` component is now a truly reusable and composable component; this is not an easy feat to achieve.

If you don't ship it, it never happened. In the next chapter, we will prepare this Angular app for a production release by troubleshooting application errors, ensuring automated unit and e2e tests pass and containerizing the Angular app with Docker, so it can be published on the web.

3
Prepare Angular App for Production Release

If you don't ship it, it never happened. In the previous chapter, you created a local weather application that can retrieve current weather data. You have created some amount of value; however, if you don't put your app on the web, you end up creating zero value. Delivering something is difficult, delivering something to production is even more difficult. You want to follow a strategy that results in a reliable, high quality, and flexible release.

The app we created in `Chapter 2`, *Create a Local Weather Web Application*, is fragile, has failing unit and **end-to-end** (e2e) tests, and emits console errors. We need to fix the unit tests and harden the application by intentionally introducing errors so that you can see the side-effects of real-life conditions in action using debugging tools. We also need to be able to deliver the frontend app separately from the backend app, which is a very important decoupling to retain the flexibility of being able to push separate app and server updates. In addition, decoupling will ensure that as the various tools and technologies in your application stack inevitably falls out of support or favor, you will be able to replace your frontend or backend without a full rewrite of your system.

In this chapter, you will learn to do the following:

- Run Angular unit and e2e
- Troubleshoot common Angular errors using Chrome Developer Tools
- Guard against null data
- Containerize the app using Docker
- Deploy the app on the web using Zeit Now

Required software is as listed:

- Docker Community Edition Version 17.12
- Zeit Now Account

Angular unit tests

Just because your Angular app launches using `npm start` and seems to work fine, it doesn't mean it is error free or production ready. As covered earlier in Chapter 2, *Create a Local Weather Web Application*, Angular CLI creates a unit test file as you create new components and services, such as `current-weather.component.spec.ts` and `weather.service.spec.ts`.

At their most basic, these unit default unit tests ensure that your new components and services can be properly instantiated in the test harness. Take a look at the following spec file and observe the `should create` test. The framework asserts that component of the `CurrentWeatherComponent` type to not be null or undefined, but be truthy:

src/app/current-weather/current-weather.component.spec.ts
```
describe('CurrentWeatherComponent', () => {
  let component: CurrentWeatherComponent
  let fixture: ComponentFixture<CurrentWeatherComponent>

  beforeEach(
    async(() => {
      TestBed.configureTestingModule({
        declarations: [CurrentWeatherComponent],
      }).compileComponents()
    })
  )

  beforeEach(() => {
    fixture = TestBed.createComponent(CurrentWeatherComponent)
    component = fixture.componentInstance
    fixture.detectChanges()
  })

  it('should create', () => {
    expect(component).toBeTruthy()
  })
})
```

The WeatherService spec contains a similar test. However, you'll note that both types of tests are set up slightly differently:

src/app/weather/weather.service.spec.ts
```
describe('WeatherService', () => {
  beforeEach(() => {
    TestBed.configureTestingModule({
      providers: [WeatherService],
    })
  })

  it('should be created', inject([WeatherService], (service:
WeatherService) => {
      expect(service).toBeTruthy()
    })
  )
})
```

In the WeatherService spec's beforeEach function, the class under test is being configured as a provider and then injected into the test. On the other hand, the CurrentWeatherComponent spec has two beforeEach functions. The first, the beforeEach function declares and compiles the component's dependent modules asynchronously, while the second, the beforeEach function creates a test fixture and starts listening to changes in the component, ready to run the tests once the compilation is complete.

Unit test execution

Angular CLI uses the Jasmine unit testing library to define unit tests and the Karma test runner to execute them. Best of it all, these testing tools are configured to be run out of the box. You may execute the unit tests with the following command:

```
$ npm test
```

The tests will be run by the Karma test runner in a new Chrome browser window. The main benefit of Karma is that it brings live-reloading capabilities similar to what Angular CLI achieves with WebPack when developing your application. You should observe the last message on the **Terminal** to be **Executed 5 of 5 (5 FAILED) ERROR**. This is normal, because we haven't been paying attention to the tests at all, so let's fix them all.

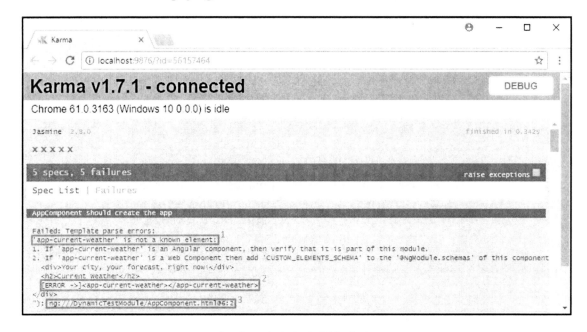

Karma Runner showing Jasmine Unit Test Results

Keep the Karma Runner window open side-by-side with VS Code so that you can instantly see the results of your changes.

Declarations

The **AppComponent should create the app** test is failing. If you observe the error details, you'll see that AppComponent is failing to be created, because **'app-current-weather' is not a known element.** Further, the error occurs if pointed out with a **[ERROR ->]** tag, and the last line spells things out for us, similar to the error originating from line 6 in AppComponent.html.

Include `CurrentWeatherComponent` in the declarations of `app.component.spec.ts`:

src/app/app.component.spec.ts
```
...
TestBed.configureTestingModule({
  declarations: [AppComponent, CurrentWeatherComponent],
}).compileComponents()
...
```

Providers

You'll note that the number of errors didn't go down. Instead, `AppComponent` and `CurrentWeatherComponent` are failing to be created due to a missing provider for `WeatherService`. So, let's add the provider for `WeatherService` to the spec files for both components.

1. Provide the `WeatherService` in the declarations in `app.component.spec.ts`
2. Apply the same code change in `current-weather.component.spec.ts`, as shown:

src/app/app.component.spec.ts
src/app/current-weather/current-weather.component.spec.ts
```
...
  beforeEach(
    async(() => {
      TestBed.configureTestingModule({
        declarations: [...],
        providers: [WeatherService],
        ...
```

You may wonder why `AppComponent` is needing a provider, since the component constructor is not injected with the `WeatherService`. This is happening because `CurrentWeatherComponent` is a hard-coded dependency of `AppComponent`. It is possible to decouple the two components further in two ways: one way is to inject the component dynamically using an `ng-container`, and the other would be to leverage Angular Router and `router-outlet`. The latter option is how you will be structuring the vast majority of your applications and will be covered in the later chapters, and implementing the former option to properly decouple the components is left as an exercise for the reader.

Imports

You still have errors remaining. Let's start by fixing the errors with the WeatherService error first, since it's a dependency of other components. The test is reporting a missing provider for HttpClient. However, we don't want our unit test to make calls over HTTP, so we shouldn't provide the HttpClient, like we did in the previous section. Angular provides a test double for HttpClient named HttpClientTestingModule. In order to leverage it, you must import it, and it will then be automatically provided to the service for you.

Import HttpClientTestingModule below the providers:

src/app/weather/weather.service.spec.ts
```
import { HttpClientTestingModule } from '@angular/common/http/testing'
...
describe('WeatherService', () => {
  beforeEach(() => {
    TestBed.configureTestingModule({
        imports: [HttpClientTestingModule],
        ...
```

Similar to HttpClientTestingModule, there's also a RouterTestingModule and a NoopAnimationsModule that are mock versions of the real services, so the unit tests can focus on only testing the component or service code that you write. In the later chapters, we will also cover how you can write your own mocks.

Now you should only see errors related to AppComponent and CurrentWeatherComponent. These components are failing even though you have provided their dependencies. To understand why this happens and how you can resolve it, you must also understand how to work with test doubles.

Test doubles

Only the code in the class-under-test should be exercised. In case of the CurrentWeatherComponent, we need to ensure that the service code is not executed. For this reason, you should *never* provide the actual implementation of the service. This is also why we used HttpClientTestingModule in the previous section. Since this is our custom service, we must provide our own implementation of a test double.

In this case, we will implement a fake of the service. Since the fake of the `WeatherService` will be used in tests for multiple components, your implementation should be in a separate file. For the sake of maintainability and discoverability of your code base, one class per file is a good rule of thumb to follow. Keeping classes in separate files will save you from committing certain coding sins, like mistakenly creating or sharing global state or standalone functions between two classes, keeping your code properly decoupled in the process:

1. Create a new file `weather/weather.service.fake.ts`

   We need to ensure that APIs for the actual implementation and the test double don't go out of sync over time. We can accomplish this by creating an interface for the service.

2. Add `IWeatherService` to `weather.service.ts`, as shown:

   src/app/weather/weather.service.ts
   ```
   export interface IWeatherService {
     getCurrentWeather(city: string, country: string):
   Observable<ICurrentWeather>
   }
   ```

3. Update `WeatherService` so that it implements the new interface:

   src/app/weather/weather.service.ts
   ```
   export class WeatherService implements IWeatherService
   ```

4. Implement a basic fake in `weather.service.fake.ts`, as follows:

   src/app/weather/weather.service.fake.ts
   ```
   import { Observable, of } from 'rxjs'

   import { IWeatherService } from './weather.service'
   import { ICurrentWeather } from '../interfaces'

   export class WeatherServiceFake implements IWeatherService {
     private fakeWeather: ICurrentWeather = {
       city: 'Bursa',
       country: 'TR',
       date: 1485789600,
       image: '',
       temperature: 280.32,
       description: 'light intensity drizzle',
     }
   ```

```
public getCurrentWeather(city: string, country: string):
Observable<ICurrentWeather> {
    return of(this.fakeWeather)
  }
}
```

We're leveraging the existing `ICurrentWeather` interface that our fake data is correctly shaped, but we must also turn it into an `Observable`. This is easily achieved using `of`, which creates an observable sequence, given the provided arguments.

Now you're ready to provide the fake to `AppComponent` and `CurrentWeatherComponent`.

5. Update providers for both components to use `WeatherServiceFake` so that the fake will be used instead of the actual service:

src/app/app.component.spec.ts
src/app/current-weather/current-weather.component.spec.ts

```
  ...
  beforeEach(
    async(() => {
      TestBed.configureTestingModule({
        ...
        providers: [{ provide: WeatherService, useClass:
WeatherServiceFake}],
        ...
```

As your services and components get more complicated, it's easy to provide an incomplete or inadequate test double. You may see errors such as **NetworkError: Failed to execute 'send' on 'XMLHttpRequest'**, **Can't resolve all parameters**, or **[object ErrorEvent] thrown**. In case of the latter error, click on the **Debug** button in Karma to discover the view error details, which may look like **Timeout - Async callback was not invoked within timeout specified by jasmine**. Unit tests are designed to run in milliseconds, so it should be impossible to actually hit the default 5-second timeout. The issue is almost always with the test setup or configuration.

We have successfully resolved all configuration and setup related issues with our unit tests. Now, we need to fix the unit tests that were generated with the initial code.

Jasmine specs

There are two failing unit tests. In Jasmine lingo, unit tests are called specs, implemented by the `it` function; `it` functions are organized under the `describe` functions that contains helper methods that can execute before or after each test and handle the overall configuration needs of specs. Your app has five specs that have been generated for you, and two of them are now failing.

The first is `AppComponent should have as title 'app'`; however, we deleted this property from `AppComponent`, because we are not using it. In this rare case, we need to do this:

1. Delete the `should have as title 'app'` unit test.

The error message is descriptive enough to let you know what test is failing quickly. This happens, because the description provided to the `describe` function is `'AppComponent'`, and the description provided to the `it` function is `'should have as title "app"'`. Jasmine then appends any parent object's description to the description of the spec. As you write new tests, it is up to you to maintain readable descriptions for your specs.

The next error, `AppComponent should render title in a h1 tag`, is one that we must fix. We render the words `LocalCast Weather` in the h1 tag now.

2. Update the `should render title in a h1 tag` test as shown:

src/app/app.component.spec.ts

```
. . .
it(
  'should render title in a h1 tag',
    . . .
  expect(compiled.querySelector('h1').textContent).toContain('LocalCa
st Weather')
    . . .
```

All unit tests are now successfully passing. We should be performing atomic commits, so let's commit the code changes.

3. Commit your code changes.

In order to achieve effective unit test coverage, you should focus on testing the correctness of functions that contain business logic. This means that you should pay extra attention to adhering to the Single Responsibility and Open/Closed Principles, the S and O in SOLID principles.

Angular e2e tests

In addition to unit tests, Angular CLI also generates and configures e2e tests for your application. While unit tests focus on isolating the class-under-test, e2e tests are about integration testing. Angular CLI leverages Protractor along with WebDriver, so you can write **automated acceptance tests (AAT)** from the perspective of a user interacting with your application on a browser. As a rule of thumb, you should always write an order of magnitude more unit tests than AATs, because your app changes frequently and as a result, AATs are vastly more fragile and expensive to maintain compared to unit tests.

 If the term web driver sounds familiar, it's because it is an evolution of the canonical Selenium WebDriver. As of March 30th, 2017, WebDriver has been proposed as an official web standard at the W3C. You read more about it at `https://www.w3.org/TR/webdriver`. If you're familiar with Selenium from before, you will feel right at home, since a lot of the patterns and practices are near identical.

The CLI provides e2e tests for the initial `AppComponent` and depending on the complexity and the feature set of your application, it is up to you to follow the provided pattern to better organize your tests. There two files generated per component under the `e2e` folder:

```
e2e/app.e2e-spec.ts
import { AppPage } from './app.po'

describe('web-app App', () => {
  let page: AppPage

  beforeEach(() => {
    page = new AppPage()
  })

  it('should display welcome message', () => {
    page.navigateTo()
    expect(page.getParagraphText()).toEqual('Welcome to app!')
  })
})
```

`app.e2e-spec.ts` is written in Jasmine and implements acceptance tests. The
dependent upon the page object (`po`) file, which is defined beside the `spec` file

e2e/app.po.ts
```
import { browser, by, element } from 'protractor'

export class AppPage {
  navigateTo() {
    return browser.get('/')
  }

  getParagraphText() {
    return element(by.css('app-root h1')).getText()
  }
}
```

The page object file encapsulates web driver implementation specifics from the `spec` file.
AATs are the most. This results in easy-to-maintain, human-readable spec files. By
separating concerns at this level, you isolate fragility of AATs to one location. By leveraging
class inheritance, you can build a robust collection of page objects that can be easier to
maintain over time.

e2e test execution

You may execute the e2e tests with the following command in the terminal; ensure that the
`npm test` process is not running:

```
$ npm run e2e
```

You will note that the test execution is different as compared to unit tests.
While you can configure a watcher to continually execute unit tests with
Karma, due to the user-driven and stateful nature of e2e tests, it is not a
good practice to attempt a similar configuration with e2e tests. Running
the tests once and stopping the test harness ensures a clean state with
every run.

e2e spec

After executing the e2e tests, you should see an error message similar to the one here:

```
***************************************************
* Failures *
***************************************************

1) web-app App should display welcome message
   - Expected 'LocalCast Weather' to equal 'Welcome to app!'.

Executed 1 of 1 spec (1 FAILED) in 1 sec.
```

This error is similar to the unit test you fixed earlier:

1. Update the `spec` to expect the correct header as follows:

   e2e/app.e2e-spec.ts
   ```
   expect(page.getParagraphText()).toEqual('LocalCast Weather')
   ```

2. Rerun the tests and they should be passing now:

   ```
   Jasmine started

     web-app App
       √ should display welcome message

   Executed 1 of 1 spec SUCCESS in 1 sec.
   ```

3. Commit your code changes.

Troubleshooting common Angular errors

Our unit tests and e2e tests are now working. In this section, you intentionally introduce an easy-to-make mistake so that you can become familiar with real-life errors that can be happen while developing your applications and gain a solid understanding of the tooling that makes make you an effective developer.

Let's pretend that we made an innocent mistake when copying and pasting the URL from the API documentation page on OpenWeatherMap.org and forgot to add http:// in front of it. This is an easy mistake to make:

src/app/weather/weather.service.ts

```
...
return this.httpClient
   .get<ICurrentWeatherData>(
 `api.openweathermap.org/data/2.5/weather?q=${city},${country}&appid=${envir
onment.appId}`
   ).pipe(map(data => this.transformToICurrentWeather(data)))
...
```

Your app will compile successfully, but when you inspect the results in the browser, you won't see any weather data. In fact, it seems like the CurrentWeather component is not rendering at all, as you can see in the image below:

LocalCast Weather

Your city, your forecast, right now!

Current Weather

CurrentWeather Does Not Render

To find out why, you will need to debug your Angular app.

Debugging with Chrome Developer Tools

As a developer, I use the Google Chrome browser because of its cross-platform and consistent developer tools with helpful extensions.

Open Chrome Developer Tools (dev tools) on macOS by pressing *option* + ⌘ + *I* or on Windows by pressing *F12* or *Ctrl* + *Shift* + *I*.

As a best practice, I code with VS Code and the browser open side by side, while the dev tools are also open in the browser. There are several good reasons for practicing side-by-side development:

- **Fast feedback loops**: With live-reloading, you see the end result of your changes very quickly
- **Laptops**: A lot of developers now do most of their development on a laptop and a second monitor is a luxury
- **Attention to responsive design**: As I have limited space to work with, I constantly pay attention to mobile-first development, fixing desktop layout issues after the fact
- **Awareness of network activity**: To enable me to quickly see any API call errors and also ensure that the amount of data that is being requested remains in line within my expectations
- **Awareness of console errors**: To enable me to quickly react and troubleshoot when new errors are introduced

Observe how side-by-side development looks like:

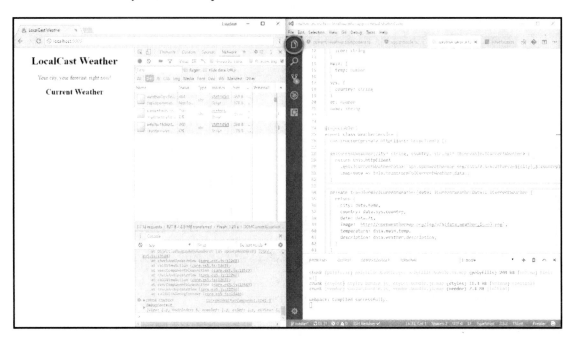

Side-by-side development with live-reloading running

Ultimately, you should do what works best for you. With the side-by-side setup, I frequently find myself toggling VS Code's Explorer on and off and resizing the dev tools pane to a larger or smaller size depending on the specific task at hand. To toggle VS Code's Explorer, click on the Explorer icon circled in the preceding screenshot.

Just as you can do side-by-side development with live-reloading using npm start, you can get the same kind of fast feedback loops for unit testing using npm test.

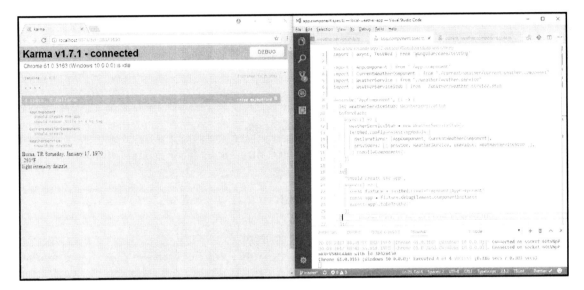

Side-by-side development with unit testing

With the side-by-side unit testing setup, you can become very effective in developing unit tests.

Optimizing Chrome Dev Tools

For the side-by-side development with live-reloading to work well, you need to optimize the default dev tools experience.

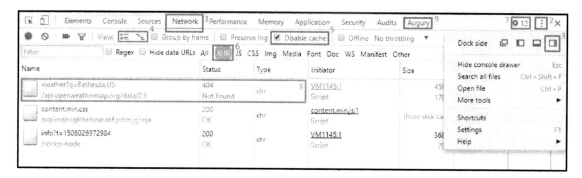

Optimized Chrome Developer Tools

Looking at the preceding figure, you will note that numerous settings and information radiators are highlighted:

1. Have the **Network** tab open by default so that you can see network traffic flowing.

2. Open the dev tools settings by clicking on the ⋮ button.

3. Click on the **right-hand side icon** so that dev tools dock on the right-hand side of Chrome. This layout gives more vertical space, so you can see more network traffic and console events at once. As a side benefit, the left-hand side takes the rough size and shape of a mobile device.

4. **Toggle on** large request rows and **toggle off** overview to see more of the URL and parameters for each request and gain more vertical space.

5. Check the option to **Disable cache**, which will force reload every resource when you refresh a page while the dev tools are open. This prevents bizarre caching errors from ruining your day.

6. You will mostly be interested in seeing XHR calls to various APIs, so click on **XHR** to filter results.

7. Note that you can glance the number of console errors in the upper-right corner as **12**. The ideal number of console errors should be **0** at all times.

8. Note that the top item in the request row is indicating that there's an error with status code **404 Not Found**.

9. Since we are debugging an Angular application, the **Augury** extension has been loaded. I will cover this tool in more detail in `Chapter 7`, *Create a Router-First Line-of-Business App*, when you will be building a far more complicated app.

With your optimized dev tools environment, you can now effectively troubleshoot and resolve the application error from earlier.

Troubleshooting network issues

There are three visible issues with the app at this state:

- The component details aren't displaying
- There are numerous console errors
- The API call is returning a **404 not found** error

Begin by inspecting any network errors, since network errors usually cause knock-on effects:

1. Click on the failing URL in the **Network** tab
2. In the **Details** pane that opens to the right of the URL, click on the **Preview** tab
3. You should see this:

```
Cannot GET /api.openweathermap.org/data/2.5/weather
```

By just observing this error message, you will likely miss the fact that you forgot to add the `http://` prefix to the URL. The bug is subtle and certainly not glaringly obvious.

4. Hover over the URL and observe the full URL, as shown:

Inspecting Network Errors

As you can see, now the bug is glaringly obvious. In this view, we get to see the full URL, and it becomes clear that the URL defined in `weather.service.ts` is not fully qualified, so Angular is attempting to load the resource from its parent server, hosted on `localhost:5000`, instead of going over the web to the right server.

Investigating console errors

Before you fix this issue, it is worthwhile to understand the knock-on effects of the failing API call:

    1. Observe the console errors:

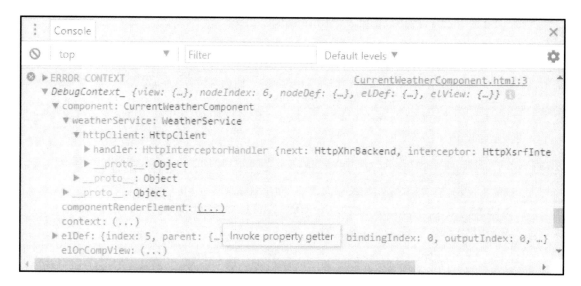

Dev Tools Console Error Context

The first element of note here is the **ERROR CONTEXT** object, which has a property named **DebugContext_**. The **DebugContext_** contains a detailed snapshot of the current state of your Angular application when the error happened. The information contained within **DebugContext_** is light years ahead of the amount of mostly unhelpful error messages AngularJS generates.

Properties that have the value (**...**) are property getters, and you must click on them to load their details. For example, if you click on the ellipsis for **componentRenderElement**, it will be populated with the **app-current-weather element**. You can expand the element to inspect the runtime condition of the component.

2. Now scroll to the top of the console
3. Observe the first error:

> **ERROR TypeError: Cannot read property 'city' of undefined**

You have probably encountered the `TypeError` before. This error is caused by trying to access the property of an object that is not defined. In this case, `CurrentWeatherComponent.current` is not assigned to with an object, because the http call is failing. Since `current` is not initialized and the template blindly tries to bind to its properties like `{{current.city}}`, we get a message saying **property 'city' of undefined** cannot be read. This is the kind of knock-on effect that can create many unpredictable side-effects in your application. You must proactively code to prevent this condition.

Karma, Jasmine, and Unit Testing errors

When running tests with the `ng test` command, you will encounter some high-level errors that can mask the root cause of the actual underlying errors.

The general approach to resolving errors should be inside out, resolving child component issues first and leaving parent and root components for last.

NetworkError

Network errors can be caused by a multitude of underlying issues:

> **NetworkError: Failed to execute 'send' on 'XMLHttpRequest': Failed to load 'ng:///DynamicTestModule/AppComponent.ngfactory.js'.**

Working inside out, you should implement test doubles of services and provide the fakes to the appropriate components, as covered in the previous section. However, in parent components, you may still encounter errors even if you correctly provided fakes. Refer to the section on dealing with generic error events to uncover the underlying issues.

Generic ErrorEvents

Error events are generic errors that hide the underlying cause:

```
[object ErrorEvent] thrown
```

To expose the root cause of a generic error, implement a new `test:debug` script:

1. Implement `test:debug`, as shown, in `package.json`:

   package.json
   ```
   ...
   "scripts": {
     ...
     "test:debug": "ng test --sourcemaps=false",
     ...
   }
   ```

2. Execute `npm run test:debug`
3. Now the Karma runner will likely reveal the underlying issue
4. If necessary, follow the stack trace to find the child component that may be causing the issue

If this strategy is not helpful, you may be able to glean more information on what's going wrong by break point debugging your unit tests.

Debugging with Visual Studio Code

You can also debug your Angular application, Karma, and Protractor tests from directly within Visual Studio Code. First, you need to configure the debugger to work with a Chrome debugging environment, as illustrated:

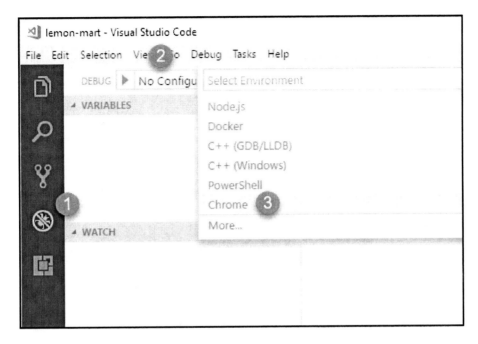

VS Code Debugging Setup

1. Click on the **Debug** pane
2. Expand the **No Configurations** dropdown and click on **Add Configuration...**
3. In the **Select Environment** select box, select **Chrome**

   This will create a default configuration in the `.vscode/launch.json` file. We will modify this file to add three separate configurations.

4. Replace the contents of `launch.json` with the following configuration:

   .vscode/launch.json

```
{
  "version": "0.2.0",
  "configurations": [
    {
      "name": "npm start",
      "type": "chrome",
      "request": "launch",
      "url": "http://localhost:5000/#",
      "webRoot": "${workspaceRoot}",
      "runtimeArgs": [
        "--remote-debugging-port=9222"
        ],
```

```
          "sourceMaps": true
        },
        {
          "name": "npm test",
          "type": "chrome",
          "request": "launch",
          "url": "http://localhost:9876/debug.html",
          "webRoot": "${workspaceRoot}",
          "runtimeArgs": [
            "--remote-debugging-port=9222"
            ],
          "sourceMaps": true
        },
        {
          "name": "npm run e2e",
          "type": "node",
          "request": "launch",
          "program":
    "${workspaceRoot}/node_modules/protractor/bin/protractor",
          "protocol": "inspector",
          "args": ["${workspaceRoot}/protractor.conf.js"]
        }
      ]
    }
```

5. Execute the relevant CLI command like `npm start`, `npm test`, or `npm run e2e` before you start the debugger

6. On the **Debug** page, in the **Debug** dropdown, select **npm start** and click on the green play icon

7. Observe that a Chrome instance has launched

8. Set a break point on a `.ts` file

9. Perform the action in the app to trigger the break point

10. If all goes well, Chrome will report that the code has been **Paused in Visual Studio Code**

 At the time of publication, this method of debugging doesn't reliably work. I had to manually set a break point in **Chrome Dev Tools | Sources** tab, finding the same `.ts` file under the `webpack://.` folder, which correctly triggered the break point in VS Code. However, this renders the entire benefit of using VS Code to debug code useless. For more information, follow the Angular CLI section on VS Code Recipes on GitHub at https://github.com/Microsoft/vscode-recipes.

Null guarding in Angular

In JavaScript, the `undefined` and `null` values are a persistent issue that must be proactively dealt with every step of the way. There are multiple ways to guard against `null` values in Angular:

1. Property Initialization
2. Safe Navigation Operator `?.`
3. Null Guarding with `*ngIf`

Property initialization

In statically-typed languages such as Java, it is drilled into you that proper variable initialization/instantiation is the key to error free operation. So let's try that in `CurrentWeatherComponent` by initializing current with default values:

`src/app/current-weather/current-weather.component.ts`
```
constructor(private weatherService: WeatherService) {
  this.current = {
    city: '',
    country: '',
    date: 0,
    image: '',
    temperature: 0,
    description: '',
  }
}
```

The outcome of these changes will reduce console errors from 12 to 3, at which point you will only be seeing API call related errors. However, the app itself will not be in a presentable state, as you can see below:

LocalCast Weather

Your city, your forecast, right now!

Current Weather

, Wednesday, December 31, 1969
0°F

Results of Property Initialization

To make this view presentable to user, we will have to code for default values on every property on the template. So by fixing the null guarding issue by initialization, we created a default value handling issue. Both the initialization and the default value handling are $O(n)$ scale tasks for developers. At its best, this strategy will be annoying to implement and at its worst, highly ineffective and error prone, requiring, at minimum, $O(2n)$ effort per property.

Safe navigation operator

Angular implements the safe navigation operation ?. to prevent unintended traversals of undefined objects. So, instead of writing initialization code and having to deal with template values, let's just update the template:

```
src/app/current-weather/current-weather.component.html
<div>
  <div>
    <span>{{current?.city}}, {{current?.country}}</span>
    <span>{{current?.date | date:'fullDate'}}</span>
  </div>
  <div>
    <img [src]='current?.image'>
    <span>{{current?.temperature}}°F</span>
  </div>
  <div>
    {{current?.description}}
  </div>
</div>
```

This time, we didn't have to make up defaults, and we let Angular deal with displaying undefined bindings. You will note that just like the initialization fix, the errors have been reduced from 12 to 3. The app itself is in a somewhat better shape. There's no more confusing data being displayed; however, it still is not in a presentable state, as shown below:

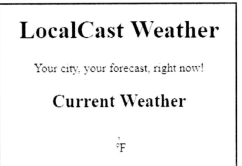

Results of Safe Navigation Operator

You can probably imagine ways where the safe navigation operator can come in handy, in far more complicated scenarios. However, when deployed at scale, this type of coding still requires, at minimum, *O(n)* level of effort to implement.

Null guarding with *ngIf

The idea strategy will be to use `*ngIf`, which is a structural directive, meaning Angular will stop traversing DOM tree elements beyond a falsy statement.

In the `CurrentWeather` component, we can easily check to see whether the `current` variable is null or undefined before attempting to render the template:

1. Update the topmost `div` element with `*ngIf` to check whether `current` is an object, as shown:

   src/app/current-weather/current-weather.component.html
   ```
   <div *ngIf="current">
     ...
   </div>
   ```

Now observe the console log and that no errors are being reported. You always ensure that your Angular application reports zero console errors. If you're still seeing errors in the console log, ensure that you have correctly reverted the OpenWeather URL to its correct state or kill and restart your npm start process. I highly recommend that you resolve any console errors before moving on. Once you've fixed all errors, ensure that you commit your code again.

2. Commit your code.

Containerizing the app using Docker

Docker docker.io is an *open platform* for developing, shipping, and running applications. Docker combines a *lightweight* container virtualization platform with workflows and tooling that help manage and deploy applications. The most obvious difference between **Virtual Machines (VMs)** and Docker containers are that VMs usually are dozens of gigabytes in size and require gigabytes of memory, whereas containers are megabytes in disk and memory size requirements. Furthermore, the Docker platform abstracts away host **operating system (OS)** level configuration settings, so every piece of configuration that is needed to successfully run an application is encoded within the human-readable Dockerfile format, as demonstrated here:

```
Dockerfile
FROM duluca/minimal-node-web-server:8.11.1
WORKDIR /usr/src/app
COPY dist public
```

The preceding file describes a new container that inherits from a container named duluca/minimal-node-web-server, changes the working directory to /usr/src/app, and then copies the contents of dist folder from your development environment into the container's public folder. In this case, the parent image is configured with an Express.js server to act as a web server to serve the content inside the public folder. Refer to the following diagram for a visual representation of what's happening:

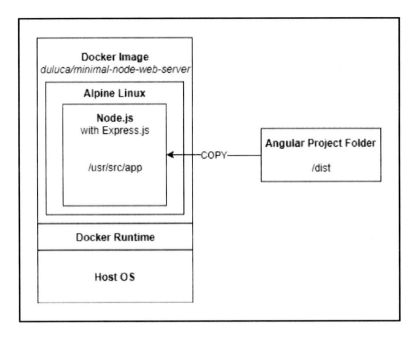

Context of a Docker Image

At the base layer is our host OS, such as Windows or macOS that runs the Docker runtime, which will be installed in the next section. The Docker runtime is capable of running self-contained Docker images, which is defined by the aforementioned `Dockerfile`. `duluca/minimal-node-web-server` is based off of the lightweight Linux operating system Alpine. Alpine is a completely pared down version of Linux that doesn't come with any GUI, drivers or even most CLI tools you may expect from a Linux system. As a result, the OS is around only ~5 MB in size. The base package then installs Node.js, which itself is around ~10 MB in size and my custom Node.js-based Express.js web server, resulting in a tiny ~15 MB image. The Express server is configured to serve the contents of the `/usr/src/app` folder. In the preceding `Dockerfile`, we merely copy the contents of the `/dist` folder in our development environment and place it into the `/usr/src/app` folder. We will later build and execute this image, which will run our Express web server containing the output of our `dist` folder.

The beauty of Docker is that you can navigate to `https://hub.docker.com`, search for `duluca/minimal-node-web-server`, read its `Dockerfile`, and trace its origins all the way back to the original base image that is the foundation of the web server. I encourage you to vet every Docker image you use in this manner to understand what exactly it brings to the table for your needs. You may find it either overkill or has features you never knew about that can make your life a lot easier. Note that the parent images require a specific version of `duluca/minimal-node-web-server` at `8.11.1`. This is quite intentional, and as the reader, you should choose the latest available version of a Docker image you find. However, if you don't specify a version number, you will always get the latest version of the image. As more versions of an image is published, you may pull a future version that may break your application. For this reason, always specify a version number for images you're depending on.

One such case is the HTTPS redirection support that is baked into `duluca/minimal-node-web-server`. You can spend countless hours trying to set up a nginx proxy to do the same thing, when all you need to do is add the following line to your Dockerfile:

```
ENV ENFORCE_HTTPS=xProto
```

Just like npm packages, Docker can bring great convenience and value, but you must take care to understand the tools you are working with.

In `Chapter 11`, *Highly-Available Cloud Infrastructure on AWS*, I mention the use of a lower footprint docker image based on Nginx. If you're comfortable configuring `nginx`, you can use `duluca/minimal-nginx-web-server` as your base image.

Installing Docker

In order to be able to build and run containers, you must first install the Docker execution environment on your computer.

Windows support of Docker can be challenging. You must have a PC with a CPU that supports virtualization extensions, which is not a guarantee on laptops. You must also have a Pro version of Windows with Hyper-V enabled. On the flip side, Windows Server 2016 has native support for Docker, which is an unprecedented amount of support shown by Microsoft toward the industry initiative to adopt Docker and containerization.

1. Install Docker by executing the following command:

   For Windows:

   ```
   PS> choco install docker docker-for-windows -y
   ```

   For macOS:

   ```
   $ brew install docker
   ```

2. Execute `docker -v` to verify the installation.

Setting up Docker scripts

Now, let's configure some Docker scripts that you can use to automated the building, testing, and publishing of your container. I have developed a set of scripts called **npm Scripts for Docker** that work on Windows 10 and macOS. You can get the latest version of these scripts at `bit.ly/npmScriptsForDocker`:

1. Sign up for a Docker Hub account on `https://hub.docker.com/`
2. Create a public (free) repository for your application

> Unfortunately, at the time of publication, Zeit doesn't support private Docker Hub repositories, so your only alternative is to publish your container publicly. If your image must remain private, I encourage you to set up an AWS ECS environment as described in `Chapter 11`, *Highly-Available Cloud Infrastructure on AWS*. You can keep tabs on the issue by visiting Zeit Now's documentation at `zeit.co/docs/deployment-types/docker`.

3. Update `package.json` to add a new config property with the following configuration properties:

   package.json
   ```
   ...
   "config": {
     "imageRepo": "[namespace]/[repository]",
     "imageName": "custom_app_name",
     "imagePort": "0000"
   },
   ...
   ```

The namespace will be your DockerHub username. You will be defining what your repository is called during creation. An example image repository variable should look like `duluca/localcast-weather`. The image name is for easy identification of your container, while using Docker commands such as `docker ps`. I will call mine just `localcast-weather`. The port will define which port should be used to expose your application from inside the container. Since we use `5000` for development, pick a different one, like `8080`.

4. Add Docker scripts to `package.json` by copy-pasting the scripts from `bit.ly/npmScriptsForDocker`. Here's an annotated version of the scripts that explains each function.

Note that with npm scripts, the `pre` and `post` keywords are used to execute helper scripts, respectively, before or after the execution of a given script and scripts are intentionally broken into smaller pieces to make it easier to read and maintain them:

package.json

```
. . .
  "scripts": {
    . . .
    "predocker:build": "npm run build",
    "docker:build": "cross-conf-env docker image build . -t
$npm_package_config_imageRepo:$npm_package_version",
    "postdocker:build": "npm run docker:tag",
    . . .
```

`npm run docker:build` will build your Angular application in `pre`, then build the Docker image using the `docker image build` command and tag the image with a version number in post:

package.json

```
    . . .
    "docker:tag": " cross-conf-env docker image tag
$npm_package_config_imageRepo:$npm_package_version
$npm_package_config_imageRepo:latest",
    . . .
```

`npm run docker:tag` will tag an already built Docker image using the version number from the `version` property in `package.json` and the `latest` tag:

package.json

```
    . . .
    "docker:run": "run-s -c docker:clean docker:runHelper",
    "docker:runHelper": "cross-conf-env docker run -e
NODE_ENV=local --name $npm_package_config_imageName -d -p
$npm_package_config_imagePort:3000 $npm_package_config_imageRepo",
    . . .
```

`npm run docker:run` will remove any existing, prior version of an image and run the already built image using the `docker run` command. Note that the `imagePort` property is used as the external port of the Docker image, which is mapped to the internal port of the image that the Node.js server listens to, port 3000:

package.json

```
    . . .
    "predocker:publish": "echo Attention! Ensure `docker login` is
correct.",
    "docker:publish": "cross-conf-env docker image push
$npm_package_config_imageRepo:$npm_package_version",
    "postdocker:publish": "cross-conf-env docker image push
$npm_package_config_imageRepo:latest",
    . . .
```

`npm run docker:publish` will publish a built image to the configured repository, in this case, Docker Hub, using the `docker image push` command. First, the versioned image is published, followed by one tagged with `latest` in post:

package.json

```
    . . .
    "docker:clean": "cross-conf-env docker rm -f
$npm_package_config_imageName",
    . . .
```

`npm run docker:clean` will remove a previously built version of the image from your system, using the `docker rm -f` command:

package.json
```
. . .
    "docker:taillogs": "cross-conf-env docker logs -f
$npm_package_config_imageName",
    . . .
```

`npm run docker:taillogs` will display the internal console logs of a running Docker instance using the `docker log -f` command, a very useful tool when debugging your Docker instance:

package.json
```
    . . .
    "docker:open:win": "echo Trying to launch on Windows && timeout
2 && start http://localhost:%npm_package_config_imagePort%",
    "docker:open:mac": "echo Trying to launch on MacOS && sleep 2
&& URL=http://localhost:$npm_package_config_imagePort && open
$URL",
    . . .
```

`npm run docker:open:win` or `npm run docker:open:mac` will wait for 2 seconds and then launch the browser with the correct URL to your application using the `imagePort` property:

package.json
```
    . . .
    "predocker:debug": "run-s docker:build docker:run",
    "docker:debug": "run-s -cs docker:open:win docker:open:mac
docker:taillogs"
  },
. . .
```

`npm run docker:debug` will build your image and run an instance of it in `pre`, open the browser, and then start displaying the internal logs of the container.

5. Install two development dependencies that are needed to ensure cross-platform functionality of the scripts:

```
$ npm i -D cross-conf-env npm-run-all
```

6. Customize the pre-build script to execute unit and e2e tests before building the image:

package.json
```
"predocker:build": "npm run build -- --prod --output-path dist && npm test -- --watch=false && npm run e2e",
```

Note that `npm run build` is provided the `--prod` argument, which achieves two things:
1. Development time payload of ~2.5 MB is optimized down to ~73kb or less
2. The configuration items defined in `src/environments/environment.prod.ts` is used at runtime

7. Update `src/environments/environment.prod.ts` to look like using your own `appId` from `OpenWeather`:

```
export const environment = {
  production: true,
  appId: '01ffxxxxxxxxxxxxxxxxxxxxxxxxxxxx',
  baseUrl: 'https://',
}
```

We are modifying how `npm test` is executed, so the tests are run only once and the tool stops executing. The `--watch=false` option is provided to achieve this behavior, as opposed to the development-friendly default continuous execution behavior. In addition `npm run build` is provided with `--output-path dist` to ensure that `index.html` is published at the root of the folder.

8. Create a new file named `Dockerfile` with no file-extensions

9. Implement the `Dockerfile`, as shown:

Dockerfile
```
FROM duluca/minimal-node-web-server:8.11.1
WORKDIR /usr/src/app
COPY dist public
```

Be sure to inspect the contents of your `dist` folder. Ensure that `index.html` is at the root of `dist`. Otherwise ensure that your `Dockerfile` copies the folder that has `index.html` at its root.

10. Execute `npm run predocker:build` to ensure that your application changes have been successful

11. Execute `npm run docker:build` to ensure that your image builds successfully

While you can run any of the provided scripts individually, you really only need to remember two of them going forward:

- **npm run docker:debug** will test, build, tag, run, tail and launch your containerize app in a new browser window for testing
- **npm run docker:publish** will publish the image you just built and test to the online Docker repository

12. Execute `docker:debug` in your terminal:

$ npm run docker:debug

You will note that the scripts display errors in the Terminal window. These are not necessarily indicators of a failure. The scripts are not polished, so they attempt both Windows and macOS compatible scripts parallelly, and during a first build, the clean command fails, because there's nothing to clean. By the time you read this, I may have published better scripts; if not, you're more than welcome to submit a pull request.

A successful `docker:debug` run should result in a new in-focus browser window with your application and the server logs being tailed in the terminal, as follows:

```
Current Environment: local.
Server listening on port 3000 inside the container
Attenion: To access server, use http://localhost:EXTERNAL_PORT
EXTERNAL_PORT is specified with 'docker run -p EXTERNAL_PORT:3000'.
See 'package.json->imagePort' for th
e default port.
GET / 304 12.402 ms - -
GET /styles.d41d8cd98f00b204e980.bundle.css 304 1.280 ms - -
GET /inline.202587da3544bd761c81.bundle.js 304 11.117 ms - -
GET /polyfills.67d068662b88f84493d2.bundle.js 304 9.269 ms - -
GET /vendor.c0dc0caeb147ad273979.bundle.js 304 2.588 ms - -
GET /main.9e7f6c5fdb72bb69bb94.bundle.js 304 3.712 ms - -
```

You should always run `docker ps` to check whether your image is running, when it was last updated, or if it is clashing with the existing images claiming the same port.

13. Execute `docker:publish` in your terminal:

```
$ npm run docker:publish
```

You should observe a successful run in the Terminal window like this:

```
The push refers to a repository [docker.io/duluca/localcast-
weather]
60f66aaaaa50: Pushed
...
latest: digest:
sha256:b680970d76769cf12cc48f37391d8a542fe226b66d9a6f8a7ac81ad77be4
f58b size: 2827
```

 Over time, your local Docker cache may grow to a significant size, that is, on my laptop, roughly 40 GB over two years. You can use the `docker image prune` and `docker container prune` commands to reduce the size of your cache. For more detailed information, refer to the documentation at `https://docs.docker.com/config/pruning`.

Let's look into an easier way to interact with Docker next.

Docker extension in VS Code

Another way to interact with Docker images and containers is through VS Code. If you have installed the `PeterJausovec.vscode-docker` Docker extension, as suggested in `Chapter 2`, *Create a Local Weather Web Application*, you will see an expandable title named **DOCKER** in the **Explorer** pane of VS Code, as pointed out with an arrow in the following screenshot:

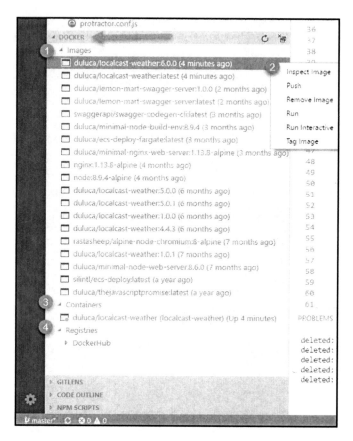

Docker extension in VS Code

Let's go through some of the functionality provided by the extension:

1. **Images** contains a list of all the container snapshots that exist on your system
2. Right-clicking on a Docker image brings up a context menu to run various operations on it, like run, push and tag

3. **Containers** list all executable Docker containers that exist on your system, which you start, stop or attach to

4. **Registries** display the registries that you're configured to connect to, like DockerHub or AWS Elastic Container Registry

While the extension makes it easier to interact with Docker, **npm Scripts for Docker** automate a lot of the chores related to building, tagging and testing and image. They are cross-platform and will work equally well in a continuous integration environment.

You may find it confusing to interact with npm scripts in general through the CLI. Let's look at VS Code's npm script support next.

NPM Scripts in VS Code

VS Code provides support for npm scripts out of the box. In order to enable npm script explorer, open VS Code settings and ensure that the `"npm.enableScriptExplorer":` `true` property is present. Once you do, you will see an expandable title named **NPM SCRIPTS** in the **Explorer** pane, as pointed out with an arrow here:

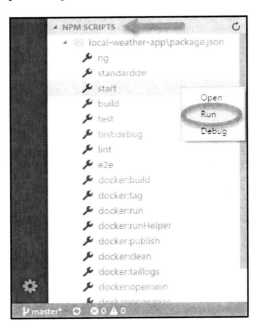

NPM Scripts in VS Code

You can click on any script to launch the line that contains the script in `package.json` or right-click and select **Run** to execute the script.

Deploying containerized app

If delivering something to production is difficult from a coding perspective, it is extremely difficult to do it right from an infrastructure perspective. In the later chapters, I will cover how to provision a world-class AWS **Elastic Container Service (ECS)** infrastructure for your applications, but that won't help if you need to quickly demonstrate an idea. Enter, Zeit Now.

Zeit Now

Zeit Now, `https://zeit.co/now`, is a multi-cloud service that enables real-time global deployments of applications directly from the CLI. Now works with applications that either correctly implement `package.json` or a `Dockerfile`. Even though we have done both, we will prefer to deploy our Docker image, because a lot more magic is applied behind the scenes to make a `package.json` deployment work, whereas your Docker image can be deployed anywhere, including AWS ECS.

Configuring the Now CLI tool

Now, let's configure Zeit Now to work on your repository:

1. Install Zeit Now by executing `npm i -g now`
2. Ensure correct installation by executing `now -v`
3. Create a new folder under `local-weather-app` called `now`
4. Create a new `Dockerfile` under the new `now` folder
5. Implement the file to pull from the image you just published:

   now/Dockerfile
   ```
   FROM duluca/localcast-weather:6.0.1
   ```

6. Finally, execute the now command in your terminal and follow the instructions to the finish configuration:

```
$ now
> No existing credentials found. Please log in:
> We sent an email to xxxxxxxx@gmail.com. Please follow the steps
provided
  inside it and make sure the security code matches XXX XXXXX.
√ Email confirmed
√ Fetched your personal details
> Ready! Authentication token and personal details saved in
"~\.now"
```

Deploying

Deploying on Zeit Now is very easy:

1. Change your working directory to now and execute the command:

   ```
   $ now --docker --public
   ```

2. In the Terminal window, the tool will report its progress and the URL from which you can access your now published app:

   ```
   > Deploying C:\dev\local-weather-app\web-app\now under duluca
   > Ready! https://xxxxxxxxxxxxx.now.sh [3s]
   > Initializing...
   > Building
   > ▲ docker build
   Sending build context to Docker daemon 2.048 kBkB
   > Step 1 : FROM duluca/localcast-weather
   > latest: Pulling from duluca/localcast-weather
   ...
   > Deployment complete!
   ```

3. Navigate to the URL listed on the second line and verify the publication of your app.

   Note that if you've made a configuration error along the way, your browser may display an error saying **This page is trying to load unsafe scripts**, allow and reload to see your app.

You can explore Zeit Now's paid features, which allow for advanced features such as automated scaling for your application.

Congratulations, you are app is live on the internet!

Summary

In this chapter, you mastered unit and e2e test configuration and setup. You optimized your troubleshooting tools and became aware of the common Angular errors you will encounter while developing applications. You learned how to best avoid Angular console errors by guarding against null data. You configured your system to work with Docker and successfully containerized your web application with its own dedicated web server. You configured your project with npm scripts for Docker that can be leveraged by any team member. Finally, you have successfully delivered a web application in the cloud.

Now you know what takes to build a production-ready Angular application that is reliable, resilient, and containerized to allow for a flexible deployment strategy. In the next chapter, we will improve the apps feature set and make it look great using Angular Material.

4
Staying Up to Date with Angular Updates

Delivering a secure, fast, and consistent experience on the web across dozens of combinations of different browsers in differing versions is not an easy feat. Angular exists to make this possible; however, the internet is a constantly evolving landscape of competing technologies and vendors. The Angular team has committed to updating the platform on a regular basis, but it's up to you to keep up to date with patch, minor and major releases of Angular.

Angular is a platform that aims to minimize the effort of upgrading from version to version, providing helpful tools and guides, most importantly in a deterministic release cadence and ample communication regarding deprecated features that allows for proper planning to remain up to date.

You must plan to keep up to date with Angular in a thoughtful and planned manner. Such a strategy will result in maximizing the benefit you gain by using a platform like Angular, keeping bugs and divergent experiences across browsers to a minimum. At its most extreme, you have a choice: either retain hundreds of testers to test your web applications across all major browsers and their recent versions and dozens of developers to maintain compatibility issues or keep your version of Angular (or your choice of framework) up to date. Keep in mind that ultimately, it's up to you to ensure the quality of the product you deliver.

Feel free to skip this chapter now and get back to it when a minor or major version of Angular is released or keep on reading to see what a potential upgrade process may look like.

In the chapter, we will go over the following topics:

- Updating Node
- Updating npm and Global Packages
- Updating Angular
- Addressing security vulnerabilities
- Updating your web server

A brief history of web frameworks

Is it important to consider why we use frameworks such as Angular or React in the first place? Before Angular, there was AngularJS and Backbone, both of which heavily relied on the framework that came before the ubiquitous jQuery. In the early days of the existence of jQuery, back in 2006, its purpose was quite obvious for web developers—to create a consistent API surface to enable DOM manipulation. Browser vendors are supposed to implement various web technologies like HTML, JavaScript/EcmaScript and CSS, as standardized by The World Wide Web Consortium (W3C). Internet Explorer, the only browser vast majority of internet users relied on at the time, acted as a vehicle to push proprietary technologies and APIs to retain its edge as the go-to browser. First, Mozilla's Firefox and then Google's Chrome browsers successfully gained significant market. However, the breakneck speed at which new browser versions started being released, competing interests and differing qualities, versions and names of implementations of draft and ratified standards created untenable conditions for developers to deliver consistent experiences on the web. So instead of repeatedly writing code to check browser versions, you could just use jQuery and you were good to go, which hid away all the complexities of vendor-specific implementations, missing features by gracefully filling in the gaps.

It was still cumbersome to create rich user experiences in jQuery, and frameworks like Backbone and AngularJS made it more cost effective to build web applications that had a native feel and speed to them. However, browsers kept changing, so did jQuery and unforeseen effects of early design decisions, as with evolving standards, resulted in two new and different approaches to building web application in Angular and React. The transition from AngularJS to Angular has been jarring experience for the entire community, including the Angular development team, but it had to be a big-bang release to create a platform that could evolve. Now, the new Angular platform is committed to stay up to date with incremental releases delivered on a regular basis to avoid the mistakes of the past.

Updating Node

Even if you are not using Node.js as a web server, you're already using it to install your dependencies through npm and execute your build and testing tasks through Node.js-based packages such as WebPack, Gulp, or Grunt. Node.js is lightweight cross-platform execution environment that makes most modern development tooling work seamlessly. Due to its nature, Node sits at the very bottom of your tech stack outside of your host operating system. It is important to keep your version of Node up-to-date to get benefits of security, speed, and feature updates.

Node.js is maintained in two branches: **Long Term Support (LTS)** version and Current. Odd numbered releases are one off, risky releases, that are not planned for an LTS phases. Even numbered releases are first released as Current, then phases in to LTS.

For maximum stability and to avoid unforeseen issues, I highly recommend sticking to the LTS version of Node:

1. Check your current version by running this:

   ```
   node -v
   v8.9.0
   ```

You can view further information on the latest release at https://nodejs. org. Apart from planned releases, this website will often contain information about out-of-band critical security patches for various Node.js releases.

2. If you're on an odd-numbered or non-LTS release channel remove your existing installation of Node:

   On Windows, ensure that you're running PowerShell with Administrative privileges:

   ```
   PS> choco uninstall node
   ```

   On macOS, if your environment is set up correctly, you shouldn't need to add sudo to your command:

   ```
   $ brew uninstall --ignore-dependencies node
   ```

3. On Windows, to upgrade to the latest LTS version, execute the following command:

```
PS> choco upgrade nodejs-lts
```

4. On macOS, if you don't already have Node 8 installed, you'll first have to execute the following:

```
$ brew install node@8
```

5. If you're already on version 8, then execute this:

```
$ brew upgrade node@8
```

 Note that version 10 is planned to be the next LTS release in October 2018, so you'll need to keep this in mind before running the brew install command.

If you're on macOS, refer to the next section for an easier way to manage your version of Node with the n tool. Otherwise, skip to the section on *Updating Npm*.

n - Node version manager for macOS

On macOS, HomeBrew doesn't have an LTS-specific channel for Node, and if the latest version is an odd-numbered version, you'll find yourself in an undesirable position. If you execute brew upgrade node by mistake and upgrade to an odd version, recovering from this mistake is annoying at best. The process includes potentially breaking other CLI tools by running a command like this:

```
$ brew uninstall --ignore-dependencies node
```

After your initial Node install through brew, I highly recommend leveraging the feature rich, and interactive Node version manager tool, n, created by ex-Node maintainer TJ Holowaychuk:

1. Install n:

```
$ npm install -g n
```

2. Execute n, which will display a list of all versions of Node previously downloaded to your computer with the current version marked:

```
$ n

    . . .
    node/8.2.1
    node/8.3.0
    node/8.4.0
  o node/8.9.0
```

3. Execute n lts to install the latest LTS build:

```
$ n lts
   install : node-v8.9.3
      mkdir : /usr/local/n/versions/node/8.9.3
      fetch :
https://nodejs.org/dist/v8.9.3/node-v8.9.3-darwin-x64.tar.gz
################################################################
##### 100.0%
   installed : v8.9.3
```

With n, you can quickly switch between Node versions.

In the section, we will go over how you can keep npm up to date.

Updating npm and Global npm packages

If Node is the lowest-level tool in your tech stack, npm and global npm packages would be considered the next layer sitting in between Angular and Node.

Every time you update your version of Node, you also get a new version of npm, which ships bundled with Node. However, npm's release schedule doesn't coincide with Node's. At times, there will be significant performance and feature gains to warrant a specific upgrade to your version of npm, such as the order of magnitude speed improvements introduced with npm v5.0.0 or the npx tool, which reduces the need for global packages, introduced with npm v5.2.0:

- On Windows, you need the `npm-windows-upgrade` tool to upgrade your version of npm:

1. Install `npm-windows-upgrade`:

   ```
   PS> npm install --global --production npm-windows-upgrade
   ```

   If you run into errors during installation of the tool, refer to the *Npm fails to install a global tool on Windows* section to resolve any issues with your system setup.

2. Execute `npm-windows-upgrade` in an elevated shell, and you will get a list of options, as shown:

   ```
   PS> npm-windows-upgrade
   npm-windows-upgrade v4.1.0
   ? Which version do you want to install?
     6.0.1-next.0
   > 6.0.0
     6.0.0-next.2
     6.0.0-next.1
     6.0.0-next.0
     5.10.0-next.0
     5.9.0-next.0
   (Move up and down to reveal more choices)
   ```

3. Select a stable release, in this case, `6.0.0`:

   ```
   PS>
   ? Which version do you want to install? 6.0.0
   Checked system for npm installation:
   According to PowerShell: C:\Program Files\nodejs
   According to npm: C:\Users\duluc\AppData\Roaming\npm
   Decided that npm is installed in C:\Program Files\nodejs
   Upgrading npm... \

   Upgrade finished. Your new npm version is 6.0.0. Have a nice day!
   ```

4. Verify your installation:

```
PS> npm -v
6.0.0
```

- On macOS, it is straightforward to upgrade your version of npm:

1. Execute npm install -g npm:

```
$ npm install -g npm
/usr/local/bin/npm -> /usr/local/lib/node_modules/npm/bin/npm-
cli.js
/usr/local/bin/npx -> /usr/local/lib/node_modules/npm/bin/npx-
cli.js
+ npm@6.0.0
updated 1 package in 18.342s
```

Note that installing global packages, as shown earlier, should not require the use of sudo.

2. If sudo is required, execute this:

```
$ which npm
/usr/local/bin/npm
```

3. Find the owner and the permissions of this folder:

```
$ ls -ld /usr/local/bin/npm
lrwxr-xr-x 1 youruser group 38 May 5 11:19 /usr/local/bin/npm ->
../lib/node_modules/npm/bin/npm-cli.js
```

As you see can see, the correct configuration looks like your own user, shown in bold as youruser, has read/write/execute rights on the folder, also shown in bold as rwx, in which npm resides. If this is not the case, use sudo chown -R $USER /usr/local/bin/npm to own the folder, followed by chmod -R o+rwx /usr/local/bin/npm to ensure that your user has full rights.

4. Verify your installation:

```
$ npm -v
6.0.0
```

It is important to keep any globally installed package up to date as well; refer to the next section on how to keep your global installs to a minimum and troubleshoot installation issues on Windows.

Global Npm packages

As mentioned earlier in this section and in Chapter 2, *Create a Local Weather Web Application*, when setting up your Angular project, you should refrain from installing any project specific tool as a global package. This includes tools like typescript, webpack, gulp, or grunt to name a few examples. The npx tool enables the conveniences of running CLI commands such as tsc using the specific version your project depends on with only a minimal hit to performance. As discussed in Chapter 2, *Create a Local Weather Web Application*, installing project-specific tools globally has adverse affects on your development environment.

I do mention a list of tools that I still continue to install globally, such as the n tool from the *Upgrading Node* section or rimraf, which is a cross-platform recursive deletion tool that comes in very handy when Windows 10 doesn't cooperate with deleting your node_modules folder. These tools are non-project specific and largely stable, that don't need frequent updates.

The reality is that unless the tool reminds you to upgrade itself, you most likely will never proactively do so. The now CLI tool we used in Chapter 3, *Prepare Angular App for Production Release*, to publish our Docker container in the cloud is a great example of a tool that remains vigilant about keeping itself up to date with a message as follows:

```
| Update available! 8.4.0 → 11.1.7                               |
| Changelog: https://github.com/zeit/now-cli/releases/tag/11.1.7 |
| Please download binaries from https://zeit.co/download         |
```

You can upgrade global tools by executing this:

```
$ npm install -g now@latest
```

 Beware that the @latest request will upgrade to the next major version, if available, without much fanfare. While major release contain exciting and useful new features, they also risk breaking old functionality that you may be depending on.

That should complete your upgrade. However, especially on Windows, it is easy to put your Node and npm installation in a broken state. The following section covers common troubleshooting steps and actions you can take to restore your Windows setup.

Npm fails to install a global tool on Windows

Npm may fail to install global tools; consider the symptom, cause, and solutions discussed as follows:

Symptom: When you attempt to install a global tool, you may get an error message containing the **Refusing to delete** message similar to the one shown here:

```
PS C:\WINDOWS\system32> npm i -g now
npm ERR! path C:\Users\duluc\AppData\Roaming\npm\now.cmd
npm ERR! code EEXIST
npm ERR! Refusing to delete
C:\Users\duluc\AppData\Roaming\npm\now.cmd:
node_modules\now\download\dist\now symlink target is not controlled
by npm C:\Users\duluc\AppData\Roaming\npm\node_modules\now
npm ERR! File exists: C:\Users\duluc\AppData\Roaming\npm\now.cmd
npm ERR! Move it away, and try again.
npm ERR! A complete log of this run can be found in:
npm ERR! C:\Users\duluc\AppData\Roaming\npm-
cache\_logs\2017-11-11T21_30_28_382Z-debug.log
```

Cause: On Windows, if you ever executed `npm install -g npm` or upgraded your version of Node using choco, your npm installation has likely been corrupted.

Solution 1: Recover your environment with the `npm-windows-upgrade` tool:

1. Execute the npm upgrade routine:

   ```
   PS> npm install --global --production npm-windows-upgrade
   PS> npm-windows-upgrade
   ```

2. Delete the offending file and directory with `rimraf`:

   ```
   PS> npm i -g rimraf
   rimraf C:\Users\duluc\AppData\Roaming\npm\now.cmd
   rimraf C:\Users\duluc\AppData\Roaming\npm\now
   ```

3. Try installing again:

```
PS> npm i -g now@latest
```

If this doesn't resolve your issue, then attempt Solution 2.

Solution 2: If you have installed non-LTS nodejs or have not configured npm correctly, try the following steps:

1. Uninstall non-LTS nodejs and reinstall it:

```
PS> choco uninstall nodejs
PS> choco install nodejs-lts --force -y
```

2. Install npm-windows-upgrade following the guide at https://github.com/npm/npm/wiki/Troubleshooting#upgrading-on-windows.

3. In Powershell, with Administrator privileges, execute this:

```
PS> Set-ExecutionPolicy Unrestricted -Scope CurrentUser -Force
PS> npm install --global --production npm-windows-upgrade
PS> npm-windows-upgrade
```

4. Execute npm-windows-upgrade:

```
PS> npm-windows-upgrade
npm-windows-upgrade v4.1.0
? Which version do you want to install? 5.5.1
Checked system for npm installation:
According to PowerShell: C:\Program Files\nodejs
According to npm: C:\Users\duluc\AppData\Roaming\npm
Decided that npm is installed in C:\Program Files\nodejs
Upgrading npm... -
Upgrade finished. Your new npm version is 5.5.1. Have a nice day!
```

5. Note the **According to npm** folder.
6. Navigate to this folder and ensure that npm or npm.cmd doesn't exist in this folder.
7. If it does, remove.

8. Ensure that this folder is in `PATH`.

Click on **Start** and search for `Environment Variables`. Click on **Edit the system environment variables**. In the **System Properties** window, click on **Environment Variables**. Select the line with **Path**. Click on **Edit**:

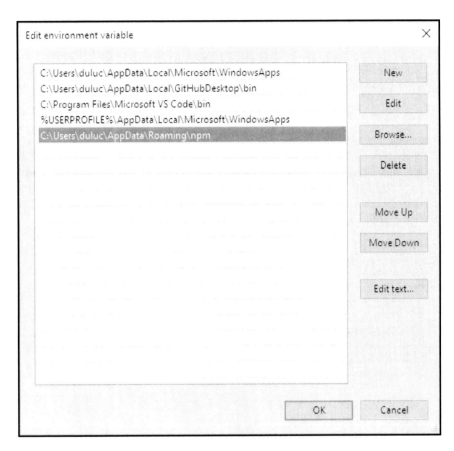

Edit environment variable dialogue

9. Try installing your global tool again.
10. If the issue persists, you may need to delete your global npm folder with PowerShell command, as shown:

```
PS> cmd /C "rmdir /S /Q C:\Users\duluc\AppData\Roaming\npm"
```

11. Navigate to the folder:

```
PS> dir C:\Users\duluc\AppData\Roaming\npm
```

12. Execute npm:

```
PS> npm@5.5.1 C:\Program Files\nodejs\node_modules\npm
```

13. Redo the npm-windows-upgrade routine:

```
PS> npm install --global --production npm-windows-upgrade
PS> npm-windows-upgrade
```

14. Reinstall the tool:

```
PS> npm i -g now
C:\Users\duluc\AppData\Roaming\npm\now ->
C:\Users\duluc\AppData\Roaming\npm\node_modules\now\download\dist\n
ow
> now@8.4.0 postinstall
C:\Users\duluc\AppData\Roaming\npm\node_modules\now
> node download/install.js
> For the source code, check out: https://github.com/zeit/now-cli
> Downloading Now CLI 8.4.0 [====================] 100%
+ now@8.4.0
```

Don't run npm i -g npm in the future.

Updating Angular

With Node and npm up-to-date, you are now ready to upgrade your version of Angular. The Angular ecosystem has been engineered to make frequent updates of your version as painless as possible. Minor version updates should be straightforward and quick and starting with version 6.0.0; major version upgrades should be easier with the new ng update command that ships with Angular CLI. Paired with the update guide published on update.angular.io and various helper tools specific to your upgrade path, updating Angular is straightforward. In this section, we will go over how you can update your Angular app presuming a scenario of upgrading from version 5.2 to 6.0. The instructions should largely remain the same, with any variance or future changes documented in https://update.angular.io/.

Keep in mind that Angular doesn't recommend skipping major version numbers when upgrading, so if you are on version 4, you're first expected to upgrade to 5 and then to 6. Do not delay updating your framework version, thinking you can gain some efficiency by leap frogging to the latest version.

Angular update guide

Follow this step-by-step guide to prepare, execute, and test your Angular version upgrade process.

Take stock of your current version

Let's first begin by inspecting package.json so that you are aware of the versions of various dependencies that you are using. All @angular packages should be on the same minor version, such as 5.2, as shown:

```
package.json
  "@angular/animations": "5.2.5",
    "@angular/cdk": "^5.2.2",
    "@angular/common": "5.2.5",
    "@angular/compiler": "5.2.5",
    "@angular/core": "5.2.5",
    "@angular/flex-layout": "^2.0.0-beta.12",
    "@angular/forms": "5.2.5",
    "@angular/http": "5.2.5",
    "@angular/material": "^5.2.2",
    "@angular/platform-browser": "5.2.5",
    "@angular/platform-browser-dynamic": "5.2.5",
```

```
    "@angular/router": "5.2.5",
    "core-js": "^2.4.1",
    ...
    "rxjs": "^5.5.6",
    "ts-enum-util": "^2.0.0",
    "zone.js": "^0.8.20"
  },
  "devDependencies": {
    "@angular/cli": "1.7.0",
    "@angular/compiler-cli": "5.2.5",
    "@angular/language-service": "5.2.5",
  ...
```

Using Angular Update Guide

Now that you are aware of your current versions, you are ready to use the Update Guide:

1. Navigate to `update.angular.io`
2. Select the complexity of your application:
     - **Basic**: No animations, no HTTP calls
     - **Medium**: If you're using Angular Material or making HTTP calls or using RxJS, largely working as 1-2 person developer team and delivering small apps
     - **Advanced**: Multi-person teams, delivering medium-to-large size apps

 Most apps will fall in the Medium complexity; I highly recommend selecting this option. If you have implemented Angular functionality beyond the surface level APIs, by leveraging functionality mentioned deep in the documentation, implement any custom behavior in the HTTP, rendering, routing—definitely scroll through the Advanced list first to ensure that you're not using a deprecated function.

3. On the update guide, select from and to versions. In this case, 5.2 to 6.0, as shown:

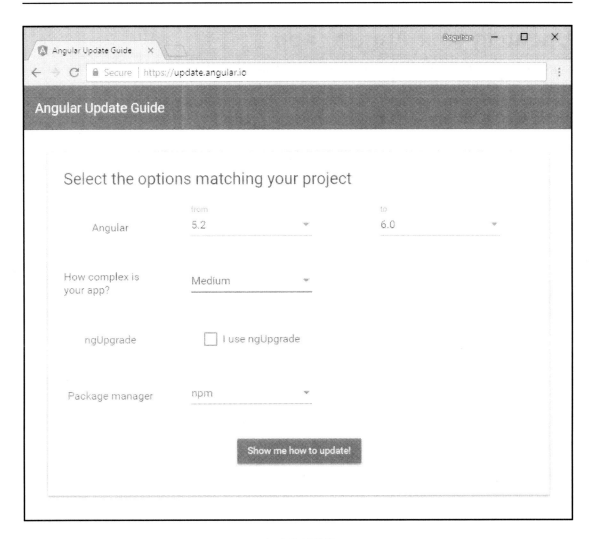

Angular Update Guide

4. Click on **Show me how to update!**
5. Observe the instructions shown on screen as three distinct sections, before updating, during, and after the update

Now for the hard part, we need to follow the instructions and apply them.

Updating your Angular app

Updating software is risky. There are several strategies to reduce your risk in updating your app. This is the primary reason you have built a barrage of automated tests in your application; however, over time, your implementation, including your CI & CD systems, can deteriorate. Version updates are a great time to reevaluate the robustness of your automated systems and make the necessary investments to shore them up. Consider the following pre-upgrade checklist before you start your update process.

Pre-upgrade checklist

Here's a handy checklist of items to run through before starting your upgrade:

1. Ensure that @angular versions all match down to the last patch.
2. Ensure your CI & CD pipeline is up and running with no failing or disabled tests.
3. Smoke test your app before upgrading. Ensure that all major functionality works and there are no console errors or warning present.
4. Address any quality issue discovered before upgrading.
5. Follow the update guide sequentially and methodically.
6. Be prepared to roll back the update.

Let's start the update process with before updating activities.

Before updating

Angular Update Guide recommends specific steps to follow under the **Before Updating** section, as shown:

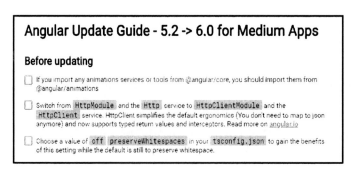

Angular Update Guide - Before updating

There can be several kinds of updates you may need to make to your code before attempting an update.

Namespace Changes: The first item on the preceding list is notifying us that the namespaces of certain animation services and tools may have changes. Such changes should be low risk and accomplished quickly with the use of the Global search tool in VS Code. Let's see how you can quickly observe all usages of `'@angular/core'` in your app. Look at the next screenshot:

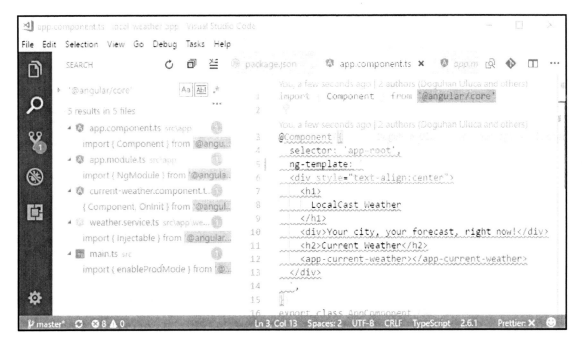

Search Results for '@angular/core'

In this case, there is no usage that is related to animations, so we can move on.

Rename and Replace Updates: In version 4, there was a requirement to replace the OpaqueTokens type with InjectionTokens. For these types of changes, once again, use the Global Search tool to find and replace the necessary codes.

When using the Global Search tool find and replace code, ensure that you enable Match Case, signified by **Aa** and Match Whole Word, signified by **Ab|**, to prevent unintended replacements. Take a look at the following screenshot for a look at the two options in their enabled state:

Match Case and Match Whole Word Enabled

Functional Changes: Deprecated features, signaled one major version ahead of time, require rewrites of the affected portions of your application code. If you have been heavily using `HttpModule` and `Http`, your code will require a serious overhaul:

1. First, discover the instances of actual usage with Global search.

2. On `angular.io`, search for the newly introduced service, in this case, **HttpClient** or **HttpClientModule**:

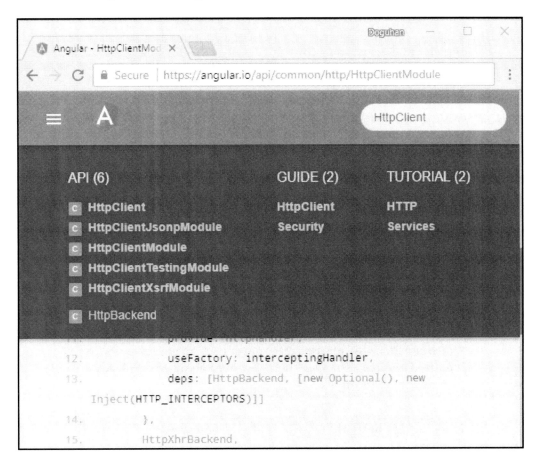

Angular.io Documentation Page

3. Click on the relevant link under the **Guide** heading, which contain rich and contextual information about the new service.

The new service usually comes along with new benefits, such as an improved coding experience, better testability, or performance.

4. Reimplement the necessary code.
5. Execute the Post Update Checklist mentioned in the next section.

Such functional changes can simultaneously be great productivity boosters but also greatly increase the friction of a timely upgrade to a new version of Angular. You can, however, lower the cost of change and reap maximum benefits of these changes by preparing ahead of time.

In this case, the LocalCast Weather app doesn't use the deprecated modules, because by chance the development of the app began right after the release of the `HttpClient` service. However, I wouldn't have known about the change if I wasn't keeping tabs on the Angular community. I highly recommend following `https://blog.angular.io` for this reason.

In addition, you can check the Angular Update tool regularly. The tool likely won't be updated quickly; however, it is a good summary resource of all upcoming changes.

In the Update tool, if you select a future version of Angular, you will get a warning message:

Warning: Plans for releases after the current major release are not finalized and may change. These recommendations are based on scheduled deprecations.

This is a great way to stay ahead of the game and plan your resources around Angular updates ahead of time.

Once you're done with the **Before Updating** phase, consider going through the Post Update Checklist before moving on to the next phase.

During the Update

Here's the **During the Update** section from the guide, which is centered around the ng update tool:

During the update

☐ Make sure you are using <u>Node 8 or later</u>

☐ Update your Angular CLI globally and locally, and migrate the configuration to the <u>new angular.json format</u> by running the following:

```
npm install -g @angular/cli
npm install @angular/cli
ng update @angular/cli
```

☐ Update any `scripts` you may have in your `package.json` to use the latest Angular CLI commands. All CLI commands now use two dashes for flags (eg `ng build --prod --source-map`) to be POSIX compliant.

☐ Update all of your Angular framework packages to v6, and the correct version of RxJS and TypeScript.

```
ng update @angular/core
```

After the update, TypeScript and RxJS will more accurately flow types across your application, which may expose existing errors in your application's typings

☐ ngModelChange is now emitted after the value/validity is updated on its control instead of before to better match expectations. If you rely on the order of these events, you will need to being tracking the old value in your component.

☐ Update Angular Material to the latest version.

```
ng update @angular/material
```

This will also automatically migrate deprecated APIs.

☐ Use `ng update` or your normal package manager tools to identify and update other dependencies.

☐ If you have TypeScript configured to be strict (if you have set `strict` to `true` in your `tsconfig.json` file), update your `tsconfig.json` to disable `strictPropertyInitialization` or move property initialization from `ngOnInit` to your constructor. You can learn more about this flag on the <u>TypeScript 2.7 release notes</u>.

Angular Update Guide - During the update

In comparison, pre-Angular 6 upgrades look like this:

☐ Update all of your dependencies to the latest Angular and the right version of TypeScript. If you are using Windows, you can use:

```
npm install @angular/animations@^5.0.0 @angular/common@^5.0.0
@angular/compiler@^5.0.0 @angular/compiler-cli@^5.0.0
@angular/core@^5.0.0 @angular/forms@^5.0.0 @angular/http@^5.0.0
@angular/platform-browser@^5.0.0 @angular/platform-browser-dynamic@^5.0.0
@angular/platform-server@^5.0.0 @angular/router@^5.0.0 typescript@2.4.2
rxjs@^5.5.2
```

```
npm install typescript@2.4.2 --save-exact
```

Angular Update Guide - Pre-Angular 6

If you are interested in learning more about manual updates, refer to the Manual Update section. In this section, I have detailed the steps that you should execute for an automated upgrade in a more comprehensive manner than the guide. In Chapter 2, *Create a Local Weather Web Application,* we avoided installing Angular CLI, and this is where this strategy pays off. You can continue working on the existing Angular 4 or Angular 5 projects without having to worry about CLI backward-compatibility issues:

1. Ensure that you have updated to the latest LTS version of Node, as shown earlier in the chapter
2. Ensure that you are on the latest version of npm, as shown earlier in the chapter
3. In your terminal, cd in to the project folder
4. Clean your node_modules folder:

   $ rimraf node_modules

    It is important to note that version changes in Node or npm can impact how your node_modules dependencies are installed or stored on your computer. After an upgrade to lower-level tools, such as Node or npm, it is prudent to wipe away node_modules and reinstall your packages in your project. In your Continuous Integration (CI) server, this means invalidating the existing cache of packages.

5. Reinstall dependencies:

```
$ npm install
```

6. Uninstall globally installed versions of @angular/cli, webpack, jasmine, or typescript:

```
$ npm uninstall -g @angular/cli webpack jasmine typescript
```

7. Update to the latest CLI version in your project:

```
$ npm i -D @angular/cli@latest
> @angular/cli@6.0.0 postinstall /Users/du/dev/local-weather-
app/node_modules/@angular/cli
> node ./bin/ng-update-message.js


====================================================================
The Angular CLI configuration format has been changed, and your
existing configuration can be updated automatically by running
the following command:
ng update @angular/cli
====================================================================
```

8. Update project configuration, as suggested by the preceding message:

```
$ npx ng update @angular/cli
          master!
          Updating karma configuration
          Updating configuration
          Removing old config file (.angular-cli.json)
          Writing config file (angular.json)
          Some configuration options have been changed, please
make sure to update any npm scripts which may have modified.
DELETE .angular-cli.json
CREATE angular.json (3644 bytes)
UPDATE karma.conf.js (1007 bytes)
UPDATE src/tsconfig.spec.json (324 bytes)
UPDATE package.json (3874 bytes)
UPDATE tslint.json (3024 bytes)
...
added 620 packages from 669 contributors in 24.956s
```

9. Try executing ng update:

```
$ npx ng update
We analyzed your package.json, there are some packages to update:

Name Version Command to update
-----------------------------------------------------------------
@angular/core 5.1.0 -> 6.0.0 ng update @angular/core
@angular/material 5.0.0 -> 6.0.0 ng update @angular/material
rxjs 5.5.2 -> 6.1.0 ng update rxjs

There might be additional packages that are outdated.
Or run ng update --all to try to update all at the same time.
```

10. Try executing ng update --all:

```
$ npx ng update --all
```

You may get an error message that says **Incompatible peer dependencies found.** with one or more specific issues listed. You will not be able to use ng update until all issues are resolved.

In the next section, I will go over strategies in resolving peer dependency errors. If you don't have these kinds of errors, feel free to skip the section.

Incompatible peer dependencies

I will go through some of incompatible peer dependency errors that I received during my upgrade process and the different strategies to resolve these errors. Note that I will start with simple cases and demonstrate the amount of research that may be required as the dependency you need may not be simply the latest released version of your package.

- Package karma-jasmine-html-reporter has a missing peer dependency of "jasmine" @ "^3.0.0".

  This is a simple error that is resolved by simply updating to the latest version of jasmine, as follows:

  ```
  $ npm i -D jasmine
  ```

- Package @angular/flex-layout has an incompatible peer dependency to "rxjs" (requires "^5.5.0", would install "6.1.0").

This error requires a bit of research and understanding of the ecosystem. As of Angular 6, we know that all libraries are version synced, so we need a 6.x version of this library. Let's discover the currently available versions with `npm info`:

```
$ npm info @angular/flex-layout
...
dist-tags:
latest: 5.0.0-beta.14 next: 6.0.0-beta.15

published a month ago by angular <devops+npm@angular.io>
```

As of publishing, this library is still in beta and the latest version is at 5.0.0, so simply updating to the latest release of `@angular/flex-layout` won't work out. In this case, we need to install the `@next` version of the package, as follows:

```
$ npm i @angular/flex-layout@next
```

You will receive a bunch of dependency warnings showing that Angular 6 packages are needed. These errors will go away once we're done with our update.

- Package "@angular/compiler-cli" has an incompatible peer dependency to "typescript" (requires ">=2.7.2 <2.8", would install "2.8.3").

Angular CLI depends on a specific version of Typescript. If you execute `npm info typescript`, the latest version of Typescript may be newer than what is required. In this case, it is `2.8.3`, as reported in the preceding error message. The error message does signal to us what version is specifically required, if you look at the requires statement. The lower bound, `2.7.2`, seems to be the correct version to install, so let's install that, as shown:

```
$ npm install -D typescript@2.7.2
```

In theory, all of our actions should have resolved all peer dependency issues. In reality, I have noted that these errors sometimes persist, when `npx ng update --all` is used, so we will continue the update by running individual update commands.

On non-macOS operating systems, you may persistently encounter an fsevents-related warning, such as **npm WARN optional SKIPPING OPTIONAL DEPENDENCY: fsevents@1.1.3**. This is an optional package that is only leveraged on macOS. An easy way to avoid seeing this error is to run `npm install --no-optional` command.

Continuing the update

We will update Angular piece by piece:

1. Let's start the update with Angular Core:

```
$ npx ng update @angular/core
Updating package.json with dependency rxjs @ "6.1.0" (was
"5.5.6")...
 Updating package.json with dependency @angular/language-service @
"6.0.0" (was "5.2.5")...
 Updating package.json with dependency @angular/compiler-cli @
"6.0.0" (was "5.2.5")...
 Updating package.json with dependency @angular/router @ "6.0.0"
(was "5.2.5")...
 Updating package.json with dependency @angular/forms @ "6.0.0"
(was "5.2.5")...
 Updating package.json with dependency @angular/platform-browser @
"6.0.0" (was "5.2.5")...
 Updating package.json with dependency @angular/animations @
"6.0.0" (was "5.2.5")...
 Updating package.json with dependency zone.js @ "0.8.26" (was
"0.8.20")...
 Updating package.json with dependency @angular/platform-browser-
dynamic @ "6.0.0" (was "5.2.5")...
 Updating package.json with dependency @angular/common @ "6.0.0"
(was "5.2.5")...
 Updating package.json with dependency @angular/core @ "6.0.0" (was
"5.2.5")...
 Updating package.json with dependency @angular/compiler @ "6.0.0"
(was "5.2.5")...
 Updating package.json with dependency @angular/http @ "6.0.0" (was
"5.2.5")...
 UPDATE package.json (5530 bytes)
 . . .
 added 12 packages from 37 contributors and updated 14 packages in
54.204s
```

Note that this command also updates rxjs.

2. Update Angular Material:

```
$ npx ng update @angular/material
Updating package.json with dependency @angular/cdk @ "6.0.0" (was
"5.2.2")...
 Updating package.json with dependency @angular/material @ "6.0.0"
(was "5.2.2")...
 UPDATE package.json (5563 bytes)
 . . .
```

Ensure that you check out the Material Update Tool and strategies to manually update Angular Material in `Chapter 5`, *Enhance Angular App with Angular Material*.

3. Update other dependencies, including typings with `npm update`:

```
$ npm update
+ codelyzer@4.3.0
+ karma-jasmine@1.1.2
+ jsonwebtoken@8.2.1
+ core-js@2.5.5
+ prettier@1.12.1
+ karma-coverage-istanbul-reporter@1.4.2
+ typescript@2.8.3
+ @types/jsonwebtoken@7.2.7
+ ts-enum-util@2.0.2
+ @types/node@6.0.108
```

Note that `typescript` was updated to its latest version, `2.8.3`, which is not acceptable for Angular 6, as covered in the preceding section. Rollback to version `2.7.2` by executing `npm install -D typescript@2.7.2`.

4. Resolve any npm errors and warnings.

You're done updating your major Angular dependencies. Consider executing the Post Update Checklist before moving on to *After the update* section.

After the update

The **After the update** phase informs changes that need to be after the updates to major Angular dependencies and sometimes inform us of the further benefits that can be gained after having upgraded our version of Angular. Observe the next steps:

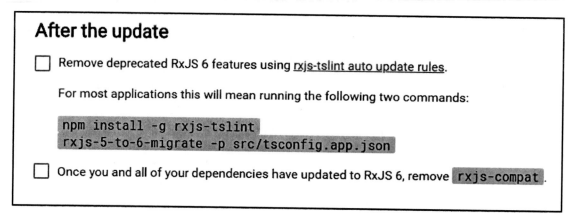

After the update

☐ Remove deprecated RxJS 6 features using rxjs-tslint auto update rules.

For most applications this will mean running the following two commands:

```
npm install -g rxjs-tslint
rxjs-5-to-6-migrate -p src/tsconfig.app.json
```

☐ Once you and all of your dependencies have updated to RxJS 6, remove `rxjs-compat`.

Angular Update Guide - After the update

In this case, we must address deprecations related to our upgrade to RxJS. Luckily, the Angular team that knows this can be a painful process, so they're suggesting an automated tool that can give us a head start:

1. Refrain from installing the tool globally
2. Execute the migration tool, as shown:

```
$ npx rxjs-tslint -p .\src\tsconfig.app.json

Running the automatic migrations. Please, be patient and wait until
the execution completes.
Found and fixed the following deprecations:

Fixed 2 error(s) in C:/dev/lemon-mart/src/app/common/common.ts
Fixed 6 error(s) in C:/dev/lemon-mart/src/app/auth/auth.service.ts
Fixed 1 error(s) in C:/dev/lemon-mart/src/app/common/ui.service.ts
. . .

WARNING: C:/dev/lemon-mart/src/app/auth/auth-http-interceptor.ts[2,
1]: duplicate RxJS import
WARNING: C:/dev/lemon-mart/src/app/auth/auth-http-interceptor.ts[4,
27]: outdated import path
```

```
WARNING: C:/dev/lemon-mart/src/app/auth/auth.service.fake.ts[2, 1]:
duplicate RxJS import
...
```

3. Resolve any warnings manually; consider this example:

```
example
import { BehaviorSubject, Observable, of } from 'rxjs'
import { ErrorObservable } from 'rxjs/observable/ErrorObservable'
import { IfObservable } from 'rxjs/observable/IfObservable'
import { catchError } from 'rxjs/operators'
```

In the preceding example, we only need to import from `'rxjs'` and `'rxjs/operators'` per RxJS 6 documentation, so remove the two other imports. In addition, the `ErrorObservable` and `IfObservable` imports are referenced by any line of code, so they're easy to identify for removal.

Some warnings may be masking errors or incompatibilities with new RxJS functions, so it is important go through them one by one.

4. Remove `rxjs-compat`:

```
$ npm uninstall rxjs-compat
```

5. Build and test your code to ensure that it builds by executing `npm run predocker:build`

`predocker:build` builds your Angular app in production mode and runs your unit and e2e tests by executing the following commands:

```
$ npm run build -- --prod && npm test -- --watch=false && npm run e2e
```

Resolve any errors. If you are getting mysterious errors that are not related to your code, try to remove `node_modules` and reinstall packages.

If everything is working correctly, congratulations, you're done with your upgrade! Before you pop the bottle of sparkling wine, execute the Post Update Checklist.

Post Update Checklist

Post Update Checklist is useful in ensuring that you haven't introduced any regressions to your code base after making sweeping code changes. You are asked to consider executing this checklist after every phase of the update process. It may not always be possible or feasible to execute the entire list, but after making significant changes to your code base, if necessary, update your unit tests, and execute the following checklist incrementally:

1. Build and smoke test your angular app
2. Commit your changes
3. With each commit, ensure that CI pipeline remains green
4. If making functional changes, it may be required to follow release-cycle procedures of your organization, which may include manual testing by a QA team
5. It is advisable to implement and deploy such changes one by one and deploy them to the production environment
6. Collect Performance data, as outlined in the following section

Committing your code after a category of changes will enable you to revert or cherry-pick further upgrade commits, if something goes wrong down the line.

For a variety of reasons, you may need to manually upgrade Angular, which is covered in the next section.

Manual update

It is good to have a general understanding of how a manual upgrade works, because you may not be able to use the version of Angular CLI that has automatic update; you may eject Angular CLI altogether from your project or the tool may contain a bug. The version numbers discussed here are examples copied from the update guide.

For the sake of this example, I will be demonstrating a potential upgrade from Angular 4 to Angular 5:

1. Follow Before updating instructions from the guide and this chapter
2. Ensure that Node and npm are up to date

3. In order to upgrade to version 5.0.0, execute the following command:

```
$ npm install @angular/animations@'^5.0.0' @angular/common@'^5.0.0'
@angular/compiler@'^5.0.0' @angular/compiler-cli@'^5.0.0'
@angular/core@'^5.0.0' @angular/forms@'^5.0.0'
@angular/http@'^5.0.0' @angular/platform-browser@'^5.0.0'
@angular/platform-browser-dynamic@'^5.0.0' @angular/platform-
server@'^5.0.0' @angular/router@'^5.0.0' typescript@2.4.2
rxjs@'^5.5.2'
```

4. This is to be followed by a `--save-exact` command so that TypeScript isn't accidentally upgraded:

```
$ npm install typescript@2.4.2 --save-exact
```

5. Ensure that your `package.json` file has been updated to the correct versions:

```
"dependencies": {
    "@angular/animations": "^5.0.0",
    "@angular/common": "^5.0.0",
    "@angular/compiler": "^5.0.0",
    "@angular/core": "^5.0.0",
    "@angular/forms": "^5.0.0",
    "@angular/http": "^5.0.0",
    "@angular/platform-browser": "^5.0.0",
    "@angular/platform-browser-dynamic": "^5.0.0",
    "@angular/platform-server": "^5.0.0",
    "@angular/router": "^5.0.0",
    "core-js": "^2.5.1",
    "rxjs": "^5.5.2",
    "zone.js": "^0.8.17"
},
"devDependencies": {
    "@angular/cli": "^1.5.0",
    "@angular/compiler-cli": "^5.0.0",
    "@angular/language-service": "^4.4.3",
    ...
    "typescript": "2.4.2"
},
```

Note that the caret and tilde has been removed from the TypeScript version, preventing any accidental upgrades, as the Angular tools are quite sensitive to the specific features of any given TypeScript release.

Note that `@angular/cli` and `@angular/compiler-cli` have been updated to their latest versions; however, the tool didn't update `@angular/language-service`. This highlights the importance of manual checks, since every tool in your tool chain is susceptible to minor bugs.

6. Update `@angular/language-service` by executing the following command:

```
$ npm install @angular/language-service@^5.0.0
```

7. Verify `package.json` has the correct version of the file:

```
"@angular/language-service": "^5.0.0",
```

You're done updating your packages.

8. Follow after the update instructions from the guide and this chapter.

After upgrading your Angular application, it is a good idea to test the impact of your changes on performance.

Testing performance

Test the performance of your Angular app before and after updates to ensure that your performance numbers remain as expected. In the following case, we automatically gain performance benefits due to platform-level improvements. First, let's compare Angular v4 to v5:

Categories	Angular 4	Angular 5	% Diff
JavaScript Assets Delivered (gzipped)	83.6 KB	72.6 KB	13% smaller
Time to first page render (Fiber)	0.57 s	0.54 s	5% faster
Time to first page render (Fast 3G)	1.27 s	1.18 s	7% faster

Angular 4.4.3 vs 5.0.0

The trend of improvement continues with Angular 6:

Categories	Angular 5	Angular 6	% Diff
JavaScript Assets Delivered (gzipped)	72.6 KB	64.1 KB	12% smaller
Time to first page render (Fiber)	0.54 s	0.32 s	40% faster
Time to first page render (Fast 3G)	1.18 s	0.93 s	21% faster

Angular 5.0.0 vs 6.0.0

This trend should continue in future updates, with a target 3 KB size using the Ivy rendering engine. We will cover the importance of these performance numbers in Chapter 5, *Enhance Angular App with Angular Material*.

Addressing security vulnerabilities

Sometimes you will be notified about security vulnerabilities in certain packages, through blogs or if you're using GitHub, you may notice warning like this on your repository:

⚠ We found a potential security vulnerability in one of your dependencies.   Dismiss

The `handlebars` dependency defined in `package-lock.json` has a known moderate severity security vulnerability in version range < 4.0.0 and should be updated.

Review vulnerable dependency

Only users who have been granted access to vulnerability alerts for this repository can see this message.
Learn more about vulnerability alerts

GitHub.com Vulnerability Scan

This is a specific issue that arose when my Angular application was on version 5.0.0 and my CLI version was on 1.5.0. If you review this dependency, you can see the dependent packages and get more detail on the issue.

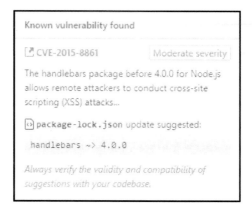

Known vulnerability found

CVE-2015-8861   Moderate severity

The handlebars package before 4.0.0 for Node.js allows remote attackers to conduct cross-site scripting (XSS) attacks...

`package-lock.json` update suggested:

  handlebars ~> 4.0.0

Always verify the validity and compatibility of suggestions with your codebase.

GitHub.com Security Bulletin

In this case, the vulnerable version of handlebars, 1.3.0 is being caused by one of Angular 5.0 packages.

Further research on Angular's GitHub issues reveals that the issue is actually caused by `@angular/cli version 1.5.0`. The reference is `https://github.com/angular/angular/issues/20654`.

This was to try an update to the latest minor version update of Angular, Material or CLI, which in this case is version 5.1.0 and 1.6.0:

```
$ npm install @angular/animations@^5.1.0 @angular/common@^5.1.0
@angular/compiler@^5.1.0 @angular/compiler-cli@^5.1.0 @angular/core@^5.1.0
@angular/forms@^5.1.0 @angular/http@^5.1.0 @angular/platform-browser@^5.1.0
@angular/platform-browser-dynamic@^5.1.0 @angular/platform-server@^5.1.0
@angular/router@^5.1.0 @angular/language-service@^5.1.0 @angular/cli@^1.6.0
```

This update resolved the security warning displayed by GitHub. If you are not able to resolve your issue by upgrading, create a new issue on GitHub and keep tabs on upcoming patch or minor releases of Angular until the issue is resolved.

Updating your web server

At the top of your stack is the web server in which you host your web application in. This is a live, production system that is likely exposed to the internet, thus one that is at most risk. It should be judiciously kept up to date.

Ideally, your release pipeline resembles the one described in Chapter 3, *Prepare Angular App for Production Release*, where your frontend application is served by a containerized low-profile instance. This can be the `minimal-node-web-server` that I publish and maintain or an Nginx-based instance. In either case, an upgrade is simple by changing version number listed next to your base image:

Dockerfile
```
FROM duluca/minimal-node-web-server:8.6.0
WORKDIR /usr/src/app
COPY dist public
```

It is always a good idea to specify the version number of the base Docker image you're using. Otherwise, it will default to a latest behavior, which in this case may mean an odd-numbered release that is not suitable for production. That said, `minimal-node-web-server` follows layers upon layers of the best security practices that reduces the attack surface and makes it incredibly difficult to mount a successful attack to compromise your web app. In line with this theme of security best practices, `minimal-node-web-server` would never push an odd numbered node version as the default behavior.

If your content is served through an installation of a web server like IIS, Apache, or Tomcat, you must follow and track security bulletins for these technologies. However, most likely another person or department altogether will be in charge upgrading this server, which may result in delays resulting from days to months, which is forever in internet time.

You're at the highest risk, if you're serving your static web content, like your SPA, through the same application server that also implements your backend APIs. Even though your architecture may be decoupled, if upgrading any tool or application in your dependency trees has side effects on any other part of your application, it means there's significant friction in your ability to secure or improve the performance of your frontend application.

A truly decoupled architecture will also allow the frontend to scale at different rate than your backend infrastructure and this can have great cost benefits. For example, suppose that your frontend serves lots of static information and rarely needs to poll the backend. At times of high load, you may need three instances of your frontend server to serve all the requests but only a single instance of the backend server since the calls are few and far in between.

Updating Docker image

After having upgrade your app and its dependencies or simply adding new features, you will need to update and publish your new Docker image.

1. In `package.json`, update the version property to `1.1.0` or match your version to your current Angular version
2. Execute `npm run docker:debug` to build and verify that your updates work correctly
3. Finally, execute `npm run docker:publish` to push your new image to a repository

After your image is published, take the necessary steps to deploy the image on a server or a cloud provider, as covered in `Chapter 3`, *Prepare Angular App for Production Release*, and `Chapter 11`, *Highly-Available Cloud Infrastructure on AWS*.

Summary

In this chapter, we covered the importance of staying up to date across your entire stack of dependencies from development tools such as Node and npm, to Angular. We looked at how you can use ng update and Angular Update Guide to make Angular updates as painless as possible. We also covered manual updates, performance testing, dealing with out-of-band security vulnerabilities and patches, including the necessity to keep your web server up to date. Maintaining a relatively up-to-date system has direct cost benefits. The smaller the delta, the less the effort to upkeep. However, as time goes on, the cost of upgrading a system raises exponentially. As non-direct benefits, we can list customer satisfaction generated from better performance, a metric that impacts companies like Amazon at the tune of millions of dollars per every 100 ms of latency. New features in tools also have a profound impact on developer productivity and happiness, which helps retention and reduces cost of newly developed features, which in return may lead to increased customer satisfaction. Saying up to date is certainly a positive feedback loop.

In the next chapter, we will go over how you can add Angular Material to your project by making your Local Weather App look great. In the process, you will learn about the negative performance impact that user control or UI component libraries can have on your application, including basic Material components, Angular Flex layout, accessibility, typography, theming, and how to update Angular Material.

5
Enhance Angular App with Angular Material

In Chapter 3, *Prepare Angular App for Production Release*, we mentioned the need to deliver a high-quality application. Currently, the app has a terrible look and feel to it, which is only fit for a website created in the late 1990s. The first impression a user or a client will get about your product or your work is very important, so we must be able to create a great looking application that also delivers a great user experience across mobile and desktop browsers.

As full-stack developers, it is difficult to focus on the polish of your application. This gets worse, as the feature set of an application rapidly grows. It is no fun to write great and modular code backing your views, but then revert to CSS hacks and inline styles in a rush to improve your application.

Angular Material is an amazing library that is developed in close coordination with Angular. If you learn how to leverage Angular Material effectively, the features you create will look and work great from the get go, whether you're working on small or large applications. Angular Material will make you a far more effective web developer, because it ships with a wide variety of user controls that you can leverage, and you won't have to worry about browser compatibility. As an added bonus, writing custom CSS will become a rarity.

In this chapter, you will learn the following:

- How to configure Angular Material
- Upgrade the UX with Angular Material

Angular Material

The goal of the Angular Material project is to provide a collection of useful and standard-setting high-quality **user interface** (UI) components. The library implements Google's Material Design specification, which is pervasive in Google's mobile apps, web properties, and Android operating system. Material Design does has a particular digital and boxy look and feel, but it is not just another CSS library, like Bootstrap is. Consider the login experience coded using Bootstrap here:

Bootstrap Login Experience

Note that input fields and their labels are on separate lines, the checkbox is a small target to hit, the error messages are displayed as an ephemeral toast notification, and the submit button just sits in the corner. Now consider the given Angular Material sample:

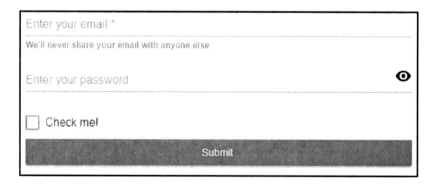

Angular Material Login Experience

The input fields and their labels are initially combined, grabbing the user's attention in a compact form factor. The checkbox is touch friendly and the **Submit** button stretches to take up the available space for a better default responsive UX. Once a user clicks on a field, the label tucks away to the top-left corner of the input field, as shown:

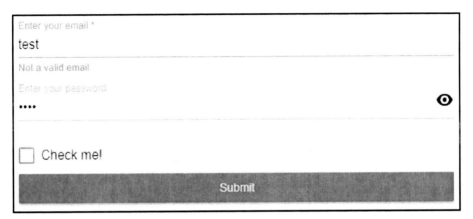

Angular Material Animations and Error

In addition, the validation error messages are shown inline, combined with a color change in the label, keeping the user's attention on the input field.

Material Design helps you design a modular UI with your own branding and styling, while also defining animations that allow for a user to have a better **user experience** (**UX**) when using your application. The human brain subconsciously keeps track of objects and their locations. Any kind of animation that aids in transitions or reactions that result from human input results in reduced cognitive load on the user, therefore allowing the user to focus on processing the content instead of trying to figure out the quirks of your particular app.

A combination of modular UI design and fluid motion creates a great UX. Look at how Angular material implements a simple button.

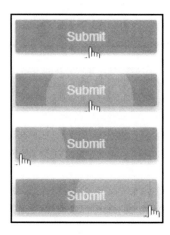

Angular Material Button Animation

In the preceding screenshot, note how the click animation on the button originates from the actual location that the user has clicked on. However subtle, this creates a continuity motion ,resulting in an appropriate reaction from a given action. This particular effect becomes more pronounced when the button is used on a mobile device, leading to an even more natural human computer interaction. Most users can't articulate what makes an intuitive UX actually intuitive, and these subtle yet crucial cues in design and experience make tremendous progress in allowing you to design such an experience for your users.

Angular Material also aims to become the reference implementation for high-quality UI components for Angular. If you intend to develop your own custom controls, the source code for Angular Material should be your first and foremost resource. The term high-quality is used often, and it's really important to quantify what that means. The Angular Material team puts it aptly on their website.

What do we mean by "high-quality"?

Internationalized and accessible so that all users can use them. Straightforward APIs that don't confuse developers and behave as expected across a wide variety of use cases without bugs. Behavior is well-tested with both unit and integration tests. Customizable within the bounds of the Material Design specification. Performance cost is minimized. Code is clean and well-documented to serve as an example for Angular devs. Browser and screen reader support.

Angular Material supports the most recent two versions of all major browsers: Chrome (including Android), Firefox, Safari (including iOS), and IE11 / Edge.

Building web applications, especially ones that are also mobile-compatible, is really difficult. There are a lot of nuances that you must be aware of. Angular Material abstracts away these nuances, including supporting all major browsers, so that you can focus on creating your application. Angular Material is no fad, and it's not to be taken lightly. If used correctly, you can greatly increase your productivity and the perceived quality of your work.

It won't always be possible to use Angular Material in your projects. I would recommend either PrimeNG, found at `https://www.primefaces.org/primeng`, or Clarity, found at `https://vmware.github.io/clarity`, as component toolkits that can satisfy your most, if not all, user control needs. The one thing to avoid here would be to pull dozens of user controls from different sources and end up with a hodgepodge library with hundreds of quirks and bugs to learn, maintain, or work around.

Angular Material setup and performance

Angular Material is configured by default to optimize the package size of your final deliverable. In Angular.JS and Angular Material 1.x, the entire dependent library would be loaded. However, with Angular Material 6, we are able to specify only the components that we intend to use, resulting in dramatic performance improvements.

In the following table, you can see improvement of the performance characteristics of a typical Angular 1.x + Angular Material 1.x vs Angular 6 + Material 6 application over a fiber connection with high speed and low latency:

Fiber Network	Angular 6 + Material 6	Angular 1.5 + Material 1.1.5	% Diff
Time to first page render*	0.61 s	1.69 s**	~2.8x faster
Base-level assets delivered*	113 KB	1,425 KB	12.6x smaller

Images or other media content has not been included in the results for a fair comparison
**Average value: Lower quality infrastructure leads to 0.9 to 2.5s in initial render times*

Under the ideal conditions of a high-speed and low-latency connection, Angular 6 + Material 6 apps load under a second. However, when we switch over to a more common moderate-speed and high-latency Fast 3G mobile network, the differences become more pronounced, as in the following table:

Fast 3G Mobile Network	Angular 6 + Material 6	Angular 1.5 + Material 1.1.5	% Diff
Time to first page render*	1.94 s	11.02 s	5.7x faster
Base-level assets delivered*	113 KB	1,425 KB	12.6x smaller

Images or other media content has not been included in the results for a fair comparison

Even though the size differences of the apps remain consistent, you can see that the additional latency introduced by a mobile network results in a dramatic slowdown of the legacy Angular application to an unacceptable level.

Adding all components to Material 6 will result in about ~1.3 MB of additional payload that will need to be delivered to the user. As you can see from the earlier comparison, this must be avoided at all costs. To deliver the smallest possible app possible, crucially in mobile and sales related scenarios, where every 100 ms of load time has an impact on user retention, you may load and include modules individually. Webpack's tree-shaking process will divide modules in to different files trimming down the initial download size. In future builds, Angular is expected to shrink further in size, potentially halving the sizes mentioned in the above table.

Installing Angular Material

Let's get started with the task and improve the UX of the weather app with Angular Material. Let's move the **Improve the UX of the app** task to **In Progress** on our Waffle.io Kanban board. Here, you can see the status of my Kanban board:

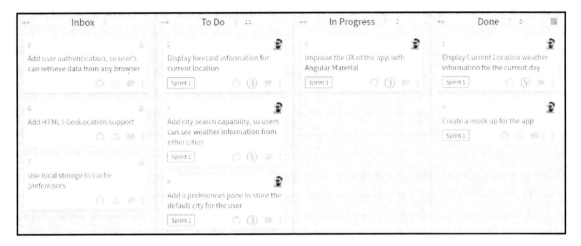

Waffle.io Kanban Board

Automatically

In Angular 6, you can automatically add Angular Material to your project, saving a lot of time in the process:

1. Execute the add command, as shown:

```
$ npx ng add @angular/material
Installing packages for tooling via npm.

+ @angular/material@6.0.1
added 1 package in 15.644s
Installed packages for tooling via npm.
UPDATE package.json (1381 bytes)
UPDATE angular.json (3694 bytes)
UPDATE src/app/app.module.ts (502 bytes)
UPDATE src/index.html (474 bytes)
UPDATE node_modules/@angular/material/prebuilt-themes/indigo-
pink.css (56678 bytes)
added 1 package in 13.031s
```

Note that the `index.html` file has been modified to add the icons library and the default font, as follows:

src/index.html
```
<head>
  <link
href="https://fonts.googleapis.com/icon?family=Material+Icons"
rel="stylesheet">
  <link
href="https://fonts.googleapis.com/css?family=Roboto:300,400,500"
rel="stylesheet">
  ...
</head>
```

Also note that `app.module.ts` has been updated to import `BrowserAnimationsModule`, as demonstrated:

src/app/app.module.ts
```
import { BrowserAnimationsModule } from '@angular/platform-
browser/animations';

@NgModule({
  declarations: [
    AppComponent
  ],
  imports: [
    ...
    BrowserAnimationsModule
  ],
```

2. Start your app and ensure that it works correctly:

$ npm start

With that, you're done. Your app should be configured with Angular Material. It is still important to understand all the various components that make up Angular Material; in the next sections, we will go over the manual installation and configuration steps. You may skip to the *Angular Flex Layout* section, but I strongly recommend skimming over the manual steps, because I introduce the concept of creating an Angular module to organize your Material modules.

Manually

We will begin by installing all required libraries. As of Angular 5, the major version of Angular Material should match the version of your Angular installation and with Angular 6, the versions should be synced:

1. In the terminal, execute `npm install @angular/material @angular/cdk @angular/animations hammerjs`

2. Observe `package.json` versions:

```
package.json
  "dependencies": {
    "@angular/animations": "6.0.0",
    "@angular/cdk": "6.0.0",
    "@angular/material": "6.0.0",
    "hammerjs": "^2.0.8",
    ...
```

In this case, all libraries have the same major and minor version at 5.0. If your major and minor versions don't match, you can rerun the `npm install` command to install a specific version or choose to upgrade your version of Angular by appending the semver version of the package to the install command:

```
$ npm install @angular/material@6.0.0 @angular/cdk@6.0.0
@angular/animations@6.0.0
```

 If you are working on a Bash-like shell, you can save some typing by using the bracket syntax to avoid having to repeat portions of the command, like `npm install @angular/{material,cdk,animations}@6.0.0`.

If you need to update your version of Angular, refer to the *Updating Angular* section in `Chapter 4`, *Staying Up to Date with Angular Updates*.

Understanding Material's components

Let's look at what we are exactly installing:

- `@angular/material` is the official Material 2 library.
- `@angular/cdk` is a peer-dependency, not something you directly use unless you intend to build your own components.

- `@angular/animations` enables some of the animations for some Material 2 modules. It can be omitted to keep app size minimal. You may use `NoopAnimationsModule` to disable animations in the modules that require this dependency. As a result, you will lose some of the UX benefits of Angular Material.
- `hammerjs` enables gesture support; it's critical if you're targeting any touch-enabled device, not just phones and tablets, but also hybrid-laptops.

Manually configuring Angular Material

Now that the dependencies are installed, let's configure Angular Material in our Angular app. Note that if you used `ng add @angular/material` to install Angular Material, some of this work will be done for you.

Importing modules

We will start by creating a separate module file to house all our Material module imports:

1. Execute the following command in the terminal to generate `material.module.ts`:

   ```
   $ npx ng g m material --flat -m app
   ```

   Note the use of the `--flat` flag, which indicates that an additional directory shouldn't be created for `material.module.ts`. Also, note that `-m`, an alias for `--module`, is specified so that our new module is automatically imported into `app.module.ts`.

2. Observe the newly created file `material.module.ts`:

   src/app/material.module.ts
   ```
   import { NgModule } from '@angular/core'
   import { CommonModule } from '@angular/common'

   @NgModule({
     imports: [CommonModule],
     declarations: [],
   })
   export class MaterialModule {}
   ```

3. Ensure that the module has been imported into `app.module.ts`:

src/app/app.module.ts
```
import { MaterialModule } from './material.module'
...
@NgModule({
    ...
    imports: [..., MaterialModule],
}
```

4. Add animations and gesture support (optional, but necessary for mobile device support):

src/app/app.module.ts
```
import 'hammerjs'
import { BrowserAnimationsModule } from '@angular/platform-browser/animations'

@NgModule({
    ...
    imports: [..., MaterialModule, BrowserAnimationsModule],
}
```

5. Modify `material.module.ts` to import basic components for Button, Toolbar, and Icon

6. Remove `CommonModule`:

src/app/material.module.ts
```
import { MatButtonModule, MatToolbarModule, MatIconModule } from '@angular/material'
import { NgModule } from '@angular/core'

@NgModule({
    imports: [MatButtonModule, MatToolbarModule, MatIconModule],
    exports: [MatButtonModule, MatToolbarModule, MatIconModule],
})
export class MaterialModule {}
```

Material is now imported into the app, let's now configure a theme and add the necessary CSS to our app.

Importing theme

A base theme is necessary in order to use Material components. We can define or change the default theme in angular.json:

```
angular.json
...
"styles": [
  {
    "input": "node_modules/@angular/material/prebuilt-themes/indigo-
pink.css"
  },
  "src/styles.css"
],
...
```

1. Choose a new option from here:
   - deeppurple-amber.css
   - indigo-pink.css
   - pink-bluegrey.css
   - purple-green.css

2. Update angular.json to use the new Material theme

 You may create your own themes as well, which is covered in the Custom Themes section of this chapter. For more information, visit https://material.angular.io/guide/theming.

Note that any CSS implemented in styles.css will be globally available throughout the application. That said, do not include view-specific CSS in this file. Every component has their own CSS file for this purpose.

Adding Material Icon font

You can get access to a good default set of iconography by adding the Material Icon web font to your application. Clocking in at 48 kb in size, this is a very lightweight library.

- For icon support, import the font in `index.html`:

src/index.html
```html
<head>
  ...
  <link
href="https://fonts.googleapis.com/icon?family=Material+Icons"
rel="stylesheet">
</head>
```

Discover and search through the icons on `https://www.google.com/design/icons/`.

For a richer set of icons, check out `MaterialDesignIcons.com`. This icon set contains the base set of Material icons, plus a rich set of third-party icons that contains useful imagery from social media sites to a rich set of actions that cover a lot of ground. This font is 118 kb in size.

Angular Flex Layout

Before you can make effective use of Material, you must be aware of its layout engine. If you have been doing web development for a while, you may have encountered Bootstrap's 12-column layout system. A mathematical barrier to my brain wired to divvy things up as parts of a 100%. Bootstrap also demands a strict adherence to a div column, div row hierarchy that must be precisely managed from your top-level HTML all the way to the bottom. This can make for a very frustrating development experience. In the following screenshot, you see can see how Bootstrap's 12-column scheme looks:

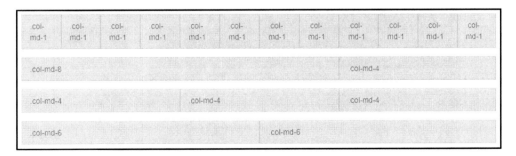

Bootstrap's 12 Column Layout Scheme

Bootstrap's custom grid-layout system was revolutionary for its time, but then CSS3 Flexbox arrived at the scene. In combination with Media Queries, these two technologies allow for creation of responsive user interfaces. However, it is very laborious to effectively leverage these technologies. As of Angular v4.1, the Angular team introduced its Flex Layout system that just works.

Angular Flex Layout documentation on GitHub aptly explains as follows:

> *Angular Flex Layout provides a sophisticated layout API using FlexBox CSS + mediaQuery. This module provides Angular (v4.1 and higher) developers with component layout features using a custom Layout API, mediaQuery observables,and injected DOM flexbox-2016 css stylings.*

Angular's excellent implementation makes it very easy to use FlexBox. As the documentation further explains:

> *The Layout engine intelligently automates the process of applying appropriate FlexBox CSS to browser view hierarchies. This automation also addresses many of the complexities and workarounds encountered with the traditional, manual, CSS-only application of Flexbox CSS.*

The library is highly capable and can accommodate any kind of grid layout you can imagine, including integration with all CSS features you may expect, such as the `calc()` function. In the next illustration, you can see how columns can be described using CSS Flexbox:

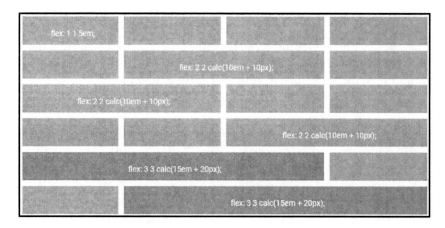

Angular Flex Layout Scheme

The great news is that Angular Flex Layout is no way coupled with Angular Material and can be used independently of it. This is very important decoupling that resolves one of the major pain points of using AngularJS with Material v1, where version updates to Material would often result in bugs in layout.

For more details, check out: `https://github.com/angular/flex-layout/wiki.`

 At the time of publication, `@angular/flex-layout` hasn't delivered a stable release. The GitHub activity on the project suggests a stable release synchronized with the launch of Angular 6. Further, CSS Grid is poised to supersede CSS Flexbox and as a result, the underlying technology that this library uses may change. My wish is that this library acts as an abstraction layer to the layout engine underneath.

Responsive layouts

All UIs you design and build should be mobile-first UIs. This is not just to serve mobile phone browsers, but also cases where a laptop user may use your application side by side with another one. There are many nuances to getting mobile-first design right.

The following is the *Mozilla Holy Grail Layout*, which demonstrates "the ability to dynamically change the layout for different screen resolutions" while optimizing the display content for mobile devices.

 You can read more about Basic concepts of Flexbox at `https://mzl.la/` `2vvxj25.`

This is a representation of how the UI looks on a large screen:

Mozilla Holy Grail Layout on Large Screen

The same layout is represented on a small screen as follows:

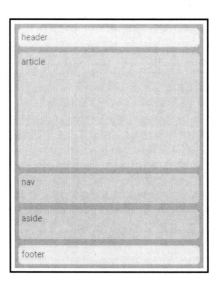

Mozilla Holy Grail Layout on Small Screen

Mozilla's reference implementation takes 85 lines of code to accomplish this kind of responsive UI. Angular Flex Layout accomplishes the same task with only half the code.

Installing Angular Flex Layout

Let's install and add Angular Flex layout to our project:

1. In the terminal, execute `npm i @angular/flex-layout`

 At the time of publishing, the current release of `@angular/flex-layout` is version `5.0.0-beta.14`, which causes numerous peer dependency errors. To get around these errors, execute `npm i @angular/flex-layout@next` to install version `6.0.0-beta.15`, as mentioned in `Chapter 4`, *Staying Up to Date with Angular Updates*.

2. Update `app.module.ts`, as shown:

   src/app.module.ts
   ```
   import { FlexLayoutModule } from '@angular/flex-layout'

   imports: [
   ...
     FlexLayoutModule,
   ],
   ```

Layout basics

Bootstrap and CSS FlexBox are different beasts than Angular Flex Layout. If you learn Angular Flex Layout, you will code a lot less layout code, because Angular Material automatically does the right thing most of the time, but you'll be in for a disappointment once you realize how much more code you have to write to get things working once you leave the protective cocoon of Angular Flex Layout. However, your skills will still translate over, since the concepts are largely the same.

Let's review the Flex Layout APIs in the coming sections.

Flex Layout APIs for DOM containers

These directives can be used on DOM containers such as `<div>` or `<span>`, like `<div fxLayout="row" fxLayoutAlign="start center" fxLayoutGap="15px">...</div>`:

HTML API	Allowed values
fxLayout	\<direction\> | \<direction\> \<wrap\> Use: row | column | row-reverse | column-reverse
fxLayoutAlign	\<main-axis\> \<cross-axis\> main-axis: start |center | end | space-around | space-between cross-axis: start | center | end | stretch
fxLayoutGap	% | px | vw | vh

Flex Layout APIs for DOM elements

These directives influence how DOM elements acts within their container, like `<div fxLayout="column"><input fxFlex /></div>`:

HTML API	Allowed values
fxFlex	"" | px | % | vw | vh | \<grow\> \<shrink\> \<basis\>
fxFlexOrder	int
fxFlexOffset	% | px | vw | vh
fxFlexAlign	start | baseline | center | end
fxFlexFill	*none*

Flex Layout APIs for any element

The following directives can be applied to any HTML element to show, hide, or change the look and feel of the said elements, such as `<div fxShow fxHide.lt-sm></div>`, which will show an element unless the screen size is less than small:

HTML API	Allowed values
`fxHide`	TRUE | FALSE | 0 | ""
`fxShow`	TRUE | FALSE | 0 | ""
`ngClass`	@extends ngClass core
`ngStyle`	@extends ngStyle core

This section covers the basics for Static Layouts. You can read more about the Static APIs at `https://github.com/angular/flex-layout/wiki/Declarative-API-Overview`. We'll cover the Responsive API in *Chapter 10, Angular App Design and Recipes*. You can read more about the Responsive APIs at `https://github.com/angular/flex-layout/wiki/Responsive-API`.

Adding Material Components to your app

Now that we have all the various dependencies installed, we can start modifying our Angular app to add Material components. We will add a toolbar, material design card element, and cover accessibility and typography concerns alongside basic layout techniques.

Angular Material schematics

With Angular 6 and the introduction of schematics, libraries like Material can provide their own code generators. At time of publication, Angular Material ships with three rudimentary generators to create Angular components with a side navigation, a dashboard layout, or a data table. You can read more about generator schematics at `https://material.angular.io/guide/schematics`.

For example, you can create a side navigation layout by executing this:

```
$ ng generate @angular/material:material-nav --name=side-nav

CREATE src/app/side-nav/side-nav.component.css (110 bytes)
CREATE src/app/side-nav/side-nav.component.html (945 bytes)
CREATE src/app/side-nav/side-nav.component.spec.ts (619 bytes)
CREATE src/app/side-nav/side-nav.component.ts (489 bytes)
UPDATE src/app/app.module.ts (882 bytes)
```

This command updates `app.module.ts`, directly importing Material modules into that file, breaking my suggested `material.module.ts` pattern from earlier. Further, a new `SideNavComponent` is added to the app as a separate component, but as mentioned in the *Side Navigation* section in Chapter 9, *Design Authentication and Authorization*, such a navigation experience needs to be implemented at the very root of your application.

In short, Angular Material Schematics hold a promise of making it a lot less cumbersome to add various Material modules and components to your Angular app; however, as provided, these schematics are not suitable for the purposes of creating a flexible, scalable, and well-architected code base, as pursued by this book.

For the time being, I would recommend using these schematics for rapid prototyping or experimentation purposes.

Now, let's start manually adding some components to LocalCast Weather.

Modifying landing page with Material Toolbar

Before we start making further changes to `app.component.ts`, let's switch the component to use inline templates and inline styles, so we don't have to switch back and forth between file for a relatively simple component.

1. Update `app.component.ts` to use an inline template
2. Remove `app.component.html` and `app.component.css`

```
src/app/app.component.ts
import { Component } from '@angular/core'

@Component({
  selector: 'app-root',
  template: `
    <div style="text-align:center">
      <h1>
```

```
        LocalCast Weather
        </h1>
        <div>Your city, your forecast, right now!</div>
        <h2>Current Weather</h2>
        <app-current-weather></app-current-weather>
      </div>

})
export class AppComponent {}
```

Let's start improving our app by implementing an app-wide toolbar:

3. Observe the h1 tag in `app.component.ts`:

   src/app/app.component.ts
   ```
   <h1>
     LocalCast Weather
   </h1>
   ```

4. Update the h1 tag with `mat-toolbar`:

   src/app/app.component.ts
   ```
   <mat-toolbar>
     <span>LocalCast Weather</span>
   </mat-toolbar>
   ```

5. Observe the result; you should see a toolbar, as illustrated:

LocalCast Weather Toolbar

6. Update `mat-toolbar` with a more attention-grabbing color:

src/app/app.component.ts
```
<mat-toolbar color="primary">
```

For a more native feeling, it is important that the toolbar touches the edges of the browser. This works well both on large- and small-screen formats. In addition, when you place clickable elements such as a hamburger menu or a help button on the far-left or far-right side of the toolbar, you'll avoid the potential that the user will click on empty space. This is why Material buttons actually have a larger hit-area than visually represented. This makes a big difference in crafting frustration-free user experiences:

src/styles.css
```
body {
  margin: 0;
}
```

This won't be applicable to this app, however, if you're building a dense application; you'll note that your content will go all the way to the edges of the application, which is not a desirable outcome. Consider wrapping your content area in a div and apply the appropriate margins using css, as shown:

src/styles.css
```
.content-margin {
  margin-left: 8px;
  margin-right: 8px;
}
```

In the next screenshot, you can see the edge-to-edge toolbar with the primary color applied to it:

LocalCast Weather with Improved Toolbar

Representing weather in Material Card

Material card is a great container to represent the current weather information. The card element is surrounded by a drop-shadow that delineates the content from its surroundings:

1. Import `MatCardModule` in `material.module`:

    src/app/material.module.ts
    ```
    import { ..., MatCardModule} from '@angular/material'
    ...
    @NgModule({
      imports: [..., MatCardModule],
      exports: [..., MatCardModule],
    })
    ```

2. In `app.component`, surround `<app-current-weather>` with `<mat-card>`:

    src/app/app.component.ts
    ```
    <div style="text-align:center">
      <mat-toolbar color="primary">
        <span>LocalCast Weather</span>
      </mat-toolbar>
      <div>Your city, your forecast, right now!</div>
      <mat-card>
        <h2>Current Weather</h2>
        <app-current-weather></app-current-weather>
      </mat-card>
    </div>
    ```

3. Observe the barely distinguishable card element, as shown:

LocalCast Weather with Indistinguishable Card

In order to lay out the screen better, we need to switch to the Flex Layout engine. Start by removing the training-wheels from the component template:

4. Remove `style="text-align:center"` from the surrounding `<div>`:

To center an element in a page, we need to create row, assign a width to the center element, and create two additional columns on either side that can flex to take the empty space, such as this:

src/app/app.component.ts
```
<div fxLayout="row">
  <div fxFlex></div>
  <div fxFlex="300px">

    ...
  </div>
  <div fxFlex></div>
</div>
```

5. Surround `<mat-card>` with the preceding HTML
6. Observe that the card element is properly centered, as follows:

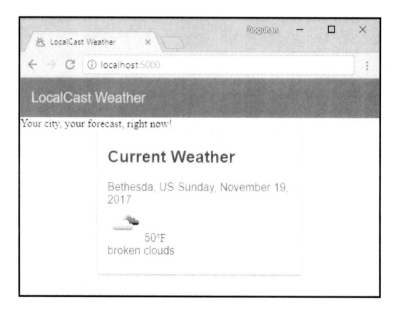

LocalCast Weather with Centered Card

Reading through the Card documentation and looking through the examples on Material's documentation site at `https://material.angular.io/components/card/overview`, you'll note that `mat-card` provides elements to house title and content. We will implement this in the upcoming sections.

 On `material.angular.io`, you can view the source code of any example by clicking on the brackets icons or launch a working example in Plunker by clicking on the arrow icon.

Accessibility

Leveraging such Material features may feel unnecessary; however, you must consider responsiveness, styling, spacing, and accessibility concerns when designing your app. The Material team has put in a lot of effort so that your code works correctly under most circumstances and can serve the largest possible user base with a high-quality user experience. This can include visually-impaired or keyboard-primary users, who must rely on specialized software or keyboard features such as tabs to navigate your app. Leveraging Material elements provides crucial metadata for these users to be able to navigate your app.

Material claims support for the following screen reader software:

- NVDA and JAWS with IE / FF / Chrome (on Windows)
- VoiceOver with Safari on iOS and Safari / Chrome on OSX
- TalkBack with Chrome on Android

Card header and content

Now, let's implement the title and content elements of `mat-card`, as shown:

src/app/app.component.ts
```
<mat-toolbar color="primary">
  <span>LocalCast Weather</span>
</mat-toolbar>
<div>Your city, your forecast, right now!</div>
<div fxLayout="row">
  <div fxFlex></div>
  <mat-card fxFlex="300px">
    <mat-card-header>
      <mat-card-title>Current Weather</mat-card-title>
    </mat-card-header>
    <mat-card-content>
```

```
        <app-current-weather></app-current-weather>
      </mat-card-content>
    </mat-card>
    <div fxFlex></div>
  </div>
```

With Material, less is always more. You'll note that we were able to remove the center `div` and directly apply the `fxFlex` on the center card. All material elements have native support for the Flex Layout engine, and this has tremendous positive maintainability implications in complicated UIs.

After we apply `mat-card-header`, you can see this result:

LocalCast Weather Card with Title and Content

Note that fonts within the card now match Material's Roboto font. However, **Current Weather** is no longer attention grabbing, like before. If you add back in the `h2` tag inside `mat-card-title`, **Current Weather** will visually look bigger; however, the font won't match the rest of your application. To fix this issue, you must understand Material's typography features.

Material typography

Material's documentation aptly puts it as follows:

Typography is a way of arranging type to make text legible, readable, and appealing when displayed.

Material offers a different level of typography that has different font-size, line-height, and font-weight characteristics that you can apply to any HTML element, not just the components provided out of the box.

In the following table are CSS classes that you can use to apply Material's typography, such as `<div class="mat-display-4">Hello, Material world!</div>`:

Class Name	Usage
`display-4`, `display-3`, `display-2` and `display-1`	Large, one-off headers, usually at the top of the page (for example, a hero header)
`headline`	Section heading corresponding to the `<h1>` tag
`title`	Section heading corresponding to the `<h2>` tag
`subheading-2`	Section heading corresponding to the `<h3>` tag
`subheading-1`	Section heading corresponding to the `<h4>` tag
`body-1`	Base body text
`body-2`	Bolder body text
`caption`	Smaller body and hint text
`button`	Buttons and anchors

You can read more about Material Typography at `https://material.angular.io/guide/typography`.

Applying typography

There are multiple ways to apply typography. One way is to leverage the `mat-typography` class and use the corresponding HTML tag like `<h2>`:

src/app/app.component.ts
```
<mat-card-header class="mat-typography">
  <mat-card-title><h2>Current Weather</h2></mat-card-title>
</mat-card-header>
```

Another way is to apply the specific typography directly on an element, like `class="mat-title"`:

src/app/app.component.ts
```
<mat-card-title><div class="mat-title">Current Weather</div></mat-card-title>
```

Note that `class="mat-title"` can be applied to `div`, `span` or an `h2` with the same results.

As a general rule of thumb, it is usually a better idea to implement the more specific and localized option, which is the second implementation.

Updating the tagline as center-aligned caption

We can center the tagline of the application using `fxLayoutAlign` and give it a subdued `mat-caption` typography, as follows:

1. Implement the layout changes and caption typography:

   src/app/app.component.ts
   ```
   <div fxLayoutAlign="center">
     <div class="mat-caption">Your city, your forecast, right now!</div>
   </div>
   ```

2. Observe the results, as shown:

LocalCast Weather Centered Tagline

Updating Current Weather card layout

There's still more work to do to make the UI look like the design, particularly the contents of the Current Weather card, which looks like this:

To design the layout, we'll leverage Angular Flex.

You'll be editing `current-weather.component.html`, which uses the `<div>` and `<span>` tags to establish elements that live on separate lines or on the same line, respectively. With the switch over to Angular Flex, we need switch all elements to `<div>` and specify rows and columns using `fxLayout`.

Implementing Layout Scaffolding

We need to start by implementing the rough scaffolding.

Consider the current state of the template:

```
src/app/current-weather/current-weather.component.html
1  <div *ngIf="current">
2   <div>
3     <span>{{current.city}}, {{current.country}}</span>
4     <span>{{current.date | date:'fullDate'}}</span>
5   </div>
6   <div>
7     <img [src]='current.image'>
8     <span>{{current.temperature | number:'1.0-0'}}°F</span>
9   </div>
10  <div>
11     {{current.description}}
12  </div>
13 </div>
```

Let's go through the file step by step and update it:

1. Update `<span>` elements to `<div>` on lines 3, 4, and 8
2. Wrap the `<img>` element with a `<div>`
3. Add the `fxLayout="row"` property to the `<div>` element that has multiple child elements on lines 2 and 6
4. The City and Country column takes roughly 2/3rds of the screen, so add `fxFlex="66%"` to the `<div>` element on line 3
5. Add `fxFlex` to the next `<div>` element on line 4 to ensure that it takes up the rest of the horizontal space
6. Add `fxFlex="66%"` to the new `<div>` element, surrounding the `<img>` element
7. Add `fxFlex` to the next `<div>` element on line 4

The final state of the template should look like this:

src/app/current-weather/current-weather.component.html

```
1  <div *ngIf="current">
2    <div fxLayout="row">
3      <div fxFlex="66%">{{current.city}},
{{current.country}}</div>
4      <div fxFlex>{{current.date | date:'fullDate'}}</div>
5    </div>
6    <div fxLayout="row">
7      <div fxFlex="66%">
8        <img [src]='current.image'>
9      </div>
10     <div fxFlex>{{current.temperature | number:'1.0-0'}}°F</div>
11   </div>
12   <div>
13     {{current.description}}
14   </div>
15 </div>
```

You can be more verbose in adding Angular Flex attributes; however, the more code you write, the more you'll need to maintain, making future changes more difficult. For example, the `<div>` element on line 12 doesn't need `fxLayout="row"`, since a `<div>` implicitly gets a new line. Similarly, on line 4 and line 7, the right-hand side column doesn't need an explicit `fxFlex` attribute, since it'll automatically be squeezed by the left-hand side element.

From a grid placement perspective, all your elements are now in the correct *cell*, as shown:

LocalCast Weather with layout scaffolding

Aligning elements

Now, we need to align and style each individual cell to match the design. The date and temperature needs to be right aligned and the description centered:

1. To right align the date and temperature, create a new css class named `.right` in `current-weather.component.css`:

   src/app/current-weather/current-weather.component.css
   ```
   .right {
     text-align: right
   }
   ```

2. Add `class="right"` to the `<div>` elements on lines 4 and 10

3. Center the `<div>` element for description in the same way you centered the app's tagline earlier in the chapter

4. Observe that the elements are aligned correctly, as follows:

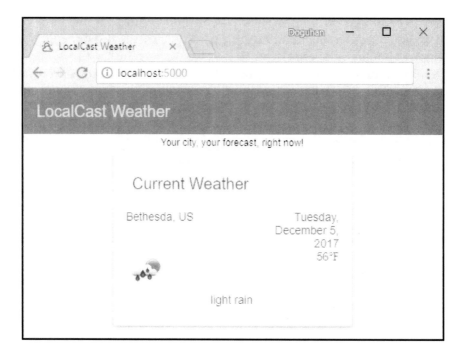

LocalCast Weather with correct alignments

Styling elements

Finalizing the styling of elements is usually the most time-consuming part of frontend development. I recommend doing multiple passes to achieve a close enough version of the design with minimal effort first and then have your client or team decide whether it's worth the extra resources to spend more time to polish the design:

1. Add a new css property:

   `src/app/current-weather/current-weather.component.css`
   ```
   .no-margin {
     margin-bottom: 0
   }
   ```

2. For the city name, on line 3, add `class="mat-title no-margin"`
3. For the date, on line 4, add `"mat-subheading-2 no-margin"` to `class="right"`
4. Change the format of the date from `'fullDate'` to `'EEEE MMM d'` to match the design
5. Modify `<img>`, on line 8 to add `style="zoom: 175%"`
6. For the temperature, on line 10, append `"mat-display-3 no-margin"`
7. For the description, on line 12, add `class="mat-caption"`

   This is the final state of the template:

   `src/app/current-weather/current-weather.component.html`
   ```
   <div *ngIf="current">
     <div fxLayout="row">
       <div fxFlex="66%" class="mat-title no-margin">{{current.city}},
   {{current.country}}</div>
       <div fxFlex class="right mat-subheading-2 no-
   margin">{{current.date | date:'EEEE MMM d'}}</div>
     </div>
     <div fxLayout="row">
       <div fxFlex="66%">
         <img style="zoom: 175%" [src]='current.image'>
       </div>
       <div fxFlex class="right mat-display-3 no-
   margin">{{current.temperature | number:'1.0-0'}}°F</div>
     </div>
     <div fxLayoutAlign="center" class="mat-caption">
       {{current.description}}
     </div>
   </div>
   ```

8. Observe that the styled output of your code changes, as illustrated:

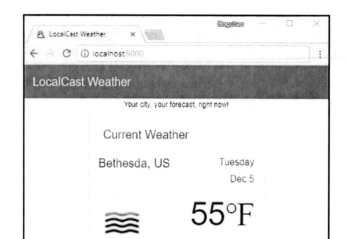

LocalCast Weather with styling

Fine-tuning styles

The tagline can benefit from some top and bottom margins. This is common CSS that we're likely to use across the application, so let's put it in `styles.css`:

1. Implement `vertical-margin`:

   src/styles.css
   ```css
   .vertical-margin {
     margin-top: 16px;
     margin-bottom: 16px;
   }
   ```

2. Apply `vertical-margin`:

   src/app/app.component.ts
   ```
   <div class="mat-caption vertical-margin">Your city, your forecast,
   right now!</div>
   ```

Current Weather has the same style as the City Name; we need to distinguish between the two.

3. In `app.component.ts`, update Current Weather with a `mat-headline` typography:

   src/app/app.component.ts
   ```
   <mat-card-title><div class="mat-headline">Current
   Weather</div></mat-card-title>
   ```

4. The image and the temperature aren't centered, so add `fxLayoutAlign="center center"` to the row surrounding those elements on line 6:

   src/app/current-weather/current-weather.component.html
   ```
   <div fxLayout="row" fxLayoutAlign="center center">
   ```

5. Observe the final design of your app, which should look like this:

LocalCast Weather final design

Tweaking to match design

This is an area where you may spend a significant amount of time. If we were following the 80-20 principal, pixel-perfect tweaks usually end up being the last 20% that takes 80% of the time to complete. Let's examine the differences between our implementation and the design and what it would take to bridge the gap:

The date needs further customization. The numeric ordinal *th* is missing; to accomplish this, we will need to bring in a third-party library such as moment or implement our own solution and bind it next to the date on the template:

1. Update `current.date` to append an ordinal to it:

   src/app/current-weather/current-weather.component.html
   ```
   {{current.date | date:'EEEE MMM d'}}{{getOrdinal(current.date)}}
   ```

2. Implement a `getOrdinal` function:

   src/app/current-weather/current-weather.component.ts
   ```
   export class CurrentWeatherComponent implements OnInit {
   ...
     getOrdinal(date: number) {
       const n = new Date(date).getDate()
       return n > 0
         ? ['th', 'st', 'nd', 'rd'][(n > 3 &amp;&amp; n < 21) || n %
   10 > 3 ? 0 : n % 10]
         : ''
     }
   ...
   }
   ```

Note that the implementation of `getOrdinal` boils down to a complicated one-liner that isn't very readable and is very difficult to maintain. Such functions, if critical to your business logic, should be heavily unit tested.

 Angular 6, at the time of writing, doesn't support new line breaks in the date template; ideally, we should be able to specify the date format as `'EEEE\nMMM d'` to ensure that the line break is always consistent.

The temperature implementation needs to separate the digits from the unit with a `<span>` element, surrounded with a `<p>`, so the superscript style can be applied to the unit, such as `<span class="unit">°F</span>`, where unit is a CSS class to make it look like a superscript element.

3. Implement a `unit` CSS class:

   src/app/current-weather/current-weather.component.css
   ```
   .unit {
     vertical-align: super;
   }
   ```

4. Apply `unit`:

   src/app/current-weather/current-weather.component.html
   ```
   ...
    7 <div fxFlex="55%">
   ...
   10 <div fxFlex class="right no-margin">
   11    <p class="mat-display-3">{{current.temperature |
   number:'1.0-0'}}
   12      <span class="mat-display-1 unit">°F</span>
   13    </p>
   ```

We need to experiment with how much of space the forecast image should have, by tweaking the `fxFlex` value on line 7. Otherwise, the temperature overflows to the next line and your setting can further be affected by the size of your browser window. For example, `60%` works well with a small browser window, but when maximized, it forces an overflow. However, `55%` seems to satisfy both conditions:

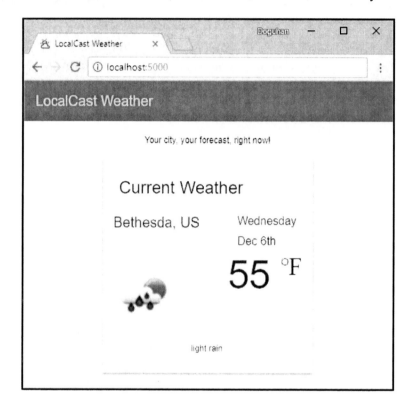

LocalCast Weather after tweaks

As always, it is possible to further tweak margins and paddings to further customize the design. However, each deviation from the library will have maintainability consequences down the line. Unless you're truly building a business around displaying weather data, you should defer any further optimizations to the end of the project, as time permits, and if experience is any guide, you will not be making this optimization.

With two negative margin-bottom hacks, you can attain a design fairly close to the original, but I will not include those hacks here and leave it as an exercise for the reader to discover on the GitHub repository. Such hacks are sometimes necessary evils, but in general, they point to a disconnect between design and implementation realities. The solution leading up to the tweaks section is the sweet spot, where Angular Material thrives:

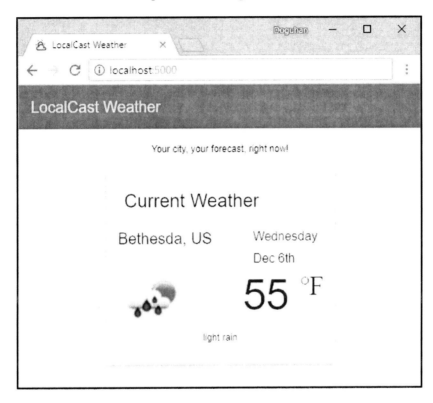

LocalCast Weather after tweaks and hacks

Updating unit tests

In order to keep your unit tests running, you will need to import `MaterialModule` to any component's `spec` file that uses Angular material:

```
*.component.spec.ts
...
  beforeEach(
    async(() => {
      TestBed.configureTestingModule({
        ...
        imports: [..., MaterialModule, NoopAnimationsModule],
      }).compileComponents()
    })
  )
```

You will also need to update any test, including e2e tests, that search for a particular HTML element.

For example, since the app's title, LocalCast Weather, is not in an `h1` tag anymore, you must update the `spec` file to look for it in a `span` element:

```
src/app/app.component.spec.ts
expect(compiled.querySelector('span').textContent).toContain('LocalCast
Weather')
```

Similarly, in e2e tests, you will need to update your page object function to retrieve the text from the correct location:

```
e2e/app.po.ts
getParagraphText() {
  return element(by.css('app-root mat-toolbar span')).getText()
}
```

Custom themes

As we previously discussed, Material ships with some default themes like deeppurple-amber, indigo-pink, pink-bluegrey, and purple-green. However, your company or product may have its own color scheme. For this, you can create a custom theme that change the look of your application.

In order to create a new theme, you must implement a new scss file:

1. Create a new file under `src` called `localcast-theme.scss`
2. Material theme guide, located at `https://material.angular.io/guide/theming`, includes an up-to-date starting file. I'll break down the contents of the file further
3. Start by including the base theming library:

   src/localcast-theme.scss
   ```
   @import '~@angular/material/theming';
   ```

4. Import the `mat-core()` mixin, which includes all common styles used by various Material components:

   src/localcast-theme.scss
   ```
   @include mat-core();
   ```

 `mat-core()` should only be included once in your application; otherwise, you'll introduce unnecessary and duplicated css payload in your application.

`mat-core()` contains the necessary scss functions to be able to inject your custom colors into Material, such as mat-palette, mat-light-theme, and mat-dark-theme.

At a minimum, we must define a new primary and an accent color. Defining new colors, however, is not a straightforward process. Material requires a palette to be defined, mat-palette, which needs to be seeded by a complicated color object that can't just be overridden by a simple hex value such as `#BFB900`.

To pick your colors, you may use the Material Design Color Tool, located at `https://material.io/color`. Here's a screenshot of the tool:

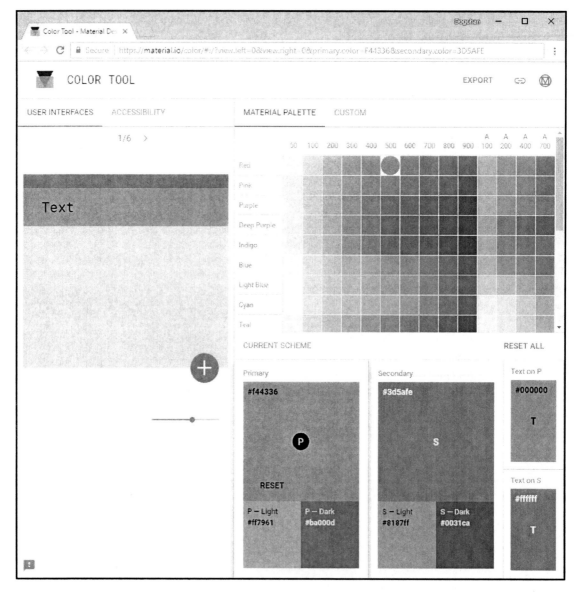

Material.io Color Tool

5. Using **Material Palette**, select a **Primary** and a **Secondary** color:
   - My primary selection is red with a hue value of 500
   - My secondary selection is indigo with a hue value of A400

6. Observe how your selections would apply to a material design app by going through the 6 prebuilt screen on the left

7. Evaluate the accessibility implications of your selections, as shown:

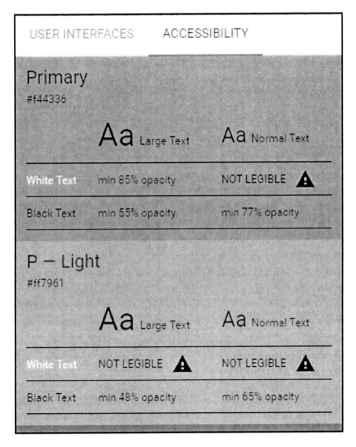

Material.io Color Tool Accessibility tab

The tool is warning us that our selections result in ineligible text, when white text is used over the primary color. You should either take care to avoid displaying white text over your primary color or change your selection.

The interface for `mat-palette` looks like this:

```
mat-palette($base-palette, $default: 500, $lighter: 100, $darker:
700)
```

8. Define the primary and secondary `mat-palette` objects using the default hue from the tool:

src/localcast-theme.scss
```
$localcast-primary: mat-palette($mat-red, 500);
$localcast-accent: mat-palette($mat-indigo, A400);
```

9. Create a new theme and apply it:

src/localcast-theme.scss
```
$localcast-app-theme: mat-light-theme($localcast-primary,
$localcast-accent);

@include angular-material-theme($localcast-app-theme);
```

10. In `angular.json`, locate the `apps.styles` attribute

11. Prepend the list with `localcast-theme.scss` while removing the `styles.input` attribute

angular.json
```
...
"styles": [
  "src/localcast-theme.scss",
  "src/styles.css"
],
...
```

Even though your theme is in scss, you may continue using css in the rest of your application. Angular CLI supports compiling both scss and css. If you would like to change the default behavior, you may switch to scss altogether by changing the `defaults.styleExt` property in the `angular.json` file from css to scss.

You may also choose to eliminate `styles.css` and merge its contents with `localcast-theme.scss` or convert `styles.css` to a sass file by simply renaming it to `styles.scss`. If you do this, don't forget to update `angular.json`.

Your application should now look like this:

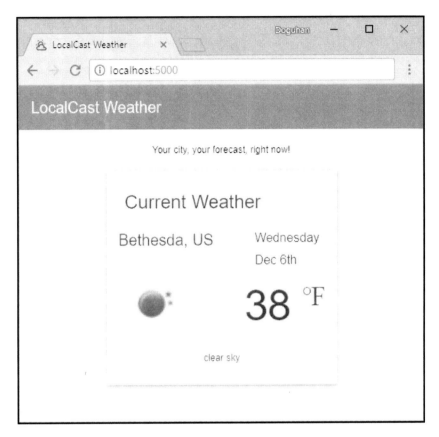

LocalCast Weather with custom theme

We can now move the UX task to the done column:

Waffle.io Kanban Board Status

Advanced themes

In order to create further customized themes, you should consider using the Material Design Theme Palette Generator at `http://mcg.mbitson.com`. This will generate the necessary code to define your custom color palette to create truly unique themes.

You may also find the Color Blender at `https://meyerweb.com/eric/tools/color-blend` to find midway points between two colors.

Updating Angular Material

In `Chapter 4`, *Staying Up to Date with Angular Updates*, we leveraged `ng update` for an automated upgrade experience and also went over a manual and methodical approach to updating packages. We will follow a similar strategy when updating Angular Material.

You can use `ng update` for a quick and painless upgrade experience, which should look like below:

```
$ npx ng update @angular/material
    Updating package.json with dependency @angular/cdk @ "6.0.0" (was
"5.2.2")...
    Updating package.json with dependency @angular/material @ "6.0.0" (was
"5.2.2")...
UPDATE package.json (5563 bytes)
```

In addition, I have discovered the `material-update-tool` published by the Angular team at `https://github.com/angular/material-update-tool`. In it's current form this tool is advertised as a specific Angular Material 5.x to 6.0 updater tool, so it may perhaps become part of `ng update` like the `rxjs-tslint` tool in the future. You may run the tool as shown below:

```
$ npx angular-material-updater -p .\src\tsconfig.app.json

√ Successfully migrated the project source files. Please check above output
for issues that couldn't be automatically fixed.
```

If you're lucky and everything goes well, feel free to skip the rest of this section. For the rest of the section I will go over a specific scenario involving release candidates and beta versions that I ran into during the development of this example, which highlights the need for a manual update. First, we will establish awareness of the current versions, then discover latest available versions, and, finally, update and test the upgrade, like we did while updating Angular manually.

Take stock of your current versions

Observe Angular Material package versions in `package.json`:

```
package.json
"dependencies": {
  "@angular/core": "^5.0.0",
  ...
  "@angular/animations": "^5.0.0",
  "@angular/cdk": "^5.0.0-rc0",
  "@angular/flex-layout": "^2.0.0-beta.10-4905443",
  "@angular/material": "^5.0.0-rc0",
  "hammerjs": "^2.0.8",
},
```

In this particular case, I had installed Material 5.0.0 during its RC phase. It is advisable to not ship Beta or RC libraries. Since our `@angular/core` package indicated that we're on Angular version 5.0.0, we will aim to upgrade to the latest 5.x.x release of Angular Material.

Check on the latest available versions

We will leverage npm CLI tool to discover the latest available versions of Angular Material:

1. Execute `npm info @angular/material` and observe the output:

```
{
  name: '@angular/material',
  description: 'Angular Material',
  'dist-tags': { latest: '5.0.0' },
  versions:
   [ ...
     '5.0.0-rc.0',
     '5.0.0-rc.1',
     '5.0.0-rc.2',
     '5.0.0-rc.3',
     '5.0.0-rc0',
     '5.0.0' ],
  ...
time: {
  created: ...
     '5.0.0-rc0': '2017-11-06T20:15:29.863Z',
     '5.0.0-rc.1': '2017-11-21T00:38:56.394Z',
     '5.0.0-rc.0': '2017-11-27T19:21:19.781Z',
     '5.0.0-rc.2': '2017-11-28T00:13:13.487Z',
     '5.0.0-rc.3': '2017-12-05T21:20:42.674Z',
     '5.0.0': '2017-12-06T20:19:25.466Z'
  }
}
```

You can observe that, combined with the time information found deeper in the output, since the `5.0.0-rc0` release 5 new releases have been pushed, the final version is the major 5.0.0 release of the library.

If there are other major versions of the Material library available, such as 6.0.0, you should still stick to the 5.x.x version, since our `@angular/core` version is at 5.x.x. As rule of thumb, you should aim to keep Angular and Material on the same major versions.

2. Research the latest available versions of
   `@angular/core`, `@angular/animations`, `@angular/cdk`, `@angular/flex-layout`, `@angular/material`, **and** `hammerjs`

3. To reduce the amount of information you need to weed through, execute `npm info <package-name>` versions for each package

4. Document your findings in a table similar to the following; we'll discuss how to determine your target version here:

Package	Current	Latest	Target
@angular/core	5.0.0	5.1.0	5.0.0
@angular/animations	5.0.0	5.1.0	5.0.0
@angular/cdk	5.0.0-rc0	5.0.0	5.0.0
@angular/flex-layout	2.0.0-beta.10-4905443	2.0.0-rc.1	2.x.x
@angular/material	5.0.0-rc0	5.0.0	5.0.0
hammerjs	2.0.8	2.0.8	2.x.x

Research results reveal that a new minor version of Angular was released, which is useful information to have. In determining your target version, stay conservative. Follow the following guidance:

- Do not update Angular components while updating Material
- If you intended to also update Angular components, do it in separate phases and ensure that you execute your tests after each individual phase
- Update any Beta or RC package to its latest available version
- When new versions of packages are available, stay within the same Major release of the package
- Adhere to these guidelines, unless the documentation suggests otherwise

Updating Angular Material

Now that we know what version to upgrade to, let's go ahead and do it:

1. Execute the following command to update Material and its related components to their target versions:

   ```
   $ npm install @angular/material@^5.0.0 @angular/cdk@^5.0.0
   @angular/animations@^5.0.0 @angular/flex-layout@^2.0.0-rc.1
   ```

2. Verify your `package.json` to ensure that the versions match the expected version

3. Address any NPM Warnings (as detailed in `Chapter 4`, *Staying Up to Date with Angular Updates*, in the *Updating Angular* section)

In this specific instance, I receive impossible-to-meet peer dependency warnings by the `@angular/flex-layout` package. Further investigation on GitHub (`https://github.com/angular/flex-layout/issues/508`) reveals that this is a known issue and in general to be expected from a Beta or RC package. This means it is safe to ignore these warnings.

After your upgrade is complete, ensure that you execute the Post Update Checklist, as detailed in `Chapter 4`, *Staying Up to Date with Angular Updates.*

Summary

In this chapter, you learned what Angular Material is, how to use the Angular Flex layout engine, the impact of UI libraries on performance, and how to apply specific Angular Material components to your application. You became aware of pitfalls of overly-optimizing UI design and how to add a custom theme to your application. We also went over how you can keep Angular Material up-to-date.

In the next chapter, we will update the weather app to respond to user input with reactive forms and keep our components decoupled, while also enabling data exchange between them using `BehaviorSubject`. After the next chapter, we will be done with the weather app and shift our focus on building larger, line-of-business applications.

6
Reactive Forms and Component Interaction

So far, you've been working with putting together the basic elements that make up an Angular application, such as modules, components, pipes, services, RxJS, unit testing, environment variables, and even going a step ahead by learning how to deliver your web application using Docker and make it look polished with Angular Material.

In order to build truly dynamic applications, we need to build features that enable rich user interactions and leverage modern web functionality such as `LocalStorage` and `GeoLocation`. You also need to become proficient with new Angular syntax to effectively leverage binding, conditional layouts, and repeating elements.

You need to be able to work with Angular Forms to create input fields with validation messages, create engaging search experiences with search-as-you-type functionality, provide users a way to customize their preferences, and be able to persist this information both locally and on a server. Your applications will likely have multiple components sharing data.

As your app matures and you involve more people to work on it with you or communicate your ideas to your colleagues, it becomes increasingly difficult to do so with just a hand-drawn sketch. This means we need a more professional mock-up, preferably an interactive one, to best demonstrate the planned UX for the app.

In this chapter, you will do the following:

1. Become aware of these:
   - Two-way binding
   - Template driven forms

2. Become proficient in interactions between components

3. Be able to create these:
   - Interactive prototype
   - Input field and validation using Angular Reactive Forms

Interactive prototype

Appearances do matter. Whether you're working on a development team or as a freelancer, your colleagues, bosses, or clients will always take a well put together presentation more seriously. In `Chapter 2`, *Create a Local Weather Web Application*, I mentioned the time and information management challenges of being a full-stack developer. We must pick a tool that can achieve the best results with the least amount of work. This usually means going down the paid-tool route, but UI/UX design tools are rarely free or cheap.

A prototyping tool will help you create a better, more professional looking, mock up of the app. Whatever tool you choose should also support the UI framework you choose to use, in this case, Material.

If a picture is worth a 1,000 words, an interactive prototype of your app is worth a 1,000 lines of code. An interactive mock-up of the app will help you vet ideas before you write a single line of code and save you a lot of code writing.

MockFlow WireFramePro

I've picked MockFlow WireFramePro, `https://mockflow.com`, as an easy-to-use, capable, and online tool that supports Material design UI elements and allows you to create multiple pages, which can then be linked together to create the illusion of a working application.

Most importantly, at the time of publishing, MockFlow allows one free project forever with the full feature set and capabilities available. This will give you a chance to truly vet the usefulness of the tool without artificial limits or a trial period that always seems to go by much quicker than you expect.

Balsamiq is the better-known wireframing tool. However, `https://balsamiq.com` doesn't offer any free usage, but if you are looking for a tool without a monthly cost, I would highly recommend Balsamiq's desktop application Mockups, which has a one-time purchase cost.

Building the mock-up

We start by adding a new task to create an interactive prototype and at the end of the task, I'll attach all artifacts to this task so that they're stored on GitHub where it is accessible to all team members and also can be linked from the Wiki page for persistent documentation. Let's pull this new task to the **In Progress** column and take a look at the status of our Kanban board from Waffle.io:

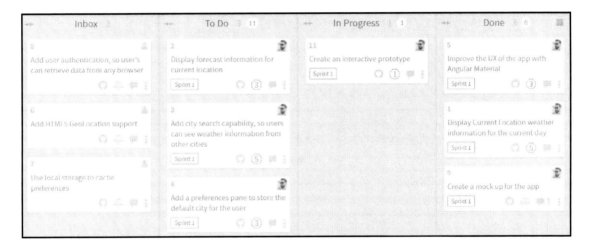

WireframePro is pretty intuitive as a drag and drop design interface, so I won't go into the details of how the tool works, but I will highlight some tips:

1. Create your project
2. Select a component pack, either **Hand Drawn UI** or **Material design**

3. Add each screen as a new page, as shown:

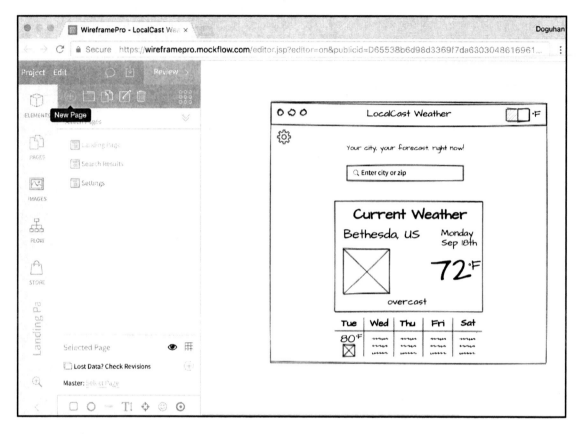

MockFlow.com WireFrame Pro

I would recommend sticking to the hand-drawn UI look and feel, because it sets the right expectation with your audience. If you present a very high quality of a mock-up on your first meeting with a client, your first demo will be an understatement. You will, at best, merely meet expectations and, at worst, underwhelm your audience.

Home screen

Here's the new mock-up of the home screen:

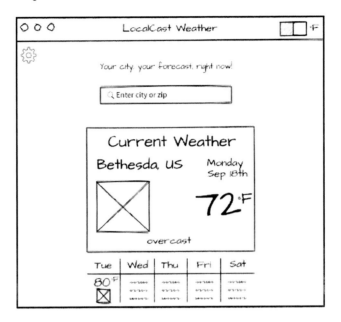

LocalCast Weather Wireframe

You'll note some differences, such as the app toolbar being conflated with the browser bar and the intentional vagueness of the repeating elements. I have made these choices to reduce the amount of design time I would need to spend on each screen. I simply used horizontal and vertical line objects to create the grid.

Search results

The search screen similarly remains intentionally vague to avoid having to maintain any kind of detailed information. Surprisingly, your audience is far more likely to focus on what your test data is rather than focusing on the design elements.

By being vague, we intentionally keep the audiences attention on what matters. Here's the search screen mock-up:

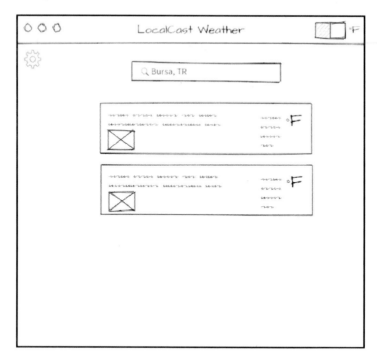

LocalCast Weather Search Wireframe

Settings pane

The settings pane is a separate screen with the elements from the home screen copied over and applied 85% opacity to create a model-like experience. The settings pane itself is just a rectangle with a black border and a solid white background.

Take a look at the following mock-up:

LocalCast Weather Settings Wireframe

Adding interactivity

Being able to click around a mock-up and get a feel for the navigational workflow is an indispensable tool to get early user feedback. This will save you and your clients a lot of frustration, time, and money.

To link elements together, do as follows:

1. Select a clickable element such as the *gear* icon on the Home Screen
2. Under the **Link** subheading, click on **Select Page**
3. On the pop-over window, select **Settings**

4. Click on **Create Link**, as shown in this screenshot:

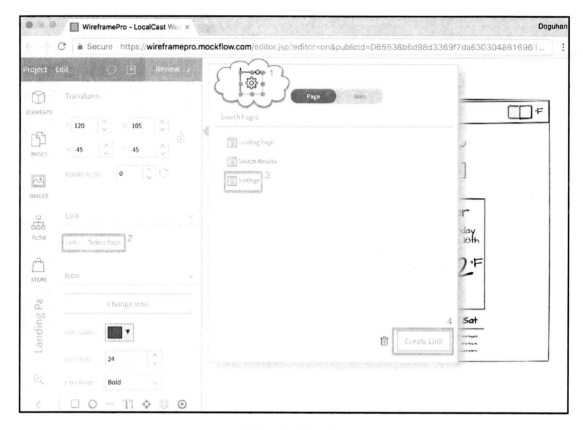

WireFrame Pro - Adding a Link

Now, when you click on the *gear* icon, the tool will display the **settings** page, which will create the effect of the sidebar actually displayed on the same page. To go back to the home screen, you can link the gear icon and the section outside of the sidebar back to that page so that the user can navigate back and forth.

Exporting the functional prototype

Once your prototype is completed, you can export it as various formats:

1. Select the **Export wireframe** button, as shown:

WireFrame Pro - Export wireframe

2. Now select your file format, as follows:

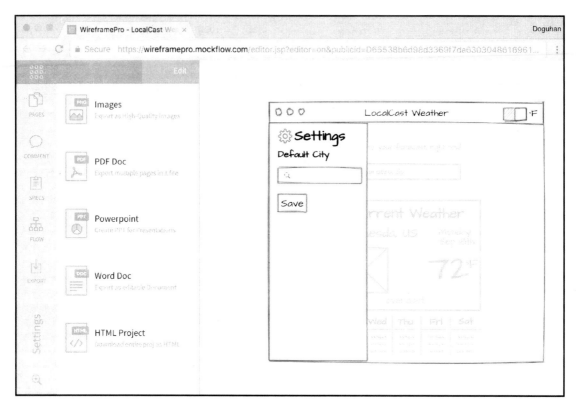

WireFrame Pro - File formats

I prefer the HTML format, for flexibility; however, your workflow and needs will differ.

3. If you selected HTML, you will get to download a ZIP bundle of all the assets.

4. Unzip the bundle and navigate to it using your browser; you should get an interactive version of your wireframe, as illustrated:

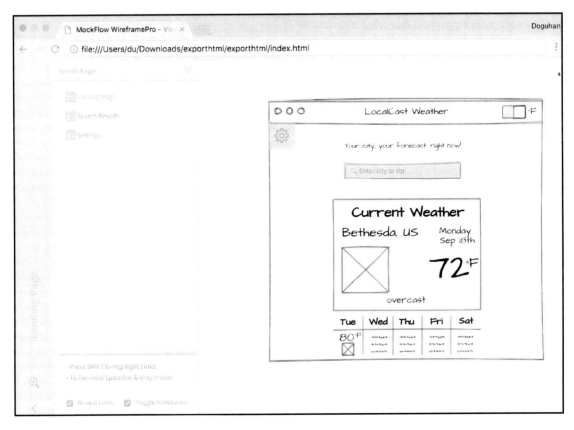

WireFrame Pro - Interactive Wireframe

The interactive elements are highlighted in yellow in the following screenshot. You can enable or disable this behavior with the `Reveal Links` option on the bottom-left corner of the screen.

You can even containerize the prototype HTML project using `minimal-nginx-server` or `minimal-node-server` and host it on Zeit Now, using the exact same techniques discussed in `Chapter 3`, *Prepare Angular App for Production Release*.

Now add all assets to a comment on the GitHub issue, including the ZIP bundle, and we are ready to move on to the next task. Let's move **Add city search card ...** to **In Progress**, as shown in our Kanban board:

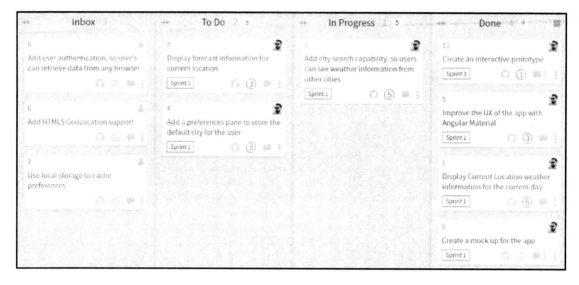

Waffle.io Kanban Board

Searching with user input

Now, we'll implement the search bar on the home screen of the application. The user story states **display forecast information for current location**, which may be taken to imply an inherit GeoLocation functionality. However, as you may note, GeoLocation is listed as a separate task. The challenge is that with native platform features such as GeoLocation, you are never guaranteed to receive the actual location information. This may be due to signal loss issues on mobile devices or the user may simply refuse to give permission to share their location information.

First and foremost, we must deliver a good baseline UX and implement value-add functionality such as GeoLocation only afterwards. We will be implementing a search-as-you-type functionality, while providing feedback to the user, if the service is unable to retrieve the expected data.

Initially, it may be intuitive to implement a type-ahead search mechanism; however, OpenWeatherMap APIs don't provide such an endpoint. Instead, they provide bulk data downloads, which are costly and are in the multiples of megabytes range.

We will need to implement our own application server to expose such an endpoint so that our app can effectively query, while using minimal amounts of data.

The free endpoints for OpenWeatherMap does pose an interesting challenge, where a two-digit country code may accompany either a city name or zip code for the most accurate results. This is a good opportunity to implement a feedback mechanism to the user if more than one result is returned for a given query.

We want every iteration of the app to be a potentially releasable increment and avoid doing too much at any given one time.

We will do the following:

1. Add Angular Form Control
2. Use Angular Material Input as documented at `https://material.angular.io/components/input`
3. Create the search bar as its own component
4. Extend the existing endpoint to accept zip code and make country code optional in `weather.service`
5. Throttle requests

Adding Angular Reactive Forms

You may wonder why we're adding Angular Forms, since we are adding just a single input field and not a form with multiple inputs. As a general rule of thumb, any time you add any input field, it should be wrapped in a `<form>` tag . The `Forms` module contains the `FormControl` that enables you to write the backing code behind the input field to respond to user inputs, and provide the appropriate data or the validation or message in response.

There are two types of Forms in Angular:

- **Template Driven:** These forms are similar to what you may be familiar from AngularJS, where the form logic is mostly inside the HTML template. I'm personally not a fan of this approach, because it is harder to test these behaviors, and fat HTML templates become difficult to maintain quickly.
- **Reactive:** The behavior of Reactive forms is driven by TypeScript code written in the controller. This means that your validation logic can be unit tested and, better yet, reused across your application. Read more about Reactive forms at `https://angular.io/guide/reactive-forms`.

Let's start by importing the `ReactiveFormsModule` into our app:

src/app/app.module.ts
```
...
import { FormsModule, ReactiveFormsModule } from '@angular/forms'
...
@NgModule({
  ...
  imports: [
    ...
    FormsModule,
    ReactiveFormsModule,
    ...
```

Reactive forms is the core technology that will enable the Angular Material team to write richer tools, like one that can autogenerate an input form based off of a TypeScript interface in the future.

Adding and verifying components

We will be creating a `citySearch` component using Material form and input modules:

1. Add `MatFormFieldModule` and `MatInputModule` to `material.module` so that it becomes available for use in the app:

    src/app/material.module.ts
    ```
    import {
      ...
      MatFormFieldModule,
      MatInputModule,
    } from '@angular/material'
    ...
    @NgModule({
      imports: [
        ...
        MatFormFieldModule,
        MatInputModule,
      ],
      exports: [
        ...
        MatFormFieldModule,
        MatInputModule,
      ],
    })
    ```

We're adding `MatFormFieldModule`, because each input field should be wrapped in a `<mat-form-field>` tag to get the most out of Angular Material functionality. At a high-level, `<form>` encapsulates numerous default behaviors for keyboard, screen-reader, and browser extension users; `<mat-form-field>` enables easy two-way data binding, a technique that should be used in moderation and also allows for graceful label, validation, and error message display.

2. Create the new `citySearch` component:

   ```
   $ npx ng g c citySearch --module=app.module
   ```

   Since we added the `material.module.ts` file, `ng` can't guess what feature module citySearch should be added to, resulting in an error such as **More than one module matches**. Therefore, we need to provide the module that we want `citySearch` to be added to, with the `--module` option. Use the `--skip-import` option to skip importing the component into any module.

3. Create a basic template:

   src/app/city-search/city-search.component.html
   ```html
   <form>
     <mat-form-field>
       <mat-icon matPrefix>search</mat-icon>
       <input matInput placeholder="Enter city or zip" aria-label="City or Zip" [formControl]="search">
     </mat-form-field>
   </form>
   ```

4. Import and instantiate an instance of `FormControl`:

   src/app/city-search/city-search.component.ts
   ```ts
   import { FormControl } from '@angular/forms'
   ...
   export class CitySearchComponent implements OnInit {
     search = new FormControl()
     ...
   ```

Reactive forms have three levels of controls:

- `FormControl` is the most basic element that has a one-to-one relationship with an input field
- `FormArray` represents repetitive input fields that represent a collection of objects
- `FormGroup` is used to register individual `FormControl` or `FormArray` objects as you add more input fields to a form

Finally, the `FormBuilder` object is used to more easily orchestrate and maintain the actions of a `FormGroup`, which will be covered in Chapter 10, *Angular App Design and Recipes*.

5. Add `app-city-search` to `app.component` in between the caption on the out row that contains `app-current-weather`:

src/app/app.component.ts

```
...
  </div>
  <div fxLayoutAlign="center">
    <app-city-search></app-city-search>
  </div>
  <div fxLayout="row">
...
```

6. Test the integration of components by checking out the app in the browser, as shown:

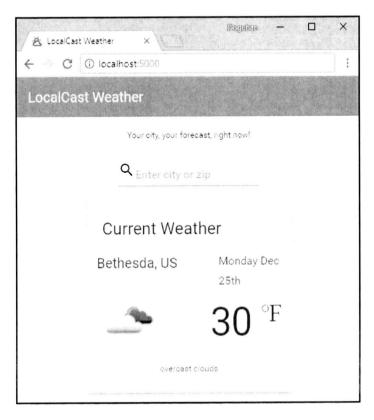

LocalWeather App with Search Field

If you've no errors, now we can start adding the `FormControl` elements and wire them to a search endpoint.

Adding search to weather service

So far, we have been passing parameters to get the weather for a city using its name and country code. By allowing users to enter zip codes, we must make our service more flexible to accept both types of inputs.

OpenWeatherMap's API accepts URI parameters, so we can refactor the existing `getCurrentWeather` function using a TypeScript union type and using a type guard, we can supply different parameters, while preserving type checking:

1. Refactor the `getCurrentWeather` function in `weather.service` to handle both zip and city inputs:

app/src/weather/weather.service.ts
```
getCurrentWeather(
  search: string | number,
  country?: string
): Observable<ICurrentWeather> {
  let uriParams = ''
  if (typeof search === 'string') {
    uriParams = `q=${search}`
  } else {
    uriParams = `zip=${search}`
  }

  if (country) {
    uriParams = `${uriParams},${country}`
  }

  return this.getCurrentWeatherHelper(uriParams)
}
```

We renamed the city parameter to `search`, since it can either be a city name or a zip code. We then allowed its type to be either a `string` or a `number`, and depending on what the type is at runtime, we will either use `q` or `zip`. We also made `country` optional and only append it to the query if it exists.

`getCurrentWeather` now has business logic embedded into it and thus is a good target for unit testing. Following the Single Responsibility Principle, from SOLID principles, we will refactor the HTTP call to its own function, called `getCurrentWeatherHelper`.

2. Refactor the HTTP call into `getCurrentWeatherHelper`.

In the next sample, note the use of a back-tick character ` instead of a single-quote character ', which leverages the template literals functionality that allows embedded expressions in JavaScript:

src/app/weather/weather.service.ts
```
private getCurrentWeatherHelper(uriParams: string):
Observable<ICurrentWeather> {
```

```
        return this.httpClient
          .get<ICurrentWeatherData>(
    `${environment.baseUrl}api.openweathermap.org/data/2.5/weather?` +
          `${uriParams}&appid=${environment.appId}`
          )
          .pipe(map(data => this.transformToICurrentWeather(data)))
      }
```

As a positive side effect, `getCurrentWeatherHelper` adheres to the Open/Closed principle, because it is open to extension by our ability to change the function's behavior by supplying different `uriParams` and is closed to modification, because it won't have to be changed frequently.

To demonstrate the latter point, let's implement a new function to get the current weather by latitude and longitude.

3. Implement `getCurrentWeatherByCoords`:

   src/app/weather/weather.service.ts
   ```
   getCurrentWeatherByCoords(coords: Coordinates):
   Observable<ICurrentWeather> {
     const uriParams =
   `lat=${coords.latitude}&lon=${coords.longitude}`
     return this.getCurrentWeatherHelper(uriParams)
   }
   ```

   As you can see, `getCurrentWeatherHelper` can easily be extended without any modification.

4. Ensure that you update `IWeatherService` with the changes made earlier.

As a result of adhering to SOLID design principles, we make it easier to robustly unit test flow-control logic and ultimately end up writing code that is more resilient to bugs and is cheaper to maintain.

Implementing search

Now, let's connect the new service method to the input field:

1. Update `citySearch` to inject the `weatherService` and subscribe to input changes:

   src/app/city-search/city-search.component.ts
   ```
   ...
   ```

```
export class CitySearchComponent implements OnInit {
  search = new FormControl()
  constructor(private weatherService: WeatherService) {}
  ...
  ngOnInit() {
    this.search.valueChanges
      .subscribe(...)
  }
```

We are treating all input as string at this point. The user input can be a city, zip code or a city and country code, or zip code and country code separated by a comma. While city or zip code is required, country code is optional. We can use the String.split function to parse any potential comma separated input and then trim any whitespace out from the beginning and the end of the string with String.trim. We then ensure that we trim all parts of the string by iterating over them with Array.map.

We then deal with the optional parameter with ternary operator ?:, only passing in a value if it exists, otherwise leaving it undefined.

2. Implement the search handler:

    src/app/city-search/city-search.component.ts
    ```
    this.search.valueChanges
      .subscribe((searchValue: string) => {
        if (searchValue) {
          const userInput = searchValue.split(',').map(s => s.trim())
          this.weatherService.getCurrentWeather(
            userInput[0],
            userInput.length > 1 ? userInput[1] : undefined
          ).subscribe(data => (console.log(data)))
        }
      })
    ```

3. Add a hint for the user about the optional country functionality:

    src/app/city-search/city-search.component.html
    ```
    ...
      <mat-form-field>
        ...
        <mat-hint>Specify country code like 'Paris, US'</mat-hint>
      </mat-form-field>
    ...
    ```

At this point, the subscribe handler will make calls to the server and log its output to the console.

Observe how this works with Chrome Dev Tools. Note how often the `search` function is run and also that we are not handling service errors.

Limiting user inputs with throttle/debounce

As is, we submit a request to the server with every keystroke. This is not a desirable behavior, because it can lead to a bad user experience, drain battery life, result in wasted network requests, and create performance issues both on the client and server side. Users make typos; they can change their mind about what they are inputting and rarely ever, the first few characters of information input result in useful results.

We can still listen to every keystroke, but we don't have to react to every keystroke. By leveraging throttle/debounce, we can limit the number of events generated to a predetermined interval and still maintain the type-as-you-search functionality.

Note that `throttle` and `debounce` are not functional equivalents, and their behavior will differ from framework to framework. In addition to throttling, we expect to capture the last input that the user has typed. In the `lodash` framework, the throttle function fulfills this requirement, whereas in RxJS, debounce fulfills it. Beware that this discrepancy may be fixed in future framework updates.

It is very easy to inject throttling into the observable stream using `RxJS/debounceTime`.

Implement `debounceTime` with `pipe`:

src/app/city-search/city-search.component.ts
```
import { debounceTime } from 'rxjs/operators'

    this.search.valueChanges
      .pipe(debounceTime(1000))
      .subscribe(...)
```

`debounceTime` will, at a maximum, run a search every second, but also run a last search after the user has stopped typing. In comparison, `RxJS/throttleTime` will only run a search every second, on the second, and will not necessarily capture the last few characters the user may have input.

RxJS also has the `throttle` and `debounce` functions, which you can use to implement custom logic to limit input that is not necessarily time-based.

Since this is a time- and event-driven functionality, break point debugging is not feasible. You may monitor the network calls within the **Chrome Dev Tools | Network** tab, but to get a more real-time feeling of how often your search handler is actually being invoked, add a `console.log` statement.

It is not a good practice to check in code with active `console.log` statements. As covered in `Chapter 3`, *Prepare Angular App for Production Release*, `console.log` is a poor-man's debugging method. The statements make it difficult to read the actual code, which itself bears a high cost of maintainability. So, whether they are commented out or not, do not check in code with `console.log` statements.

Implementing input validation and error messaging

`FormControl` is highly customizable. It allows you to set a default initial value, add validators, or listen to changes on blur, change, and submit events, as follows:

example
```
new FormControl('Bethesda', { updateOn: 'submit' })
```

We won't be initializing the `FormControl` with a value, but we need to implement a validator to disallow one character inputs:

1. Import `Validators` from `@angular/forms`:

   src/app/city-search/city-search.component.ts
   ```
   import { FormControl, Validators } from '@angular/forms'
   ```

2. Modify `FormControl` to add a minimum length validator:

   src/app/city-search/city-search.component.ts
   ```
   search = new FormControl('', [Validators.minLength(2)])
   ```

3. Modify the template to show a validation error message:

   src/app/city-search/city-search.component.html
   ```
   ...
   <form style="margin-bottom: 32px">
     <mat-form-field>
       ...
       <mat-error *ngIf="search.invalid">
         Type more than one character to search
   ```

```
        </mat-error>
      </mat-form-field>
  </form>
  . . .
```

 Note the addition of some extra margin to make room for lengthy error messages.

If you are handling different kinds of errors, the `hasError` syntax in the template can get repetitive. You may want to implement a more scalable solution that can be customized through code, as shown:

example
```
<mat-error *ngIf="search.invalid">{{getErrorMessage()}}</mat-error>

getErrorMessage() {
    return this.search.hasError('minLength') ? 'Type more than one
character to search' : '';
}
```

4. Modify the `search` function to not execute a search with invalid input:

src/app/city-search/city-search.component.ts
```
this.search.valueChanges.pipe(debounceTime(1000)).subscribe((search
Value: string) => {
        if (!this.search.invalid) {
            . . .
```

Instead of doing a simple check to see whether `searchValue` is defined and not an empty string, we can tap in to the validation engine for a more robust check by calling `this.search.invalid`.

Template driven forms with two-way binding

The alternative to Reactive forms are Template driven forms. If you're familiar with `ng-model` from AngularJS, you'll find that the new `ngModel` directive is an API compatible replacement for it.

Behind the scenes, `ngModel` implements a `FormControl` that can automatically attach itself to a `FormGroup`. `ngModel` can be used at the `<form>` level or individual `<input>` level. You can read more about `ngModel` at `https://angular.io/api/forms/NgModel`.

In the Local Weather app, I have included a commented-out component in `app.component.ts` named `app-city-search-tpldriven`. You can uncomment this component in `app.component` to experiment with it. Let's see how the alternate template implementation looks like:

src/app/city-search-tpldriven/city-search-tpldriven.component.html

```
...
  <input matInput placeholder="Enter city or zip" aria-label="City or
Zip"
      [(ngModel)]="model.search" (ngModelChange)="doSearch($event)"
      minlength="2" name="search" #search="ngModel">
...
  <mat-error *ngIf="search.invalid">
    Type more than one character to search
  </mat-error>
...
```

Note the `[()]` "box of bananas" two-way binding syntax being used with `ngModel`.

The differences in the component are implemented as follows:

src/app/city-search-tpldriven/city-search-tpldriven.component.ts

```
import { NgModel, Validators} from '@angular/forms'
...
export class CitySearchTpldrivenComponent implements OnInit {
  model = {
    search: '',
  }
  ...
  doSearch(searchValue) {
    const userInput = searchValue.split(',').map(s => s.trim())
    this.weatherService
      .getCurrentWeather(userInput[0], userInput.length > 1 ? userInput[1]
: undefined)
      .subscribe(data => console.log(data))
  }
```

As you can see, most of the logic is implemented in the template, and the programmer is required to maintain an active mental model of what's in the template and the controller and switch back and forth between the two files to make changes to event handlers and validation logic.

Furthermore, we have lost the input limiting and the ability to prevent service calls when the input is in an invalid state. It is, of course, possible to still implement these features, but they require convoluted solutions and do not neatly fit into the new Angular syntax and concepts.

Enabling component interaction

In order to update current weather information, we need the `city-search` component to interact with the `current-weather` component. There are four main techniques to enable component interaction in Angular:

- Global events
- Parent components listening for information bubbling up from children components
- Sibling, parent, or children components within a module that work off of similar data streams
- Parent components passing information to children components

Global events

This a technique that's been leveraged since the early days of programming in general. In JavaScript, you may have achieved this with global function delegates or jQuery's event system. In AngularJS, you may have created a service and stored values in it.

In Angular, you can still create a root level service, store values in it, use Angular's `EventEmitter` class, which is really meant for directives, or use an `rxjs/Subscription` to create a fancy messaging bus for yourself.

As a pattern, global events are open to rampant abuse and rather than helping maintain a decoupled application architecture, it leads to global state over time. Global state or even localized state at the controller level, where functions read and write to variables in any given class, is enemy number one of writing maintainable and unit testable software.

Ultimately, if you're storing all your application data or routing all events in one service to enable component interaction, you're merely inventing a better mouse trap. This is an anti-pattern that should be avoided at all costs. In a later section, you will find that essentially we will still be using services to enable component interaction; however, I want to point out that there's a fine line that exists between a flexible architecture that enables decoupling and the global or centralized decoupling approach that does not scale well.

Child-parent relationships with event emitters

Your child component should be completely unaware of its parent. This is key to creating reusable components.

We can implement the communication between the city search component and the current weather component leveraging app component as a parent element and let the app module controller orchestrate the data.

Let's see how this implementation will look:

1. The `city-search` component exposes an `EventEmitter` through an `@Output` property:

   src/app/city-search/city-search.component.ts
   ```
   import { Component, Output, EventEmitter } from '@angular/core'

   export class CitySearchComponent implements OnInit {
     ...
     @Output() searchEvent = new EventEmitter<string>()

     ...
   this.search.valueChanges.debounceTime(1000).subscribe(((searchValue:
   string) => {
       if (!this.search.invalid) {
         this.searchEvent.emit(this.searchValue)
       }
     })
     ...
   }
   ```

2. The app component consumes that and calls the `weatherService`, setting the `currentWeather` variable:

   src/app/app.component.ts
   ```
   template: `
     ...
   ```

```
        <app-city-search (searchEvent)="doSearch($event)"></app-city-
search>
    ...


export class AppComponent {
  currentWeather: ICurrenWeather
  constructor() { }

  doSearch(searchValue) {
    const userInput = searchValue.split(',').map(s => s.trim())
    this.weatherService
      .getCurrentWeather(userInput[0], userInput.length > 1 ?
userInput[1] : undefined)
      .subscribe(data => this.currentWeather = data)
  }
}
```

We have been able to successfully bubble up the information, but now we must be able to pass it down to the `current-weather` component.

Parent-child relationships with input binding

By definition, your parent component will be aware of what child components it is working with. Since the `currentWeather` property is bound to the `current` property on the `current-weather` component, the results pass down to be displayed. This is achieved by creating an `@Input` property:

src/app/current-weather/current-weather.component.ts
```
import { Component, Input } from '@angular/core'
...
export class CurrentWeatherComponent implements OnInit {
 @Input() current: ICurrentWeather
  ...
}
```

You can then update `app` component to bind the data to `current` weather:

src/app/app.component.ts
```
template: `
  ...
    <app-current-weather [current]="currentWeather"></app-current-weather>
  ...
```

This approach may be appropriate in cases where you are creating well-coupled components or user controls and no outside data is being consumed. A good example might be adding forecast information to the `current-weather` component, as shown:

Tue	Wed	Thu	Fri	Sat
80°F ⊠				

Weather Forecast Wireframe

Each day of the week can be implemented as a component that is repeated using `*ngFor`, and it will be perfectly reasonable for `current-weather` to retrieve and bind this information to its children component:

example
```
<app-mini-forecast *ngFor="let dailyForecast of forecastArray
  [forecast]="dailyForecast">
</app-mini-forecast>
```

In general, if you're working with data-driven components, the parent-child or child-parent communication pattern results in an inflexible architecture, making it very difficult to reuse or rearrange your components. Given the ever-changing business requirements and design, this is an important lesson to keep in mind.

Sibling interactions with subjects

The main reason for components to interact is to send or receive updates to data either provided by the user or received from the server. In Angular, your services expose `RxJS.Observable` endpoints, which are data-streams that your components can subscribe to. `RxJS.Observer` compliments `RxJS.Observable` as a consumer of events emitted by `Observable`. `RxJS.Subject` brings the two sets of functionalities together, in an easy to work with object. You can essentially describe a stream that belongs to a particular set of data, such as the current weather data that is being displayed, with subjects:

src/app/weather/weather.service.ts
```
import { Subject } from 'rxjs'
...
export class WeatherService implements IWeatherService {
  currentWeather: Subject<ICurrentWeather>
  ...
}
```

`currentWeather` is still a data stream and does not simply represent one data point. You can subscribe to changes to `currentWeather` data with subscribe, or you can publish changes to it as follows:

example
```
currentWeather.subscribe(data => (this.current = data))
currentWeather.next(newData)
```

The default behavior of `Subject` is very much like generic pub/sub mechanisms, such as jQuery events. However, in an asynchronous world where components are loaded or unloaded in ways that are unpredictable, using the default `Subject` is not very useful.

There are three different types of Subjects:

- `ReplaySubject`: It will remember and cache all data points occurred within the data stream so that a subscriber can replay all events at any given time
- `BehaviorSubject`: It remembers only the last data point, while continuing to listen for new data points
- `AsyncSubject`: This is for one-time only events that are not expected to reoccur

`ReplaySubject` can have severe memory and performance implications on your application, so it should be used with care. In the case of `current-weather`, we are only interested in displaying the latest weather data received, but through user input or other events we are open to receiving new data, so we can keep the `current-weather` component up to date. The `BehaviorSubject` would be the appropriate mechanism to meet these needs:

1. Define `BehaviorSubject` in `weatherService` and set a default value:

   app/src/weather/weather.service.ts
   ```
   import { BehaviorSubject } from 'rxjs'
   . . .
   export class WeatherService implements IWeatherService {
     currentWeather = new BehaviorSubject<ICurrentWeather>({
       city: '--',
       country: '--',
       date: Date.now(),
       image: '',
       temperature: 0,
       description: '',
     })
     . . .
   }
   ```

2. Update the `current-weather` component to subscribe to the new BehaviorSubject:

app/src/current-weather/current-weather.component.ts

```
...
ngOnInit() {
  this.weatherService.currentWeather.subscribe(data =>
(this.current = data))
}
...
```

3. Update the `city-search` component to publish the data it receives to BehaviorSubject:

app/src/city-search/city-search.component.ts

```
...
this.weatherService
  .getCurrentWeather(
    userInput[0],
    userInput.length > 1 ? userInput[1] : undefined
  )
  .subscribe(data => this.weatherService.currentWeather.next(data))
...
```

4. Test your app in the browser; it should look as follows:

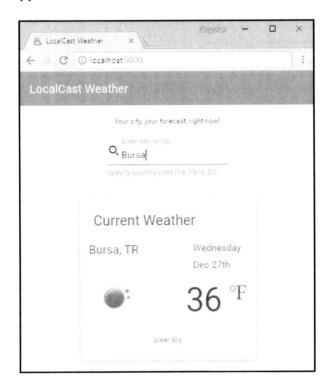

Weather Information for Bursa, Turkey

When you type in a new city, the component should update for the current weather information for that city.

There's still room for improvement; the default experience looks broken when the app first loads. There are at least two different ways to handle this. The first is at the app component level to hide the entire component if there's no data to display. For this to work, we will have to inject weatherService to the app component, ultimately leading to a less flexible solution. Another way is to be able to better handle missing data within the current-weather component.

To make the app better, you can implement geolocation to get weather for the user's current location at launch of the app. You can also leverage `window.localStorage` to store the city that was last displayed or the last location that was retrieved from `window.geolocation` on initial launch.

Don't forget to execute `npm test` and `npm run e2e` before moving on. It is left as an exercise for the reader to fix the unit and end-to-end tests.

Summary

This chapter completes our work on the Local Weather App. We can move the **City Search capability** task to the `done` column, as shown in our Kanban board:

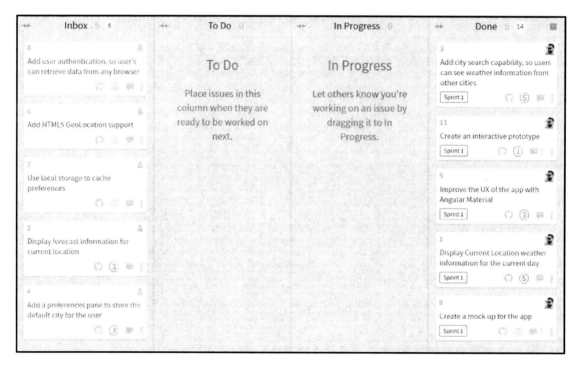

Waffle.io Kanban Board Status

In this chapter, you learned how to create an interactive prototype without writing a single line of code. You then created a search-as-you-type functionality using `MatInput`, validators, reactive forms, and data stream driven handlers. You also learned about different strategies to enable inter-component interactions and data sharing. Finally, you became aware of two-way binding and template-driven forms.

LocalCast Weather is a straightforward application that we used to cover the basic concepts of Angular. As you saw, Angular is great for building such small and dynamic applications, while delivering a minimal amount of framework code to the end user. You should consider leveraging Angular for even quick and dirty projects, which is also a great practice when building larger applications. In the next chapter, you will be creating a far more complicated **line-of-business (LOB)** application, using a router-first approach to designing and architecting scalable Angular applications with first-class authentication and authorization, user experience, and numerous recipes that cover a vast majority of requirements that you may find in LOB applications.

7

Create a Router-First Line-of-Business App

Line-of-Business (**LOB**) applications are the bread and butter of the software development world. As defined in Wikipedia, LOB is a general term, which refers to a product or a set of related products that serve a particular customer transaction or business need. LOB apps present a good opportunity to demonstrate a variety of features and functionality without getting into contorted or specialized scenarios that large enterprise applications usually require. In a sense, they are the 80-20 learning experience. I must, however, point out a curious thing about LOB apps—if you end up building a semi-useful LOB app, the demand for it will grow uncontrollably, and you will quickly become the victim of your own success. This is why you should treat the start of every new project as an opportunity, a coding-kata if you will, to get better at creating more flexible architectures.

In this chapter and the remaining chapters, we'll set up a new application with rich features that can meet the demands of an LOB application with a scalable architecture and engineering best practices that will help you start small and be able to grow your solution quickly if there's demand. We will follow the Router-first design pattern, relying on reusable components to create a grocery store LOB named LemonMart.

In this chapter, you will learn to do the following:

- Effectively use CLI to create major Angular Components and CLI Scaffolds
- Learn how to build Router-first Apps
- Branding, Custom and Material Iconography
- Debug complicated apps with Augury
- Enable lazy loading
- Create a walking skeleton

The code samples provided in this book require Angular version 5 and 6. Angular 5 code is runtime compatible with Angular 6. Angular 6 will be supported in LTS until October 2019. The most up-to-date versions of the code repositories may be found at the following URLs:

- For Chapters 2 to 6, LocalCast Weather at `Github.com/duluca/local-weather-app`
- For Chapters 7 to 12, LemonMart at `Github.com/duluca/lemon-mart`

Angular cheat sheet

Before we dive in to creating our LOB app, I have included a cheat sheet for you to familiarize yourself with common Angular syntax and CLI commands, because going forward, this syntax and these commands will be used without their purpose explicitly explained. Take some time to review and orient yourself with new Angular syntax, major components, CLI scaffolds, and common pipes. You may find the list especially useful if your background is with AngularJS, since you will need to unlearn some old syntax.

Binding

Binding, or data binding, refers to an automatic, one or two-way connection between a variable in code and a value displayed or input in an HTML template or another component:

Type	Syntax	Data direction

Interpolation
Property
Attribute
Class
Style
	`{{expression}}`
	`[target]="expression"`
	`bind-target="expression"`
		One-way
		from data source
		to view target

Event	`(target)="statement"` `on-target="statement"`	One-way from view target to data source
Two-way	`[(target)]="expression"` `bindon-target="expression"`	Two-way

Source: `https://angular.io/guide/template-syntax#binding-syntax-an-overview`

Built-in directives

Directives encapsulate coded behaviors that can be applied as attributes to HTML elements or other components:

Name	Syntax	Purpose
Structural Directives	`*ngIf` `*ngFor` `*ngSwitch`	Controls structural layout of the HTML and if elements get added or removed from the DOM
Attribute Directives	`[class]` `[style]` `[(model)]`	Listens to and modifies the behavior of other HTML elements, attributes, properties, and components, such as CSS classes, HTML styles, and HTML form elements

Structural Directives Source: `https://angular.io/guide/structural-directives`

Attribute Directives Source: `https://angular.io/guide/template-syntax#built-in-attribute-directives`

Common pipes

Pipes modify how a data-bound value is displayed in the HTML template.

Name	Purpose	Usage
Date	Formats a date according to locale rules	`{{date_value	date[:format]}}`
Text Transformation	Transforms text to uppercase, lowercase, or title case	`{{value	uppercase}}` `{{value	lowercase}}` `{{value	titlecase }}`
Decimal	Formats a number according to locale rules	`{{number	number[:digitInfo]}}`
Percent	Formats a number as a percentage according to locale rules	`{{number	percent[:digitInfo]}}`
Currency	Formats a number as currency with currency code and symbol according to locale rules	`{{number	currency[:currencyCode [:symbolDisplay[:digitInfo]]]}}`

Pipes Source: `https://angular.io/guide/pipes`

Starter commands, major components, and CLI scaffolds

Starter commands help generate new projects or add dependencies. Angular CLI commands help create major components by automatically generating boilerplate scaffolding code with ease. For the list of full set of commands, visit `https://github.com/angular/angular-cli/wiki`:

Name	Purpose	CLI Command
New	Creates a new Angular application with initialized git repository, package.json, and routing already configured. Run from parent folder.	`npx @angular/cli new project-name --routing`
Update	Updates Angular, RxJS, and Angular Material dependencies. Rewrites code, if necessary, to maintain compatibility.	`npx ng update`
Add Material	Installs and configures Angular Material dependencies.	`npx ng add @angular/material`
Module	Creates a new `@NgModule` class. Uses `--routing` to add routing for submodules. Optionally, import new module into a parent module using `--module`.	`ng g module new-module`
Component	Creates a new `@Component` class. Uses `--module` to specify parent module. Optionally, use `--flat` to skip directory creation, `-t` for an inline template, and `-s` for an inline style.	`ng g component new-component`
Directive	Creates a new `@Directive` class. Optionally, uses `--module` to scope directives for a given submodule.	`ng g directive new-directive`
Pipe	Creates a new `@Pipe` class. Optionally, use `--module` to scope pipes for a given submodule.	`ng g pipe new-pipe`

Service	Creates a new `@Injectable` class. Uses `--module` to provide a service for a given submodule. Services are not automatically imported to a module. Optionally use `--flat` false to create service under a directory.	`ng g service new-service`
Guard	Creates a new `@Injectable` class, which implements the Route lifecycle hook `CanActivate`. Uses `--module` to provide a guard for a given submodule. Guards are not automatically imported to a module.	`ng g guard new-guard`
Class	Creates a bare-bones class.	`ng g class new-class`
Interface	Creates a bare-bones interface.	`ng g interface new-interface`
Enum	Creates a bare-bones enum.	`ng g enum new-enum`

In order to properly scaffold some of the components listed earlier under a custom module, such as `my-module`, you can prepend the module name before the name of what you intend to generate, for example, `ng g c my-module/my-new-component`. Angular CLI will properly wire up and place the new component under the `my-module` folder.

Configure Angular CLI autocomplete

You get an autocomplete experience when working with Angular CLI. Execute the appropriate command for your `*nix` environment:

- For bash shell:

```
$ ng completion --bash >> ~/.bashrc
$ source ~/.bashrc
```

- For zsh shell:

```
$ ng completion --zsh >> ~/.zshrc
$ source ~/.zshrc
```

- For Windows users using git bash shell:

```
$ ng completion --bash >> ~/.bash_profile
$ source ~/.bash_profile
```

Router-first architecture

The Angular router, shipped in the `@angular/router` package, is a central and critical part of building **single-page-applications (SPAs)** that act and behave like regular websites that are easy to navigate using browser controls or the zoom or microzoom controls.

Angular Router has advanced features such as lazy loading, router outlets, auxiliary routes, smart active link tracking, and the ability to be expressed as an `href`, which enables a highly flexible Router-first app architecture leveraging stateless data-driven components using RxJS `SubjectBehavior`.

Large teams can work against a single-code base, with each team responsible of a module's development, without stepping on each other's toes, while enabling easy continuous integration. Google, with its billions of lines of code, works against a single code base for a very good reason. Integration, after the fact, is very expensive.

Small teams can remix their UI layouts on the fly to quickly respond to changes without having to rearchitect their code. It is easy to underestimate the amount of time wasted due to late game changes in layout or navigation. Such changes are easier to absorb by larger teams but a costly endeavor for small teams.

With lazy-loading, all developers benefit from sub-second first meaningful paints, because the file size of the core user experience that's delivered to the browser is kept at a minimum at build time. The size of a module impacts download and loading speed, because the more a browser has to do, the longer it will take for a user to see the first screen of the app. By defining lazy-loaded modules, each module can be packaged as separated files, which can be downloaded and loaded individually and as needed. Smart active link tracking results in a superior developer and user experience, making it very easy to implement highlighting features to indicate to the user the current tab or portion of the app that is currently active. Auxiliary routes maximize the reuse of components and help pull off complicated state transitions with ease. With auxiliary routes, you can render multiple master and detail views using only a single outer template. You can also control how the route is displayed to the user in the browser's URL bar and compose routes using `routerLink`, in templates, and `Router.navigate`, in code, driving complicated scenarios.

In order to pull off a router-first implementation, you need to do this:

1. Define user roles early on
2. Design with lazy loading in mind
3. Implement a walking-skeleton navigation experience
4. Design around major data components
5. Enforce a decoupled component architecture
6. Differentiate between user controls and components
7. Maximize code reuse

User roles normally indicate the job function of a user, such as a manager or data-entry specialist. In technical terms, they can be thought of as a group of actions that a particular class of user is allowed to execute. Defining user roles help identify sub modules that can then be configured to be lazy loaded. After all, a data-entry specialist won't ever see most of the screens that a manager can, so why deliver those assets to those users and slow down their experience? Lazy loading is critical in creating a scalable application architecture, not only from an application perspective, but also from a high-quality and efficient development perspective. Configuring lazy loading can be tricky, which is why it is important to nail down a walking-skeleton navigation experience early on.

Identifying major data components that your users will work with, such as invoice or people objects, will help you avoid over-engineering your application. Designing around major data components will inform API design early on and help define `BehaviorSubject` data anchors that you will use to achieve a stateless, data-driven design to ensure a decoupled component architecture, as detailed in `Chapter 6`, *Reactive Forms and Component Interaction*.

Finally, identify self-contained user controls that encapsulate unique behaviors that you wish to create for your app. User controls will likely be created as directives or components that have data-binding properties and tightly-coupled controller logic and templates. Components, on the other hand, will leverage router life cycle events to parse parameters and perform CRUD operations on data. Identifying these component reuses early on will result in creating more flexible components that can be reused in multiple contexts as orchestrated by the router, maximizing code reuse.

Creating LemonMart

LemonMart will be a mid-sized line-of-business application with over 90 code files. We will start our journey by creating a new Angular app with routing and Angular Material configured from the get go.

Creating a Router-first app

With the Router-first approach, we will want to enable routing early on in our application:

1. You can create the new application with routing already configured by executing this command:

   Ensure that @angular/cli is not installed globally, or you may run into errors:

   ```
   $ npx @angular/cli new lemon-mart --routing
   ```

2. A new AppRoutingModule file has been created for us:

   src/app/app-routing.modules.ts
   ```
   import { NgModule } from '@angular/core';
   import { Routes, RouterModule } from '@angular/router';

   const routes: Routes = [];

   @NgModule({
     imports: [RouterModule.forRoot(routes)],
     exports: [RouterModule]
   })
   export class AppRoutingModule { }
   ```

We will be defining routes inside the routes array. Note that routes array is passed in to be configured as the root routes for the application, the default root route being /.

When configuring your RouterModule, you can pass in additional options to customize the default behavior of the Router, such as when you attempt to load a route that is already being displayed, instead of taking no action, you can force a reload of the component. To enable this behavior, create your router like RouterModule.forRoot(routes, { onSameUrlNavigation: 'reload' }).

3. Finally, `AppRoutingModule` is registered with `AppModule`, as shown:

src/app/app.module.ts

```
...
import { AppRoutingModule } from './app-routing.module';

@NgModule({
  ...
  imports: [
    AppRoutingModule
    ...
  ],
  ...
```

Configuring Angular.json and Package.json

Here's a quick summary of configuration steps covered in Chapters 2-6. If you're unfamiliar with a step, refer to prior chapters. You should complete these steps before moving forward:

1. Modify `angular.json` and `tslint.json` to enforce your settings and coding standards
2. Install `npm i -D prettier`
3. Add `prettier` settings to `package.json`
4. Configure your development serve port to other than `4200`, such as `5000`
5. Add the `standardize` script and update `start` and `build` scripts
6. Add **npm Scripts for Docker** to `package.json`
7. Establish dev norms and document it in your project, `npm i -D dev-norms` then `npx dev-norms create`
8. If you use VS Code, set up the `extensions.json` and `settings.json` files

You may configure the TypeScript Hero extension to auto organize and prune import statements, but adding `"typescriptHero.imports.organizeOnSave": true` to `settings.json`. If combined with the setting `"files.autoSave": "onFocusChange"` you may find that the tool aggressively cleans unused imports as you are trying to type them out. Ensure that this setting works for you and doesn't collide with any other tools or VS Code's own import organization feature.

9. Execute `npm run standardize`

Refer to `Chapter 3`, *Prepare Angular App for Production Release,* for further configuration details.

You can get the npm Scripts for Docker at `bit.ly/npmScriptsForDocker` and npm Scripts for AWS at `bit.ly/npmScriptsForAWS`.

Configuring Material and Styles

We will also need to set up Angular Material and configure a theme to use, as covered in `Chapter 5`, *Enhance Angular App with Angular Material*:

1. Install Angular Material:

```
$ npx ng add @angular/material
$ npm i @angular/flex-layout hammerjs
$ npx ng g m material --flat -m app
```

2. Import and export `MatButtonModule`, `MatToolbarModule`, and `MatIconModule`

3. Configure your default theme and register other Angular dependencies

4. Add common css to `styles.css` as shown below,

src/styles.css

```
body {
  margin: 0;
}

.margin-top {
```

```
    margin-top: 16px;
  }

  .horizontal-padding {
    margin-left: 16px;
    margin-right: 16px;
  }

  .flex-spacer {
    flex: 1 1 auto;
  }
```

Refer to `Chapter 5`, *Enhance Angular App with Angular Material,* for further configuration details.

Designing LemonMart

It is important to build a rudimentary road map to follow, from the database to the frontend, while also avoiding over-engineering. This initial design phase is critical to the long-term health and success of your project, where any existing silos between teams must be broken down and an overall technical vision well understood by all members of the team. This is easier said than done, and there are volumes of books written on the topic.

In engineering, there's no one right answer to a problem, so it is important to remember that no one person can ever have all the answers nor a crystal clear vision. It is important that technical and non-technical leaders create a safe space with opportunities for open discussion and experimentation as part of the culture. The humility and empathy that comes along with being able to court such uncertainty as a team is as important as any single team member's technical capabilities. Every team member must be comfortable with checking their egos out at the door, because our collective goal will be to grow and evolve an application to ever-changing requirements during the development cycle. You will know that you have succeeded if individual parts of the software you created is easily replaceable by anyone.

Identifying user roles

The first step of our design will be to think about you using the application and why.

We envision four user states or roles for LemonMart:

- Authenticated, any authenticated user would have access to their profile
- Cashier, whose sole role is to check out customers
- Clerk, whose sole role is to perform inventory-related functions
- Manager, who can perform all actions a cashier and a clerk can perform but also have access to administrative functions

With this in mind, we can start a high-level design of our app.

Identifying high-level modules with site map

Develop a high-level site map of your application, as shown:

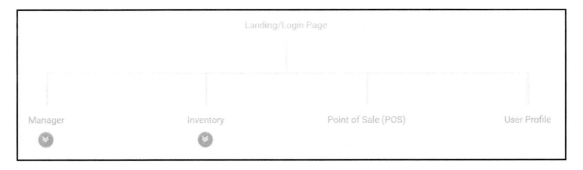

Landing pages for users

 I used MockFlow.com's SiteMap tool to create the site map shown at `https://sitemap.mockflow.com`.

Upon first examination, three high-level modules emerge as lazy-loading candidates:

1. **Point of Sale (POS)**
2. **Inventory**
3. **Manager**

Cashier will only have access to the POS module and component. The Clerk will only have access to the **Inventory** module, which will include additional screen for **Stock Entry**, **Products**, and **Categories** management components.

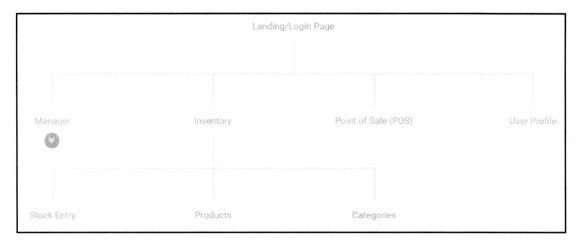

Inventory pages

Finally, the **Manager** will be able to access all three modules with the **Manager** module, including User management and Receipt lookup components.

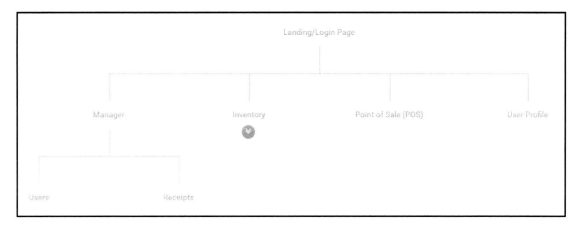

Manager pages

There's great benefit to enable lazy-loading for all three modules, since cashiers and clerks will never use components belonging to other user roles, there's no reason to send those bytes down to their devices. This means as the **Manager** module gains more advanced reporting features or new roles are added to the application, the **POS** module will be unaffected by the bandwidth and memory impact of an otherwise growing application. This means less support calls and consistent performance on the same hardware for a much longer period of time.

Generating router-enabled modules

Now that we have our high-level components defined as **Manager**, **Inventory**, and **POS**, we can define them as modules. These modules will be different from the ones you've created so far, for routing and Angular Material. We can create the user profile as a component on the app module; however, note that user profile will only ever be used for already authenticated users, so it makes sense to define a fourth module only meant for authenticated users in general. This way, you will ensure that your app's first payload remains as minimal as possible. In addition, we will create a Home component to contain the landing experience for our app so that we can keep implementation details out of `app.component`:

1. Generate `manager`, `inventory`, `pos`, and `user` modules, specifying their target module and routing capabilities:

    ```
    $ npx ng g m manager -m app --routing
    $ npx ng g m inventory -m app --routing
    $ npx ng g m pos -m app --routing
    $ npx ng g m user -m app --routing
    ```

    As discussed in `Chapter 1`, *Setting Up Your Development Environment*, if you have configured `npx` to automatically recognize `ng` as a command, you can save some more keystrokes so that you won't have to append `npx` to your commands every time. Do not globally install `@angular/cli`. Note the abbreviate command structure, where `ng generate module manager` becomes `ng g m manager`, and similarly, `--module` becomes `-m`.

2. Verify that you don't have CLI errors.

   Note that using `npx` on Windows may encounter an error such as **Path must be a string. Received undefined**. This error doesn't seem to have any effect on the successful operation of the command, which is why it is critical to always inspect what the CLI tool generated.

3. Verify the folder and the files are created:

```
/src/app
|     app-routing.module.ts
|     app.component.css
|     app.component.html
|     app.component.spec.ts
|     app.component.ts
|     app.module.ts
|     material.module.ts
|————inventory
|           inventory-routing.module.ts
|           inventory.module.ts
|————manager
|           manager-routing.module.ts
|           manager.module.ts
|————pos
|           pos-routing.module.ts
|           pos.module.ts
└————user
            user-routing.module.ts
            user.module.ts
```

4. Examine how `ManagerModule` has been wired.

   A child module implements an `@NgModule` similar to `app.module`. The biggest difference is that a child module does not implement the `bootstrap` property, which is required for your root module, to initialize your Angular app:

src/app/manager/manager.module.ts
```
import { NgModule } from '@angular/core'
import { CommonModule } from '@angular/common'

import { ManagerRoutingModule } from './manager-routing.module'

@NgModule({
  imports: [CommonModule, ManagerRoutingModule],
  declarations: [],
```

```
})
export class ManagerModule {}
```

Since we have specified the -m option, the module has been imported into app.module:

src/app/app.module.ts
```
...
import { ManagerModule } from './manager/manager.module'
...
@NgModule({
  ...
  imports: [
    ...
    ManagerModule
  ],
...
```

In addition, because we also specified the --routing option, a routing module has been created and imported into ManagerModule:

src/app/manager/manager-routing.module.ts
```
import { NgModule } from '@angular/core'
import { Routes, RouterModule } from '@angular/router'

const routes: Routes = []

@NgModule({
  imports: [RouterModule.forChild(routes)],
  exports: [RouterModule],
})
export class ManagerRoutingModule {}
```

Note that RouterModule is being configured using forChild, as opposed to forRoot, which was the case for the AppRouting module. This way, the router understands the proper relationship between routes defined in different modules' contexts and can correctly prepend /manager to all child routes in this example.

The CLI doesn't respect your tslint.json settings. If you have correctly configured your VS Code environment with prettier, your Code Styling preferences will be applied as you work on each file or, globally, when you run the prettier command.

Designing the home route

Consider the following mock-up as the landing experience for LemonMart:

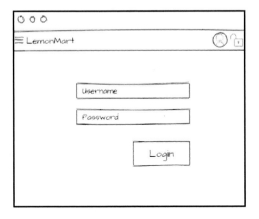

LemonMart Landing Experience

Unlike the `LocalCastWeather` app, we don't want all this markup to be in the `App` component. The `App` component is the root element of your entire application; therefore, it should only contain elements that will persistently appear throughout your application. In the following annotated mock-up, the toolbar marked as **1** will be persistent throughout the app.

The area marked as **2** will house the home component, which itself will contain a login user control, marked as **3**:

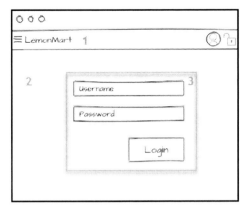

LemonMart Layout Structure

It is a best practice to create your default or landing component as a separate element in Angular. This helps reduce the amount of code that must be loaded and logic executed in every page, but it also results in a more flexible architecture when utilizing the router:

Generate the home component with inline template and styles:

```
$ npx ng g c home -m app --inline-template --inline-style
```

Now, you are ready to configure the router.

Setting up default routes

Let's get started with setting up a simple route for LemonMart:

1. Configure your home route:

   src/app/app-routing.module.ts
   ```
   ...
   const routes: Routes = [
     { path: '', redirectTo: '/home', pathMatch: 'full' },
     { path: 'home', component: HomeComponent },
   ]
   ...
   ```

   We first define a path for 'home' and inform the router to render HomeComponent by setting the component property. Then, we set the default path of the application '' to be redirected to '/home'. By setting the pathMatch property, we always ensure that this very specific instance of the home route will be rendered as the landing experience.

2. Create a pageNotFound component with an inline template
3. Configure a wildcard route for PageNotFoundComponent:

   src/app/app-routing.module.ts
   ```
   ...
   const routes: Routes = [
     ...
     { path: '**', component: PageNotFoundComponent }
   ]
   ...
   ```

This way, any route that is not matched will be directed to the PageNotFoundComponent.

RouterLink

When a user lands on the `PageNotFoundComponent`, we would like them to be redirected to the `HomeComponent` using the `RouterLink` direction:

1. Implement an inline template to link back to home using `routerLink`:

   src/app/page-not-found/page-not-found.component.ts

   ```
   ...
   template: `
       <p>
          This page doesn't exist. Go back to <a
   routerLink="/home">home</a>.
       </p>
       `,
   ...
   ```

 This navigation can also be done via an `<a href>` tag implementation; however, in more dynamic and complicated navigation scenarios, you will lose features such as automatic active link tracking or dynamic link generation.

The Angular bootstrap process will ensure that `AppComponent` is inside the `<app-root>` element in your `index.html`. However, we must manually define where we would like `HomeComponent` to render, to finalize the router configuration.

Router outlet

`AppComponent` is considered a root element for the root router defined in `app-routing.module`, which allows us to define outlets within this root element to dynamically load any content we wish using the `<router-outlet>` element:

1. Configure `AppComponent` to use inline template and styles
2. Add the toolbar for your application
3. Add the name of your application as a button link so that it takes the user to the home page when clicked on

4. Add `<router-outlet>` for the content to render:

src/app/app.component.ts

```
...
template: `
    <mat-toolbar color="primary">
      <a mat-button routerLink="/home"><h1>LemonMart</h1></a>
    </mat-toolbar>
    <router-outlet></router-outlet>
  `,
```

Now, the contents of home will render inside `<router-outlet>`.

Branding, Custom, and Material Icons

In order to construct an attractive and intuitive toolbar, we must introduce some iconography and branding to the app so that the users can easily navigate through the app with the help of familiar icons.

Branding

In terms of branding, you should ensure that your web app should have custom color palette and integrate with desktop and mobile browser features to bring forward your app's name and iconography.

Color palette

Pick a color palette using the Material Color tool, as discussed in Chapter 5, *Enhance Angular App with Angular Material*. Here's the one I picked for LemonMart:

```
https://material.io/color/#!/?view.left=0&view.right=0&primary.color=2E7D32
&secondary.color=C6FF00
```

Implementing browser manifest and icons

You need to ensure that the browser shows the correct title text and icon in a **Browser** tab. Further, a manifest file should be created that implements specific icons for various mobile operating systems, so that if a user pins your website, a desirable icon is displayed similar to other app icons on a phone. This will ensure that if a user favorites or pin your web app on their mobile device's home screen, they'll get a native-looking app icon:

1. Create or obtain an SVG version of your website's logo from a designer or site like `https://www.flaticon.com`

2. In this case, I will be using a particular lemon image:

LemonMart's signature logo

When using images you find on the internet, pay attention to applicable copyrights. In this case, I have purchased a license to be able to publish this lemon logo, but you may grab your own copy at the following URL, given that you provide the required attribution to the author of the image: `https://www.flaticon.com/free-icon/lemon_605070`.

3. Generate `favicon.ico` and manifest files using a tool such as `https://realfavicongenerator.net`

4. Adjust settings for iOS, Android, Windows Phone, macOS, and Safari to your liking

5. Ensure that you set a version number, favicons can be notorious with caching; a random version number will ensure that users always get the latest version

6. Download and extract the generated `favicons.zip` file into your `src` folder

7. Edit the `angular.json` file to include the new assets in your app:

angular.json
```
"apps": [
  {
    ...
      "assets": [
        "src/assets",
        "src/favicon.ico",
        "src/android-chrome-192x192.png",
        "src/favicon-16x16.png",
        "src/mstile-310x150.png",
```

```
"src/android-chrome-512x512.png",
"src/favicon-32x32.png",
"src/mstile-310x310.png",
"src/apple-touch-icon.png",
"src/manifest.json",
"src/mstile-70x70.png",
"src/browserconfig.xml",
"src/mstile-144x144.png",
"src/safari-pinned-tab.svg",
"src/mstile-150x150.png"
]
```

8. Insert the generated code in the `<head>` section of your `index.html`:

src/index.html
```
<link rel="apple-touch-icon" sizes="180x180" href="/apple-touch-
icon.png?v=rMlKOnvxlK">
<link rel="icon" type="image/png" sizes="32x32"
href="/favicon-32x32.png?v=rMlKOnvxlK">
<link rel="icon" type="image/png" sizes="16x16"
href="/favicon-16x16.png?v=rMlKOnvxlK">
<link rel="manifest" href="/manifest.json?v=rMlKOnvxlK">
<link rel="mask-icon" href="/safari-pinned-tab.svg?v=rMlKOnvxlK"
color="#b3ad2d">
<link rel="shortcut icon" href="/favicon.ico?v=rMlKOnvxlK">
<meta name="theme-color" content="#ffffff">
```

9. Ensure that your new favicon displays correctly

To further your branding, consider configuring a custom Material theme and leveraging `https://material.io/color`, as discussed in *Chapter 5, Enhance Angular App with Angular Material*.

Custom icons

Now, let's add your custom branding inside your Angular app. You will need the svg icon you used to create your favicon:

1. Place the image under `src/app/assets/img/icons`, named `lemon.svg`

2. Import `HttpClientModule` to `AppComponent` so that the `.svg` file can be requested over HTTP

3. Update `AppComponent` to register the new svg file as an icon:

src/app/app.component.ts
```
import { DomSanitizer } from '@angular/platform-browser'
...
export class AppComponent {
  constructor(iconRegistry: MatIconRegistry, sanitizer:
DomSanitizer) {
    iconRegistry.addSvgIcon(
      'lemon',
sanitizer.bypassSecurityTrustResourceUrl('assets/img/icons/lemon.sv
g')
    )
  }
}
```

4. Add the icon to the toolbar:

src/app/app.component.ts
```
template: `
    <mat-toolbar color="primary">
      <mat-icon svgIcon="lemon"></mat-icon>
      <a mat-button routerLink="/home"><h1>LemonMart</h1></a>
    </mat-toolbar>
    <router-outlet></router-outlet>
  `,
```

Now let's add the remaining icons for menu, user profile, and logout.

Material icons

Angular Material works out of the box with Material Design icons, which can be imported into your app as a web font in your `index.html`. It is possible to self-host the font; however, if you go down that path, you also don't get the benefit of the user's browser having already cached the font when they visited another website, saving the speed and latency of downloading a 42-56 KB file in the process. The complete list of icons can be found at `https://material.io/icons/`.

Now let's update the toolbar with some icons and setup the home page with a minimal template for a fake login button:

1. Ensure Material icons `<link>` tag has been added to `index.html`:

   src/index.html
   ```html
   <head>
     ...
     <link
   href="https://fonts.googleapis.com/icon?family=Material+Icons"
   rel="stylesheet">
   </head>
   ```

    Instructions on how to self-host can be found under the **Self Hosting** section at `http://google.github.io/material-design-icons/#getting-icons`.

   Once configured, working with Material icons is easy.

2. Update the toolbar to place a **Menu** button to the left of the title.
3. Add an `fxFlex` so that the remaining icons are right aligned.
4. Add user profile and logout icons:

   src/app/app.component.ts
   ```
   template: `
     <mat-toolbar color="primary">
       <button mat-icon-button><mat-icon>menu</mat-icon></button>
       <mat-icon svgIcon="lemon"></mat-icon>
       <a mat-button routerLink="/home"><h1>LemonMart</h1></a>
       <span class="flex-spacer"></span>
       <button mat-icon-button><mat-icon>account_circle</mat-
   icon></button>
       <button mat-icon-button><mat-icon>lock_open</mat-
   icon></button>
     </mat-toolbar>
     <router-outlet></router-outlet>
     `,
   ```

5. Add a minimal template for a login:

src/app/home/home.component.ts
```
styles: [`
  div[fxLayout] {margin-top: 32px;}
`],
template: `
  <div fxLayout="column" fxLayoutAlign="center center">
    <span class="mat-display-2">Hello, Lemonite!</span>
    <button mat-raised-button color="primary">Login</button>
  </div>
`
```

Your app should look similar to this screenshot:

LemonMart with minimal login

There's still some work to be done, in terms of implementing and showing/hiding the menu, profile, and logout icons, given the user's authentication status. We will cover this functionality in Chapter 9, *Design Authentication and Authorization*. Now that you've set up basic routing for your app, you need to learn how to debug your Angular app before we move on to setting up lazily loaded modules with subcomponents.

Angular Augury

Augury is a Chrome Dev Tools extension for debugging and profiling Angular applications. It is a purpose-built tool to help developers visually navigate the component tree, inspect the state of the router, and enable break point debugging by source-mapping between the generated JavaScript code and the TypeScript code that the developer coded in. You can download Augury from augury.angular.io. Once installed, when you open Chrome Dev Tools for your Angular app, you'll note a new tab for Augury, as illustrated:

Chrome Dev Tools Augury

Augury provides useful and critical information in understanding how your Angular app is behaving at runtime:

1. Current Angular version is listed, in this case, as version **5.1.2**
2. **Component Tree**
3. **Router Tree** shows all the routes that have been configured in the app
4. **NgModules** shows the AppModule and Sub-Modules of the app

Component Tree

The **Component Tree** tab shows how all app components are related and how they interact with each other:

1. Select a particular component, such as `HomeComponent`, as follows:

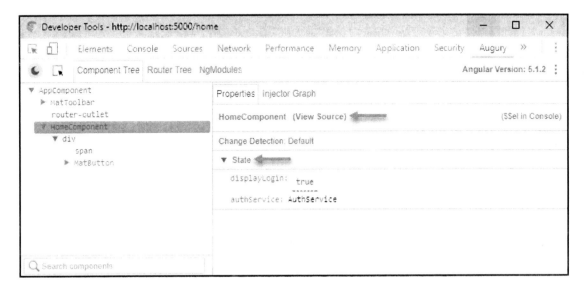

Augury Component Tree

The **Properties** tab on the right-hand side will display a link called **View Source**, which you can use to debug your component. Further below, you will be able to observe the state of properties of the component, such as the **displayLogin** boolean, including services that you have injected into the component and their state.

You can change the value of any property by double-clicking on the value. For example, if you would like to change the value of **displayLogin** to `false`, simply double-click on the blue box that contains the true value and type in false. You will be able to observe the effects of your changes in your Angular app.

In order to observe the runtime component hierarchy of `HomeComponent`, you can observe the Injector Graph.

2. Click on the **Injector Graph** tab, as shown:

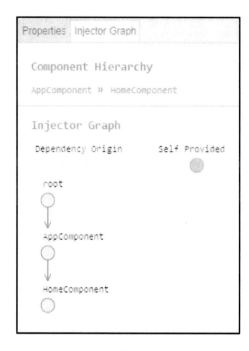

Augury Injector Graph

This view shows how your selected component came to be rendered. In this case, we can observe that `HomeComponent` was rendered within `AppComponent`. This visualization can be very helpful in tracking down the implementation of a particular component in an unfamiliar code base or where a deep component tree exists.

Break point debugging

Let me restate, for the record, that `console.log` statements shall never be checked in to your repository. In general, they are a waste of your time, because it requires editing code and later cleaning up your code. Furthermore, Augury already provides the state of your components, so in straightforward cases, you should be able to leverage it observe or coerce state.

There are some niche use cases, where `console.log` statements can be useful. These are mostly asynchronous workflows that operate in parallel and are dependent on timely user interaction. In these cases, console logs can help you better understand the flow of events and interaction between various components.

Augury is not yet sophisticated enough to resolve asynchronous data or data returned via functions. There are other common cases, where you would like to observe the state of properties as they are being set, and even be able to change their values on the fly to force your code to execute branching logic in `if-else` or `switch` statements. For these cases, you should be using break point debugging.

Let's presume that some basic logic exists on `HomeComponent`, which sets a `displayLogin` `boolean`, based on an `isAuthenticated` value retrieved from an `AuthService`, as demonstrated:

```
src/app/home/home.component.ts
...
import { AuthService } from '../auth.service'
...
export class HomeComponent implements OnInit {
  displayLogin = true
  constructor(private authService: AuthService) {}

  ngOnInit() {
    this.displayLogin = !this.authService.isAuthenticated()
  }
}
```

Now observe the state of the value of `displayLogin` and the `isAuthenticated` function as they are being set, then observe the change in the value of `displayLogin`:

1. Click on the **View Source** link on `HomeComponent`
2. Drop a break point on the first line inside the `ngOnInit` function
3. Refresh the page

4. Chrome Dev Tools will switch over to the **Source** tab, and you'll see your break point hit, as highlighted in blue here:

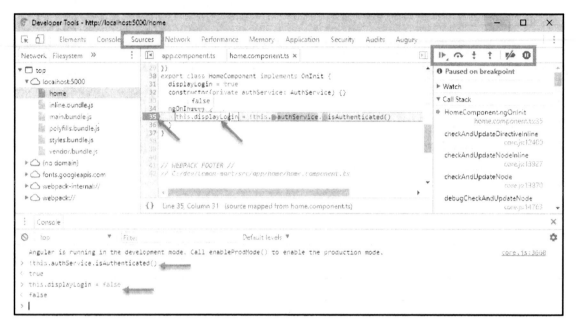

Chrome Dev Tools break point debugging

5. Hover over `this.displayLogin` and observe that its value is set to `true`

6. If hovering over `this.authService.isAuthenticated()`, you will not be able to observe its value

   While your break point is hit, you can access the current scope of the state in the console, which means you can execute the function and observe its value.

7. Execute `isAuthenticated()` in the console:

   ```
   > !this.authService.isAuthenticated()
   true
   ```

You'll observe that it returns `true`, which is what `this.displayLogin` is set to. You can still coerce the value of `displayLogin` in the console.

8. Set `displayLogin` to `false`:

```
> this.displayLogin = false
false
```

If you observe the value of `displayLogin`, either by hovering over it or retrieving it from the control, you'll see that the value is set to `false`.

Leveraging break point debugging basics, you can debug complicated scenarios without changing your source code at all.

Router Tree

The **Router Tree** tab will display the current state of the router. This can be a very helpful tool in visualizing the relationship between routes and components, as shown:

Augury Router Tree

The preceding router tree demonstrates a deeply nested routing structure with master-detail views. You can see the absolute path and parameters required to render a given component by clicking on the circular node.

As you can see, for `PersonDetailsComponent`, it can get complicated to determine, exactly, the set of parameters needed to render this detail portion of a master-detail view.

NgModules

The **NgModules** tab displays the `AppModule` and any other submodule that is currently loaded into memory:

1. Launch the `/home` route of the app
2. Observe the **NgModules** tab, as follows:

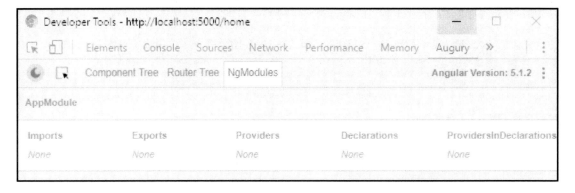

Augury NgModules

You'll note that only the `AppModule` is loaded. However, since our application has a lazy-loaded architecture, none of our other modules are yet loaded.

3. Navigate to a page in the `ManagerModule`
4. Then, navigate to a page in the `UserModule`
5. Finally, navigate back to the `/home` route

6. Observe the **NgModules** tab, as shown:

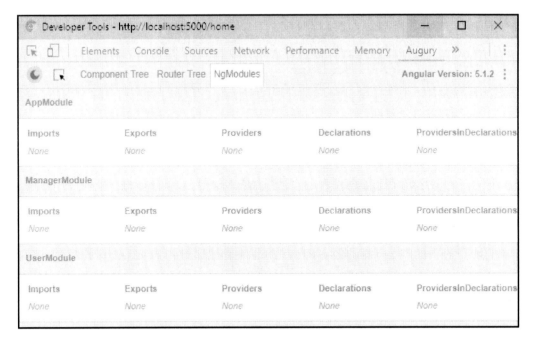

Augury NgModules with Three Modules

7. Now, you'll observe that three modules have been loaded into memory.

NgModules is an important tool to visualize the impact of your design and architecture.

Submodules with lazy loading

Lazy loading allows the Angular build process, powered by webpack, to separate our web application into different JavaScript files called chunks. By separating out portions of the application into separate submodules, we allow these modules and their dependencies to be bundled into separate chunks, thus keeping the initial JavaScript bundle size to a minimum. As the application grows, the time to first meaningful paint remains a constant, instead of consistently increasing over time. Lazy loading is critical to achieving a scalable application architecture.

We will now go over how to set up a submodule with components and routes. We will also use Augury to observe the effects of our various router configurations.

Configuring submodules with components and routes

The manager module needs a landing page, as shown in this mock-up:

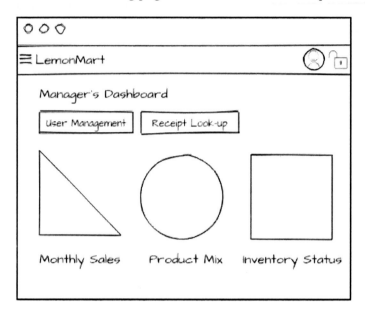

Manager's Dashboard

Let's start by creating the home screen for the `ManagerModule`:

1. Create the `ManagerHome` component:

   ```
   $ npx ng g c manager/managerHome -m manager -s -t
   ```

   In order to create the new component under the `manager` folder, we must prefix `manager/` in front of the component name. In addition, we specify that the component should be imported and declared with the `ManagerModule`. Since this is another landing page, it is unlikely to be complicated enough to require separate HTML and CSS files. You can use `--inline-style` (alias `-s`) and/or `--inline-template` (alias `-t`) to avoid creating additional files.

2. Verify that your folder structure looks as follows:

```
/src
├──────app
│  │
│  ├──────manager
│  │  │  manager-routing.module.ts
│  │  │  manager.module.ts
│  │  │
│  │  └──────manager-home
│  │  manager-home.component.spec.ts
│  │  manager-home.component.ts
```

3. Configure the `ManagerHome` component's route with `manager-routing.module`, similar to how we configured the `Home` component with `app-route.module`:

src/app/manager/manager-routing.module.ts
```typescript
import { ManagerHomeComponent } from './manager-home/manager-home.component'
import { ManagerComponent } from './manager.component'

const routes: Routes = [
  {
    path: '',
    component: ManagerComponent,
    children: [
      { path: '', redirectTo: '/manager/home', pathMatch: 'full' },
      { path: 'home', component: ManagerHomeComponent },
    ],
  },
]
```

You will note that `http://localhost:5000/manager` doesn't actually resolve to a component yet, because our Angular app isn't aware that `ManagerModule` exists. Let's first try the brute-force, eager-loading approach to import `manager.module` and register the manager route with our app.

Eager loading

This section is purely an exercise to demonstrate how the concepts we have learned so far in importing and registering routes doesn't result in a scalable solution, regardless of eagerly or lazily loading components:

1. Import the `manager.module` to `app.module`:

   src/app/app.module.ts
   ```
   import { ManagerModule } from './manager/manager.module'
     ...
     imports: [
     ...
       ManagerModule,
     ]
   ```

   You will note that `http://localhost:5000/manager` still doesn't render its home component.

2. Use **Augury** to debug the router state, as shown:

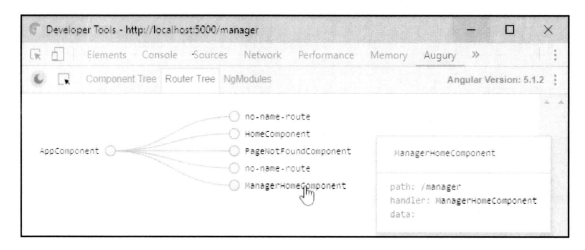

Router Tree with Eager Loading

3. It seems as if the `/manager` path is correctly registered and pointed at the correct component, `ManagerHomeComponent`. The issue here is that the `rootRouter` configured in `app-routing.module` isn't aware of the `/manager` path, so the `**` path is taking precedence and rendering the `PageNotFoundComponent` instead.

4. As a final exercise, implement the `'manager'` path in `app-routing.module` and assign `ManagerHomeComponent` to it as you would normally:

src/app/app-routing.module.ts
```
import { ManagerHomeComponent } from './manager/manager-
home/manager-home.component'
...
const routes: Routes = [
  ...
  { path: 'manager', component: ManagerHomeComponent },
  { path: '**', component: PageNotFoundComponent },
]
```

You'll now note that `http://localhost:5000/manager` renders correctly, by displaying `manager-home works!`; however, if you debug the router state through Augury, you will note that the `/manager` is registered twice.

This solution doesn't scale well, because it forces all developers to maintain a single master file to import and configure every module. It is ripe for merge conflicts and frustration, hoping that team members do not register the same route multiple times.

It is possible to engineer a solution to divide up the modules into multiple files. Instead of the standard `*-routing.module`, you can implement the Route array in `manager.module` and export it. Consider the following example:

example/manager/manager.module
```
export const managerModuleRoutes: Routes = [
  { path: '', component: ManagerHomeComponent }
]
```

These files will then need to be individually imported into `app-routing.module` and configured using the `children` attribute:

example/app-routing.module
```
import { managerModuleRoutes } from './manager/manager.module'
...
{ path: 'manager', children: managerModuleRoutes },
```

This solution will work and it is a correct solution, as demonstrated by the Augury Router tree here:

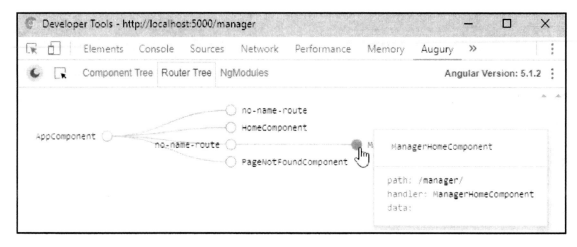

Router Tree with children routes

There are no duplicate registrations, because we removed `manager-routing.module`. In addition, we don't have to import `ManagerHomeComponent` outside of `manager.module`, resulting in a much better scalable solution. However, as the app grows, we must still register modules with `app.module`, and the submodules are still coupled to the parent `app.module` in potentially unpredictable ways. Further, this code can't be chunked, because any code that is imported using import is viewed as a hard dependency.

Lazy loading

Now that you understand how eager-loading of modules work, you will be able to better understand the code we are about to write, which may otherwise seem like black-magic, and magical (aka misunderstood) code always leads to spaghetti architectures.

We will now evolve the eager-loading solution to be a lazy-loading one. In order to load routes from a different module, we know we can't simply import them, otherwise they will be eagerly loaded. The answer lies in configuring a route using the `loadChildren` attribute with string informing the Router how to load a submodule in `app-routing.module.ts`:

1. Ensure that any module you intend to lazy load is *not* imported in `app.module`

2. Remove any routes added to `ManagerModule`

3. Ensure that `ManagerRoutingModule` is imported into `ManagerModule`

4. Implement or update the manager path with the `loadChildren` attribute:

src/app/app-routing.module.ts
```
import {
  ...
  const routes: Routes = [
    ...
    { path: 'manager', loadChildren:
'./manager/manager.module#ManagerModule' },
      { path: '**', component: PageNotFoundComponent },
    ]
  ...
```

 Lazy loading is achieved via a clever trick that avoids using an `import` statement. A string literal with two parts is defined, where the first part defines the location of the module file, such as `app/manager/manager.module`, and the second part defines the class name of the module. A string can be interpreted during the build process and at runtime, to dynamically create chunks, load the right module and instantiate the correct class. `ManagerModule` then acts as if its own Angular app and manages all of its children dependencies and routes.

5. Update the `manager-routing.module` routes, considering that manager is now their root route:

src/app/manager/manager-routing.module.ts
```
const routes: Routes = [
  { path: '', redirectTo: '/manager/home', pathMatch: 'full' },
  { path: 'home', component: ManagerHomeComponent },
]
```

We can now update the route for `ManagerHomeComponent` to a more meaningful `'home'` path. This path won't clash with the one found in `app-routing.module`, because in this context, `'home'` resolves to `'manager/home'` and, similarly, where path is empty, the URL will look like `http://localhost:5000/manager`.

6. Confirm that lazy loading is working by looking at Augury, as follows:

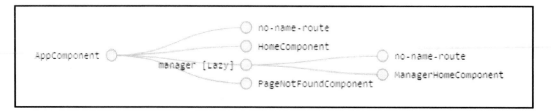

Router Tree with lazy loading

 The root node for `ManagerHomeComponent` is now named `manager [Lazy]`.

Completing the walking skeleton

Using the site map, we have created for LemonMart, from earlier in the chapter, we need to complete the walking skeleton navigation experience for the app. In order to create this experience, we will need to create some buttons to link all modules and components together. We will go at this module by module:

- Before we start, update the login button on `home.component` to link to the `Manager` module:

  src/app/home/home.component.ts
  ```
  ...
  <button mat-raised-button color="primary"
  routerLink="/manager">Login as Manager</button>
  ...
  ```

Manager module

Since we already enabled lazy loading for `ManagerModule`, let's go ahead and complete the rest of the navigational elements for it.

In the current setup, `ManagerHomeComponent` renders in the `<router-outlet>` defined in `app.component`, so when the user navigates from `HomeComponent` to `ManagerHomeComponent`, the toolbar implemented in `app.component` remains a constant. If we implement a similar toolbar that persists throughout `ManagerModule`, we can create a consistent UX for navigating subpages across modules.

For this to work, we need to replicate the parent-child relationship between `app.component` and `home/home.component`, where the parent implements the toolbar and a `<router-outlet>` so that children elements can be rendered in there:

1. Start by creating the base `manager` component:

   ```
   $ npx ng g c manager/manager -m manager --flat -s -t
   ```

The `--flat` option skips directory creation and places the component directly under the `manager` folder, just like `app.component` residing directly under the `app` folder.

2. Implement a navigational toolbar with `activeLink` tracking:

   src/app/manager/manager.component.ts
   ```
   styles: [`
     div[fxLayout] {margin-top: 32px;}
     `,`
     .active-link {
       font-weight: bold;
       border-bottom: 2px solid #005005;
     }`
   ],
   template: `
     <mat-toolbar color="accent">
       <a mat-button routerLink="/manager/home"
   routerLinkActive="active-link">Manager's Dashboard</a>
       <a mat-button routerLink="/manager/users"
   routerLinkActive="active-link">User Management</a>
       <a mat-button routerLink="/manager/receipts"
   routerLinkActive="active-link">Receipt Lookup</a>
     </mat-toolbar>
     <router-outlet></router-outlet>
     `
   ```

It must be noted that submodules don't automatically have access to services or components created in parent modules. This is an important default behavior to preserve a decoupled architecture. However, there are certain cases where it is desirable to share some amount of code. In this case, `mat-toolbar` needs to be reimported. Since the `MatToolbarModule` is already loaded in `src/app/material.module.ts`, we can just import this module into `manager.module.ts` and there will not be a performance or memory penalty for doing so.

3. `ManagerComponent` should be imported into `ManagerModule`:

   src/app/manager/manager.module.ts
   ```
   import { MaterialModule } from '../material.module'
   import { ManagerComponent } from './manager.component'
   ...
   imports: [... MaterialModule, ManagerComponent],
   ```

4. Create components for the subpages:

   ```
   $ npx ng g c manager/userManagement -m manager
   $ npx ng g c manager/receiptLookup -m manager
   ```

5. Create the parent/children routing. We know that we need the following routes to be able to navigate to our subpages, as follows:

   example
   ```
   { path: '', redirectTo: '/manager/home', pathMatch: 'full' },
   { path: 'home', component: ManagerHomeComponent },
   { path: 'users', component: UserManagementComponent },
   { path: 'receipts', component: ReceiptLookupComponent },
   ```

   In order to target the `<router-outlet>` defined in `manager.component`, we need to create a parent route first and then specify routes for the subpages:

   src/app/manager/manager-routing.module.ts
   ```
   ...
   const routes: Routes = [
     {
       path: '', component: ManagerComponent, children: [
         { path: '', redirectTo: '/manager/home', pathMatch: 'full' },
         { path: 'home', component: ManagerHomeComponent },
   ```

```
        { path: 'users', component: UserManagementComponent },
        { path: 'receipts', component: ReceiptLookupComponent },
      ]
    },
  ]
```

You should now be able to navigate through the app. When you click on the **Login as Manager** button, you will be taken to the page shown here. The clickable targets are highlighted, as shown:

Manager's Dashboard with clickable targets highlighted

If you click on **LemonMart**, you will be taken to the home page. If you click on **Manager's Dashboard**, **User Management** or **Receipt Lookup**, you will be navigated to the corresponding subpage, while active link will be bold and underlined on the toolbar.

User module

Upon login, users will be able to access their profiles and view a list of actions they can access in the LemonMart app through a side navigation menu. In Chapter 9, *Design Authentication and Authorization*, when we implement authentication and authorization, we will be receiving the role of the user from the server. Based on the role of the user, we will be able to automatically navigate or limit the options users can see. We will implement these components in this module so that they will only be loaded once a user is logged in. For the purpose of completing the walking skeleton, we will ignore authentication-related concerns:

1. Create the necessary components:

   ```
   $ npx ng g c user/profile -m user
   $ npx ng g c user/logout -m user -t -s
   $ npx ng g c user/navigationMenu -m user -t -s
   ```

2. Implement routing:

   Start with implementing the lazy loading in app-routing:

   src/app/app-routing.module.ts
   ```
   ...
     { path: 'user', loadChildren: 'app/user/user.module#UserModule' },
   ```

 Ensure that PageNotFoundComponent route is always the last route in app-routing.module.

   Now implement the child routes in user-routing:

   src/app/user/user-routing.module.ts
   ```
   ...
   const routes: Routes = [
     { path: 'profile', component: ProfileComponent },
     { path: 'logout', component: LogoutComponent },
   ]
   ```

We are implementing routing for `NavigationMenuComponent`, because it'll be directly used as an HTML element. In addition, since `userModule` doesn't have a landing page, there's no default path defined.

3. Wire up the user and logout icons:

src/app/app.component.ts

```
...
<mat-toolbar>
  ...
  <button mat-mini-fab routerLink="/user/profile"
matTooltip="Profile" aria-label="User Profile"><mat-
icon>account_circle</mat-icon></button>
  <button mat-mini-fab routerLink="/user/logout"
matTooltip="Logout" aria-label="Logout"><mat-icon>lock_open</mat-
icon></button>
</mat-toolbar>
```

Icon buttons can be cryptic, so it's a good idea to add tooltips to them. In order for tooltips to work, switch from the `mat-icon-button` directive to the `mat-mini-fab` directive and ensure that you import `MatTooltipModule` in `material.module`. In addition, ensure that you add `aria-label` for icon only buttons so that users with disabilities relying on screen readers can still navigate your web application.

4. Ensure that the app works.

You'll note that the two buttons are too close to each other, as follows:

Toolbar with icons

5. You can fix the icon layout issue by adding `fxLayoutGap="8px"` to `<mat-toolbar>`; however, now the lemon logo is too far apart from the app name, as shown:

Toolbar with padded icons

6. The logo layout issue can be fixed by merging the icon and the button:

src/app/app.component.ts

```
...
<mat-toolbar>
  ...
  <a mat-icon-button routerLink="/home"><mat-icon
svgIcon="lemon"></mat-icon><span class="mat-
h2">LemonMart</span></a>
  ...
</mat-toolbar>
```

As shown in the following screenshot, the grouping fixes the layout issue:

Toolbar with grouped and padded elements

This is a more desirable from a UX perspective as well; now users can go back to the home page by clicking on the lemon as well.

POS and inventory modules

Our walking skeleton presumes the role of the manager. To be able to access all components we are about to create, we need to enable the manager to be able to access pos and inventory modules.

Update `ManagerComponent` with two new buttons:

src/app/manager/manager.component.ts
```
<mat-toolbar color="accent" fxLayoutGap="8px">
  ...
  <span class="flex-spacer"></span>
  <button mat-mini-fab routerLink="/inventory"
matTooltip="Inventory" aria-label="Inventory"><mat-icon>list</mat-
icon></button>
    <button mat-mini-fab routerLink="/pos" matTooltip="POS" aria-
label="POS"><mat-icon>shopping_cart</mat-icon></button>
  </mat-toolbar>
```

Note that these router links will navigate use out of `ManagerModule`, so it is normal for the toolbar to disappear.

Now, it'll be up to you to implement the last two remaining modules.

POS module

POS module is very similar to the user module, except that `PosComponent` will be the default route. This will be a complicated component with some subcomponents, so ensure that it is created with a directory:

1. Create the `PosComponent`
2. Register `PosComponent` as the default route
3. Configure lazy loading for `PosModule`
4. Ensure that the app works

Inventory module

Inventory module is very similar to `ManagerModule`, as shown:

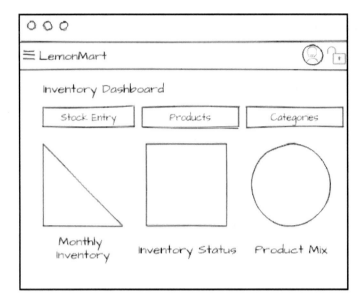

Inventory Dashboard mock-up

1. Create a base `Inventory` component
2. Register the `MaterialModule`
3. Create **Inventory Dashboard**, **Stock Entry**, **Products**, and **Categories** components
4. Configure parent-children routes in `inventory-routing.module`
5. Configure lazy loading for `InventoryModule`

6. Ensure that app works, as shown:

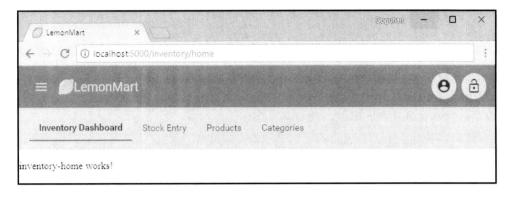

LemonMart Inventory Dashboard

Now that the walking skeleton of the app is completed, it is important to inspect the router tree to ensure that lazy loading has been configured correctly and module aren't unintentionally being eager loaded.

Inspect router tree

Navigate to the base route of the app and use Augury to inspect the router tree, as illustrated:

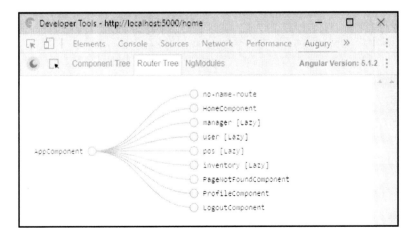

Router Tree with eager loading mistakes

Everything, but initially required components, should be denoted with the **[Lazy]** attribute. If, for some reason, routes are not denoted with **[Lazy]**, chances are that they are mistakenly being imported in `app.module` or some other component.

In the preceding screenshot, you may note that `ProfileComponent` and `LogoutComponent` are eagerly loaded, whereas the `user` module is correctly labeled as **[Lazy]**. Even multiple visual inspections through the tooling and the code base may leave you searching for the culprit. However, if you run a global search for `UserModule`, you'll quickly discover that it was being imported into `app.module`.

To be on the safe side make sure to remove any import statements for modules in `app.module` and your file should look like the one below:

src/app/app.module.ts
```
import { FlexLayoutModule } from '@angular/flex-layout'
import { BrowserModule } from '@angular/platform-browser'
import { NgModule } from '@angular/core'

import { AppRoutingModule } from './app-routing.module'
import { AppComponent } from './app.component'
import { BrowserAnimationsModule } from '@angular/platform-
browser/animations'
import { MaterialModule } from './material.module'
import { HomeComponent } from './home/home.component'
import { PageNotFoundComponent } from './page-not-found/page-not-
found.component'
import { HttpClientModule } from '@angular/common/http'

@NgModule({
  declarations: [AppComponent, HomeComponent, PageNotFoundComponent],
  imports: [
    BrowserModule,
    AppRoutingModule,
    BrowserAnimationsModule,
    MaterialModule,
    HttpClientModule,
    FlexLayoutModule,
  ],
  providers: [],
  bootstrap: [AppComponent],
})
export class AppModule {}
```

The next screenshot shows the corrected router tree:

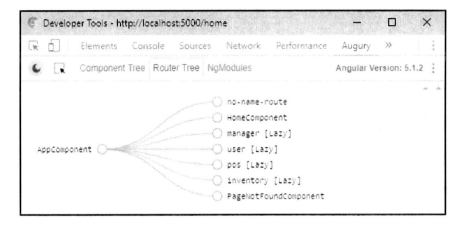

Router Tree with lazy loading

Ensure that `npm test` and `npm run e2e` executes without errors before moving on.

Common Testing Module

Now that we have a lot of modules to deal with, it becomes tedious to configure the imports and providers for each spec file individually. For this purpose, I recommend creating a common testing module to contain generic configuration that you can reuse across the board.

First start by creating a new `.ts` file.

1. Create `common/common.testing.ts`
2. Populate it with common testing providers, fakes and modules, shown as follows:

I have provided fake implementations of `ObservableMedia`, `MatIconRegistry`, `DomSanitizer`, along with arrays for `commonTestingProviders` and `commonTestingModules`.

src/app/common/common.testing.ts
```
import { HttpClientTestingModule } from '@angular/common/http/testing'
import { MediaChange } from '@angular/flex-layout'
import { FormsModule, ReactiveFormsModule } from '@angular/forms'
import { SafeResourceUrl, SafeValue } from '@angular/platform-browser'
import { NoopAnimationsModule } from '@angular/platform-browser/animations'
```

```
// tslint:disable-next-line:max-line-length
import { SecurityContext } from '@angular/platform-
browser/src/security/dom_sanitization_service'
import { RouterTestingModule } from '@angular/router/testing'
import { Observable, Subscription, of } from 'rxjs'
import { MaterialModule } from '../material.module'

const FAKE_SVGS = {
  lemon: '<svg><path id="lemon" name="lemon"></path></svg>',
}

export class ObservableMediaFake {
  isActive(query: string): boolean {
    return false
  }

  asObservable(): Observable<MediaChange> {
    return of({} as MediaChange)
  }

  subscribe(
    next?: (value: MediaChange) => void,
    error?: (error: any) => void,
    complete?: () => void
  ): Subscription {
    return new Subscription()
  }
}

export class MatIconRegistryFake {
  _document = document
  addSvgIcon(iconName: string, url: SafeResourceUrl): this {
    // this.addSvgIcon('lemon', 'lemon.svg')
    return this
  }

  getNamedSvgIcon(name: string, namespace: string = ''):
Observable<SVGElement> {
    return of(this._svgElementFromString(FAKE_SVGS.lemon))
  }

  private _svgElementFromString(str: string): SVGElement {
    if (this._document || typeof document !== 'undefined') {
      const div = (this._document || document).createElement('DIV')
      div.innerHTML = str
      const svg = div.querySelector('svg') as SVGElement
      if (!svg) {
        throw Error('<svg> tag not found')
```

```
    }
      return svg
    }
  }
}

export class DomSanitizerFake {
  bypassSecurityTrustResourceUrl(url: string): SafeResourceUrl {
    return {} as SafeResourceUrl
  }
  sanitize(context: SecurityContext, value: SafeValue | string | null):
string | null {
    return value ? value.toString() : null
  }
}

export const commonTestingProviders: any[] = [
  // intentionally left blank
]

export const commonTestingModules: any[] = [
  FormsModule,
  ReactiveFormsModule,
  MaterialModule,
  NoopAnimationsModule,
  HttpClientTestingModule,
  RouterTestingModule,
]
```

Now let's see a sample use of this shared configuration file:

src/app/app.component.spec.ts
```
import {
  commonTestingModules,
  commonTestingProviders,
  MatIconRegistryFake,
  DomSanitizerFake,
  ObservableMediaFake,
} from './common/common.testing'
import { ObservableMedia } from '@angular/flex-layout'
import { MatIconRegistry } from '@angular/material'
import { DomSanitizer } from '@angular/platform-browser'

...
TestBed.configureTestingModule({
      imports: commonTestingModules,
      providers: commonTestingProviders.concat([
        { provide: ObservableMedia, useClass: ObservableMediaFake },
```

```
        { provide: MatIconRegistry, useClass: MatIconRegistryFake },
        { provide: DomSanitizer, useClass: DomSanitizerFake },
      ]),
      declarations: [AppComponent],
    ...
```

Most other modules will just need `commonTestingModules` to be imported.

Don't move on until all your tests are passing!

Summary

In this chapter, you mastered how to effectively use Angular CLI to create major Angular components and scaffolds. You created the branding of your app, leveraging custom and built-in Material iconography. You learned how to debug complicated Angular apps with Augury. Finally, you began building Router-first apps, defining user roles early on, designing with lazy loading in mind and nailing down a walking-skeleton navigation experience early on.

To recap, in order to pull off a Router-first implementation, you need to do this:

1. Define user roles early on
2. Design with lazy loading in mind
3. Implement a walking-skeleton navigation experience
4. Design around major data components
5. Enforce a decoupled component architecture
6. Differentiate between user controls and components
7. Maximize code reuse

In this chapter, you executed steps 1-3; in the next three chapters, you will execute steps 4-7. In Chapter 8, *Continuous Integration and API Design*, we will go over designing around major data components and enable Continuous Integration to ensure a high-quality deliverable. In Chapter 9, *Design Authentication and Authorization*, we will deep dive into security considerations and design a conditional navigation experience. In Chapter 10, *Angular App Design and Recipes*, we will tie everything together by sticking to a decoupled component architecture, smartly choosing between creating user controls versus components and maximizing code reuse with various TypeScript, RxJS, and Angular coding techniques.

8
Continuous Integration and API Design

Before we start building more complicated features for our LOB app, LemonMart, we need to ensure that every code push we create has passing tests, adheres to the coding standards, and is an executable artifact that team members can run tests against, as we continue to further develop our application. Simultaneously, we need to start thinking about how our application will communicate with a backend server. Whether you, your team, or another team will be creating the new APIs, it will be important that the API design accommodates the needs of both the frontend and backend architectures. To ensure a smooth development process, a robust mechanism is needed to create an accessible, living piece of documentation for the API. **Continuous Integration (CI)** can solve the first problem and Swagger is perfect to address API design, documentation, and testing needs.

Continuous Integration is critical to ensuring a quality deliverable by building and executing tests on every code push. Setting up a CI environment can be time consuming and requires specialized knowledge of the tool being used. CircleCI is an established, cloud-based CI service with a free tier and helpful articles to get you started with as little configuration as possible. We will go over a Docker-based approach that can be run on most CI services, keeping your specific configuration knowledge relevant and CI service knowledge down to a minimum.

Another aspect of full-stack development is that you will likely be developing the frontend and backend of your application around the same time. Whether you work by yourself, as a team, or with multiple teams, it is critical to establish a data contract to ensure that you won't run into eleventh-hour integration challenges. We will use Swagger to define a data contract for a REST API and then create a mock server that your Angular application can make HTTP calls to. For backend development, Swagger can act as a great starting point to generate boilerplate code and can go forward as living documentation and testing UI for your API.

In this chapter, you will learn how to do the following:

- CI with CircleCI
- API design with Swagger

This chapter requires the following:

- A free CircleCI account
- Docker

Continuous Integration

The aim of Continuous Integration is to enable a consistent and repeatable environment to build, test, and generate deployable artifacts of your application with every code push. Before a pushing code, a developer should have a reasonable expectation that their build will pass; therefore creating a reliable CI environment that automates commands that developers can also run in their local machines is paramount.

Containerizing build environment

In order to ensure a consistent build environment across various OS platforms, developer machines, and Continuous Integration environments, you may containerize your build environment. Note that there are at least half-a-dozen common CI tools currently in use. Learning the ins and outs of each tool is almost an impossible task to achieve. Containerization of your build environment is an advanced concept that goes above and beyond of what is currently expected of CI tools. However, containerization is a great way to standardize over 90% of your build infrastructure, and can be executed in almost any CI environment. With this approach, the skills you learn and the build configuration you create becomes far more valuable, because both your knowledge and the tools you create become transferable and reusable.

There are many strategies to containerize your build environment with different levels of granularity and performance expectations. For the purpose of this book, we will focus on reusability and ease of use. Instead of creating a complicated, interdependent set of Docker images that may allow for more efficient fail-first and recovery paths, we will focus on a single and straightforward workflow. Newer versions of Docker have a great feature called multi-stage builds, which allow you to define a multi image process in an easy-to-read manner and maintain a singular `Dockerfile`.

At the end of the process, you can extract an optimized container image as our deliverable artifact, shedding the complexity of images used previously in the process.

As a reminder your single `Dockerfile` would look like the sample below:

Dockerfile
```
FROM duluca/minimal-node-web-server:8.11.1
WORKDIR /usr/src/app
COPY dist public
```

Multi-stage works by using multiple `FROM` statements in a single `Dockerfile`, where each stage can perform a task and make any resources within its instance available to other stages. In a build environment, we can implement various build-related tasks as their own stages, and then copy the end result, such as the `dist` folder of an Angular build to the final image, which contains a web server. In this case, we will implement three stages of images:

- **Builder**: Used to build a production version of your Angular app
- **Tester**: Used to run unit and e2e tests against a headless Chrome instances
- **Web Server**: The final result only containing the optimized production bits

 Multi-stage builds require Docker version 17.05 or higher. To read more about multi-stage builds, read the documentation at `https://docs.docker.com/develop/develop-images/multistage-build/`.

Start by creating a new file to implement the multi-stage configuration, named `Dockerfile.integration`, at the root of your project.

Builder

The first stage is `builder`. We need a lightweight build environment that can ensure consistent builds across the board. For this purpose, I've created a sample Alpine-based Node build environment complete with npm, bash, and git tools. For more information on why we're using Alpine and Node, refer to `Chapter 3`, *Prepare Angular App for Production Release*, in the *Containerizing the App using Docker* section:

1. Implement a new npm script to build your Angular app:

```
"scripts": {
  "build:prod": "ng build --prod",
}
```

2. Inherit from a Node.js based build environment like `node:10.1` or `duluca/minimal-node-build-env:8.11.2`

3. Implement your environment specific build script, as shown here:

 Note that at the time of publishing a bug in low-level npm tooling is preventing `node` based images from successfully installing Angular dependencies. This means that the sample `Dockerfile` below is based on an older version of Node and npm with `duluca/minimal-node-build-env:8.9.4`. In the future, when the bugs are sorted out an updated build environment will be able to leverage `npm ci` to install dependencies, which brings significant speed gains over the `npm install` command.

`Dockerfile.integration`
```
FROM duluca/minimal-node-build-env:8.9.4 as builder

# project variables
ENV SRC_DIR /usr/src
ENV GIT_REPO https://github.com/duluca/lemon-mart.git
ENV SRC_CODE_LOCATION .
ENV BUILD_SCRIPT build:prod

# get source code
RUN mkdir -p $SRC_DIR
WORKDIR $SRC_DIR
# if necessary, do SSH setup here or copy source code from local or
CI environment
RUN git clone $GIT_REPO .
# COPY $SRC_CODE_LOCATION .

RUN npm install
RUN npm run $BUILD_SCRIPT
```

In the preceding example, the source code is being pulled from GitHub by the container. I have chosen to do that for the sake of keeping the sample simple, because it works the same way in both local and remote continuous integration environments. However, your CI server will already have a copy of the source code, which you'll want to copy from your CI environment and then into the container.

Instead of the `RUN git clone $GIT_REPO .` command, you can copy source code with the `COPY $SRC_CODE_LOCATION .` command from your CI server or your local machine. If you do this, you will have to implement a `.dockerignore` file that somewhat resembles your `.gitignore` file to ensure that secrets aren't leaked, `node_modules` is not copied and the configuration is repeatable in other environments. In a CI environment, you will want to override the environment variable `$SRC_CODE_LOCATION` so that the source directory of the `COPY` command is correct. Feel free to create multiple versions of the `Dockerfile` that may fit your various needs.

In addition, I have built a minimal Node build environment `duluca/minimal-node-build-env` based on `node-alpine`, which you can observe on Docker Hub at `https://hub.docker.com/r/duluca/minimal-node-build-env`. This image is about ten times smaller than `node`. The size of Docker images have a real impact on build times, since the CI server or your team members will spend extra time pulling a larger image. Choose the environment that best fits your needs.

Debugging build environment

Depending on your particular needs, your initial setup of the builder portion of the `Dockerfile` may be frustrating. To test out new commands or debug errors, you may need to directly interact with the build environment.

To interactively experiment and/or debug within the build environment, execute the following:

```
$ docker run -it duluca/minimal-node-build-env:8.9.4 /bin/bash
```

You can test or debug commands within this temporary environment before baking them into your `Dockerfile`.

Tester

The second stage is `tester`. By default, the Angular CLI generates a testing requirement that is geared toward a development environment. This will not work in a continuous integration environment; we must configure Angular to work against a headless browser that can execute without the assistance of a GPU and further, a containerized environment to execute the tests against.

Angular testing tools are covered in `Chapter 3`, *Prepare Angular App for Production Release*.

Configuring a headless browser for Angular

The protractor testing tool officially supports running against Chrome in headless mode. In order to execute Angular tests in a continuous integration environment, you will need to configure your test runner, Karma, to run with a headless Chrome instance:

1. Update `karma.conf.js` to include a new headless browser option:

src/karma.conf.js
```
...
browsers: ['Chrome', 'ChromiumHeadless', 'ChromiumNoSandbox'],
customLaunchers: {
  ChromiumHeadless: {
        base: 'Chrome',
        flags: [
          '--headless',
          '--disable-gpu',
          // Without a remote debugging port, Google Chrome exits
immediately.
          '--remote-debugging-port=9222',
        ],
        debug: true,
      },
      ChromiumNoSandbox: {
        base: 'ChromiumHeadless',
        flags: ['--no-sandbox', '--disable-translate', '--disable-
extensions']
      }
    },
```

The `ChromiumNoSandbox` custom launcher encapsulates all the configuration elements needed for a good default setup.

2. Update `protractor` configuration to run in headless mode:

e2e/protractor.conf.js

```
...
  capabilities: {
    browserName: 'chrome',
    chromeOptions: {
      args: [
        '--headless',
        '--disable-gpu',
        '--no-sandbox',
        '--disable-translate',
        '--disable-extensions',
        '--window-size=800,600',
      ],
    },
  },
...
```

In order to test your application for responsive scenarios, you can use the `--window-size` option, as shown earlier, to change the browser settings.

3. Update the `package.json` scripts to select the new browser option in production build scenarios:

package.json

```
"scripts": {
  ...
  "test:prod": "npm test -- --watch=false"
  ...
}
```

Note that `test:prod` doesn't include `npm run e2e`. e2e tests are integration tests that take longer to execute, so think twice about including them as part of your critical build pipeline. e2e tests will not run on the lightweight testing environment mentioned in the next section, so they will require more resources and time to execute.

Configuring testing environment

For a lightweight testing environment, we will be leveraging an Alpine-based installation of the Chromium browser:

1. Inherit from `slapers/alpine-node-chromium`
2. Append the following configuration to `Docker.integration`:

Docker.integration
```
...
FROM slapers/alpine-node-chromium as tester
ENV BUILDER_SRC_DIR /usr/src
ENV SRC_DIR /usr/src
ENV TEST_SCRIPT test:prod

RUN mkdir -p $SRC_DIR
WORKDIR $SRC_DIR

COPY --from=builder $BUILDER_SRC_DIR $SRC_DIR

CMD 'npm run $TEST_SCRIPT'
```

The preceding script will copy the production build from the `builder` stage and execute your test scripts in a predictable manner.

Web server

The third and final stage generates the container that will be your web server. Once this stage is complete, the prior stages will be discarded and the end result will be an optimized sub-10 MB container:

1. Containerize your application with Docker, as discussed in `Chapter 3`, *Prepare Angular App for Production Release*
2. Append the `FROM` statement at the end of the file
3. `COPY` the production ready code from `builder` as shown here:

Docker.integration
```
...
FROM duluca/minimal-nginx-web-server:1.13.8-alpine
ENV BUILDER_SRC_DIR /usr/src
COPY --from=builder $BUILDER_SRC_DIR/dist /var/www
CMD 'nginx'
```

4. Build and test your multi-stage `Dockerfile`:

```
$ docker build -f Dockerfile.integration .
```

 If you are pulling code from GitHub, ensure that your code is committed and pushed before building the container, since it will pull your source code directly from the repository. Use the `--no-cache` option to ensure that new source code is pulled. If you are copying code from your local or CI environment, then do *not* use `--no-cache` as you won't the speed gains from being able to reuse previously built container layers.

5. Save your script as a new npm script named `build:ci` as shown:

```
package.json
"scripts": {
   ...
   "build:ci": "docker build -f Dockerfile.integration . -t
$npm_package_config_imageRepo:latest",
   ...
}
```

CircleCI

CircleCI makes it easy to get started with a free tier and great documentation for beginners and pros alike. If you have unique enterprise needs, CircleCI can be brought on premise, behind corporate firewalls, or as a private deployment in the cloud.

CircleCI has pre-baked build environments for virtual configuration of free setups, but it can also run builds using Docker containers, making it a solution that scales to user skills and needs, as mentioned in the *Containerizing Build Environment* section:

1. Create a CircleCI account at `https://circleci.com/`

2. Sign up with GitHub:

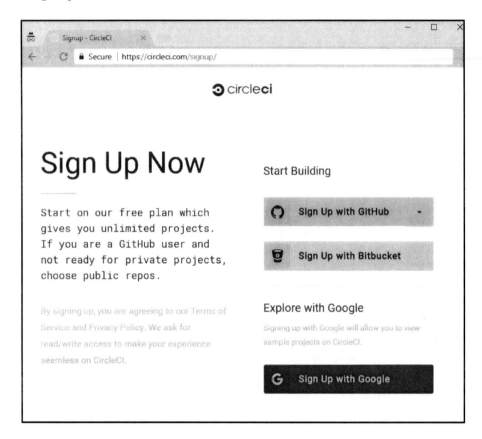

CircleCI Sign up page

3. Add a new project:

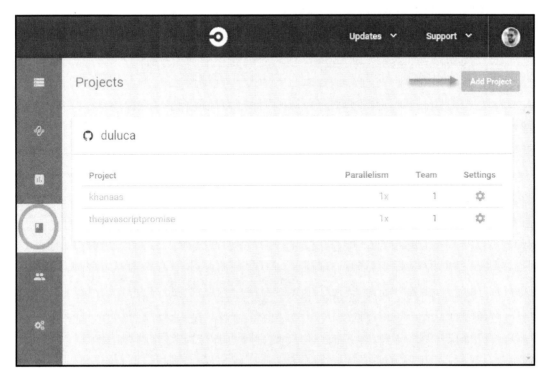

CircleCI Projects Page

On the next screen, you have an option to select **Linux** or **macOS** build environments. The macOS build environments are very useful for building iOS or macOS apps. However, there is no free-tier for those environments; only Linux instances with 1x parallelism are free.

4. Search for **lemon-mart** and click on **Setup project**
5. Select **Linux**
6. Select **Platform 2.0**
7. Select **Language** as **Other**, since we'll use a custom containerized build environment

8. In your source code, create a folder named `.circleci` and add a file named `config.yml`:

`.circleci/config.yml`
```
version: 2
jobs:
  build:
    docker:
      - image: docker:17.12.0-ce-git
    working_directory: /usr/src
    steps:
      - checkout
      - setup_remote_docker:
          docker_layer_caching: false
      - run:
          name: Build Docker Image
          command: |
            npm run build:ci
```

In the preceding file, a `build` job is defined, which is based on CircleCI's pre-built `docker:17.12.0-ce-git` image, containing the Docker and git CLI tools within itself. We then define build `steps`, which checks out the source code from GitHub with `checkout`, informs CircleCI to set up a Docker-within-Docker environment with the `setup_remote_docker` command and then executes the `docker build -f Dockerfile.integration .` command to initiate our custom build process.

In order to optimize builds, you should experiment with layer caching and copying source code from the already checked out source code in CircleCI.

9. Sync your changes to Github
10. On CircleCI, click to **Create** your project

If everything goes well, you will have passing, *green*, build. As shown in the following screenshot, build #4 was successful:

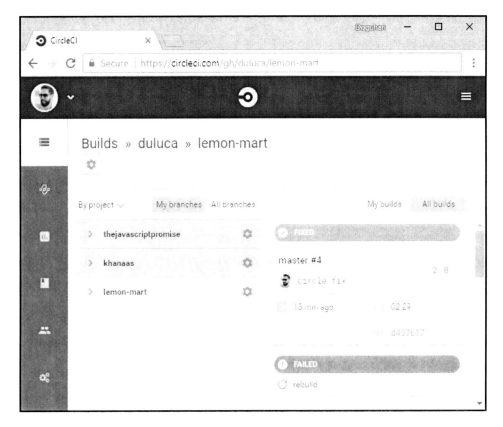

Green build on CircleCI

At the moment, the CI server is running, building the app in stage 1, then running the tests in stage 2, and then building the web server in stage 3. Note that we are not doing anything with this web server container image, such as deploying it to a server.

In order to deploy your image, you will need to implement a deploy step. In this step, you can deploy to a multitude of targets such as Docker Hub, Zeit Now, Heroku, or AWS ECS. The integration to these targets will involve multiple steps. At a highlevel, these steps are as follows:

1. Install target-specific CLI tool with a separate run step
2. Configure Docker with login credentials specific to the target environment, storing said credentials as CircleCI environment variables
3. Use `docker push` to submit the resulting web server image to the target's Docker registry
4. Execute a platform-specific `deploy` command to instruct the target to run the Docker image that was just pushed.

An example of how to configure such a deployment on AWS ECS from your local development environment is covered in `Chapter 11`, *Highly-Available Cloud Infrastructure on AWS*.

Code coverage report

A good way to understand the amount and the trends of unit tests coverage for your Angular project is through a code coverage report.

In order to generate the report for your app, execute the following command from your project folder:

```
$ npx ng test --browsers ChromiumNoSandbox --watch=false --code-coverage
```

The resulting report will be created as HTML under a folder name coverage; execute the following command to view it in your browser:

```
$ npx http-server -c-1 -o -p 9875 ./coverage
```

Here's the folder-level sample coverage report generated by `istanbul.js` for LemonMart:

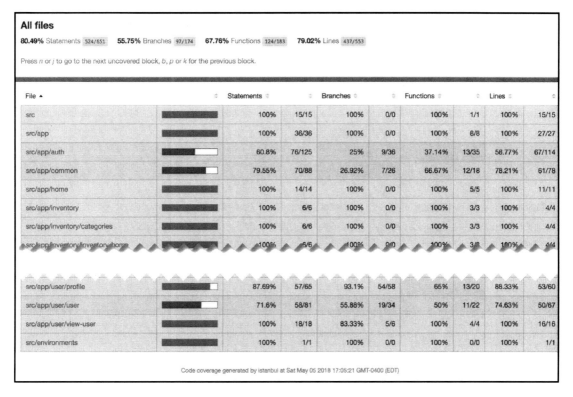

All files

80.49% Statements 324/651   **55.75%** Branches 97/174   **67.76%** Functions 124/183   **79.02%** Lines 437/553

Press *n* or *j* to go to the next uncovered block, *b*, *p* or *k* for the previous block.

File ▲		Statements		Branches		Functions		Lines	
src		100%	15/15	100%	0/0	100%	1/1	100%	15/15
src/app		100%	36/36	100%	0/0	100%	8/8	100%	27/27
src/app/auth		60.8%	76/125	25%	9/36	37.14%	13/35	58.77%	67/114
src/app/common		79.55%	70/88	26.92%	7/26	66.67%	12/18	78.21%	61/78
src/app/home		100%	14/14	100%	0/0	100%	5/5	100%	11/11
src/app/inventory		100%	6/6	100%	0/0	100%	3/3	100%	4/4
src/app/inventory/categories		100%	6/6	100%	0/0	100%	3/3	100%	4/4
src/app/inventory/inventory-home		100%	6/6	100%	0/0	100%	3/3	100%	4/4
src/app/user/profile		87.69%	57/65	93.1%	54/58	65%	13/20	88.33%	53/60
src/app/user/user		71.6%	58/81	55.88%	19/34	50%	11/22	74.63%	50/67
src/app/user/view-user		100%	18/18	83.33%	5/6	100%	4/4	100%	16/16
src/environments		100%	1/1	100%	0/0	100%	0/0	100%	1/1

Code coverage generated by istanbul at Sat May 05 2018 17:05:21 GMT-0400 (EDT)

Istanbul code coverage report for LemonMart

You can drill down on a particular folder, like `src/app/auth`, **and get a file-level report, as shown here:**

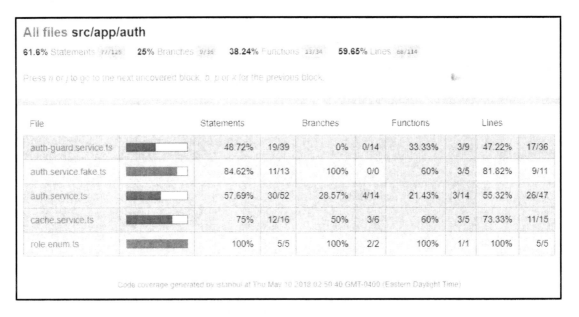

Istanbul code coverage report for src/app/auth

You can further drill down to get line-level coverage for a given file, like
`cache.service.ts`, as shown here:

All files / src/app/auth **cache.service.ts**

75% Statements 12/16 **50%** Branches 3/6 **60%** Functions 3/5 **73.33%** Lines 11/15

```
 1  1x  export abstract class CacheService {
 2  1x    protected getItem<T>(key: string): T {
 3  2x      const data = localStorage.getItem(key)
 4  2x   I  if (data && data !== 'undefined') {
 5             return JSON.parse(data)
 6          }
 7  2x      return null
 8        }
 9
10  1x    protected setItem(key: string, data: object | string) {
11  2x   I  if (typeof data === 'string') {
12           localStorage.setItem(key, data)
13          }
14  2x      localStorage.setItem(key, JSON.stringify(data))
15        }
16
17  1x    protected removeItem(key: string) {
18         localStorage.removeItem(key)
19        }
20
21  1x    protected clear() {
22         localStorage.clear()
23        }
24  1x  }
25
```

Code coverage generated by istanbul at Thu May, 10 2018 02:50:40 GMT-0400 (Eastern Daylight Time)

Istanbul Code Coverage Report for cache.service.ts

In the preceding image you can see that lines 5, 12, 17-18 and 21-22 are not covered by any test. The I icon denotes that the if path was not taken. We can increase our code coverage by implementing unit tests that exercise the functions that are contained within `CacheService`. As an exercise, the reader should attempt to atleast cover one of these functions with a new unit test and observe the code coverage report change.

Ideally, your CI server configuration should generate and host the code coverage report with every test run in a readily accessible manner. Implement these commands as script in `package.json` and execute them in your CI pipeline. This configuration is left as an exercise for the reader.

Install `http-server` as a development dependency to your project.

API design

In full-stack development, nailing down the API design early on is important. The API design itself is closely correlated with how your data contract will look. You may create RESTful endpoints or use the next-gen GraphQL technology. In designing your API, frontend and backend developers should closely collaborate to achieve shared design goals. Some high-level goals are listed as follows:

- Minimize data transmitted between client and server
- Stick to well-established design patterns (that is, pagination)
- Design to reduce business logic present in the client
- Flatten data structures
- Do not expose database keys or relationships
- Version endpoints from the get go
- Design around major data components

It is important not to reinvent the wheel and take a disciplined, if not strict, approach to designing your API. The downstream effect of missteps in API design can be profound and impossible to correct once your application goes live.

I will go into details of designing around major data components and implement a sample Swagger endpoint.

Designing around major data components

It helps to organize your APIs around major data components. This will roughly match how you consume data in various components in your Angular application. We will start off by defining our major data components by creating a rough data entity diagram and then implementing a sample API for the user data entity with swagger.

Defining entities

Let's start by taking a stab at what kind of entities you would like to store and how these entities might relate to one another.

Here's a sample design for LemonMart, created using `draw.io`:

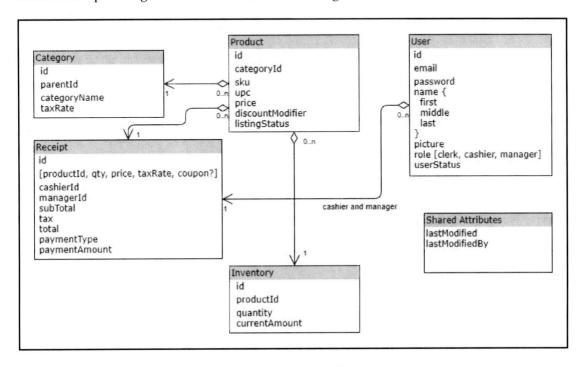

Data entity diagram for LemonMart

 At this moment, whether your entities are stored in a SQL or NoSQL database is inconsequential. My suggestion is to stick to what you know, but if you're starting from scratch, a NoSQL database like MongoDB will offer the most amount of flexibility as your implementation and requirements evolve.

Roughly speaking, you will need CRUD APIs for each entity. You can use Swagger to design your APIs.

Swagger

Swagger will allow you to design your web API. For teams, it can act as an interface between frontend and backend teams. Additionally, with API mocking, you can develop and complete API features before the implementation of the APIs even begins.

We will implement a sample Users API as we move on, to demonstrate how Swagger works.

The sample project comes with recommended extensions for VS Code. Swagger Viewer allows us to preview the YAML file without running any additional tools.

Defining a Swagger YAML file

The most widely used and supported version of the Swagger spec is `swagger: '2.0'`. The following example is given using the newer, standards-based, `openapi: 3.0.0`. The sample code repository contains both examples. However, at the time of publishing, most tooling in the Swagger ecosystem relies on version 2.0.

The sample code repository can be found at `github.com/duluca/lemon-mart-swagger-server`.

For your mock API server, you should create a separate git repository, so that this contract between your frontend and backend can be maintained separately.

1. Create a new GitHub repository, called `lemon-mart-swagger-server`
2. Start defining a YAML file with general information and target servers:

```yaml
swagger.oas3.yaml
openapi: 3.0.0
info:
  title: LemonMart
  description: LemonMart API
  version: "1.0.0"

servers:
  - url: http://localhost:3000
    description: Local environment
  - url: https://mystagingserver.com/v1
```

```
            description: Staging environment
          - url: https://myprodserver.com/v1
            description: Production environment
```

3. Under `components`, **define shared data** `schemas`:

swagger.oas3.yaml

```
...
components:
  schemas:
    Role:
      type: string
      enum: [clerk, cashier, manager]
    Name:
      type: object
      properties:
        first:
          type: string
        middle:
          type: string
        last:
          type: string
    User:
      type: object
      properties:
        id:
          type: string
        email:
          type: string
        name:
          $ref: '#/components/schemas/Name'
        picture:
          type: string
        role:
          $ref: '#/components/schemas/Role'
        userStatus:
          type: boolean
        lastModified:
          type: string
          format: date
        lastModifiedBy:
          type: string
    Users:
      type: object
      properties:
        total:
          type: number
          format: int32
```

```
      items:
        $ref: '#/components/schemas/ArrayOfUser'
    ArrayOfUser:
      type: array
      items:
            $ref: '#/components/schemas/User'
```

4. Under `components`, **add shared** `parameters`, **making it easy to reuse common patterns like paginated endpoints:**

   swagger.oas3.yaml
```
   . . .
     parameters:
       offsetParam: # <-- Arbitrary name for the definition that will
   be used to refer to it.
                     # Not necessarily the same as the parameter name.
         in: query
         name: offset
         required: false
         schema:
           type: integer
           minimum: 0
         description: The number of items to skip before starting to
   collect the result set.
       limitParam:
         in: query
         name: limit
         required: false
         schema:
           type: integer
           minimum: 1
           maximum: 50
           default: 20
         description: The numbers of items to return.
```

5. Under `paths`, **define a** `get` **endpoint for the** /`users` **path:**

```
   . . .
   paths:
     /users:
       get:
         description: |
           Searches and returns `User` objects.
           Optional query params determines values of returned array
         parameters:
           - in: query
             name: search
```

```
      required: false
      schema:
        type: string
      description: Search text
  - $ref: '#/components/parameters/offsetParam'
  - $ref: '#/components/parameters/limitParam'
responses:
  '200': # Response
    description: OK
    content: # Response body
      application/json: # Media type
        schema:
          $ref: '#/components/schemas/Users'
```

6. Under `paths`, add `get` user by ID and `update` user by ID endpoints:

swagger.oas3.yaml

```
...
  /user/{id}:
    get:
      description: Gets a `User` object by id
      parameters:
        - in: path
          name: id
          required: true
          schema:
            type: string
          description: User's unique id
      responses:
        '200': # Response
          description: OK
          content: # Response body
            application/json: # Media type
              schema:
                $ref: '#/components/schemas/User'
    put:
      description: Updates a `User` object given id
      parameters:
        - in: query
          name: id
          required: true
          schema:
            type: string
          description: User's unique id
        - in: body
          name: userData
          schema:
            $ref: '#/components/schemas/User'
```

```
        style: form
        explode: false
        description: Updated user object
  responses:
    '200':
      description: OK
      content: # Response body
        application/json: # Media type
          schema:
            $ref: '#/components/schemas/User'
```

To validate your Swagger file, you can use the online editor at `editor.swagger.io`.

Note the use of `style: form` and `explode: false`, which are the simplest way to configure an endpoint that expects basic form data. For more parameter serialization options or to simulate authentication endpoints and a slew of other possible configurations, refer to the documentation at `swagger.io/docs/specification/`.

Creating a Swagger server

Using your YAML file, you can generate a mock Node.js server using the Swagger Code Gen tool.

OpenAPI 3.0 with unofficial tooling

As mentioned in the earlier section, this section will use version 2 of the YAML file, which can generate a server using the official tooling. There are, however, other tools out there that can generate some code, but not complete enough to be easy to use:

1. If using OpenAPI 3.0 on the project folder, execute the following command:

```
$ npx swagger-node-codegen swagger.oas3.yaml -o ./server
...
Done!
Check out your shiny new API at C:\dev\lemon-mart-swagger-
server\server.
```

Under a new folder, called `server`, you should now have a Node Express server generated.

2. Install dependencies for the server:

```
$ cd server
$ npm install
```

You must then manually implement the missing stubs to complete the implementation of the server.

Swagger 2.0 with official tooling

Using official tooling and version 2.0, you can automate API creation and response generation. Once official tooling fully supports them, OpenAPI 3.0, the same instructions should apply:

1. Publish your YAML file on a URI that will be accessible by your machine:

```
https://raw.githubusercontent.com/duluca/lemon-mart-swagger-server/
master/swagger.2.yaml
```

2. In your project folder, execute the following command, replacing `<uri>` with the one pointing at your YAML file:

```
$ docker run --rm -v ${PWD}:/local swaggerapi/swagger-codegen-cli
$ generate -i <uri> -l nodejs-server -o /local/server
```

Similar to the preceding section, this will create a Node Express server under the server directory. In order to execute this server, carry on with the following steps.

3. Install the server's dependencies with `npm install`

4. Run `npm start`. Your mock server should now be up and running.

5. Navigate to `http://localhost:3000/docs`

6. Try out the API for `get /users`; you'll note that the **items** property is empty:

Request URL

```
http://localhost:3000/v1/users?limit=20
```

Response Body

```
{
  "total": 0.8008281904610115,
  "items": ""
}
```

Response Code

```
200
```

Swagger UI - Users endpoint

However, you should be receiving dummy data. We will correct this behavior.

7. Try out `get /user/{id}`; you'll see that you're receiving some dummy data back:

Request URL

```
http://localhost:3000/v1/user/1
```

Response Body

```
{
  "role": {},
  "userStatus": true,
  "lastModifiedBy": "lastModifiedBy",
  "name": {
    "middle": "middle",
    "last": "last",
    "first": "first"
  },
  "id": "id",
  "lastModified": "2000-01-23",
  "email": "email",
  "picture": "picture"
}
```

Response Code

```
200
```

Swagger UI - User by ID endpoint

The difference in behavior is because, by default, the Node Express server uses controllers generated under `server/controllers/Default.js` to read random data generated during server creation from `server/service/DefaultService.js`. However, you can disable the default controllers and force Swagger into a better default stubbing mode.

8. Update `index.js` to force the use of stubs and comment out controllers:

```
index.js
var options = {
    swaggerUi: path.join(__dirname, '/swagger.json'),
    // controllers: path.join(__dirname, './controllers'),
    useStubs: true,
}
```

9. Try out the `/users` endpoint again

As you can see here, the response is higher quality by default:

Swagger UI - Users endpoint with dummy data

In the preceding, `total` is a whole number, `role` is defined correctly, and `items` is a valid array structure.

To enable better and more customized data mocking, you can edit `DefaultService.js`. In this case, you would want to update the `usersGET` function to return an array of customized users.

Enable Cross-Origin Resource Sharing (CORS)

Before you're able to use your server from your application, you will need to configure it to allow for **Cross-Origin Resource Sharing (CORS)** so that your Angular application hosted on `http://localhost:5000` can communicate with your mock server hosted on `http://localhost:3000`:

1. Install the `cors` package:

   ```
   $ npm i cors
   ```

2. Update `index.js` to use `cors`:

   ```
   server/index.js
   ...
   var cors = require('cors')
   ...
   app.use(cors())

   // Initialize the Swagger middleware
   swaggerTools.initializeMiddleware(swaggerDoc, function(middleware)
   {
   ...
   ```

Ensure that `app.use(cors())` is called right before `initializeMiddleware`; otherwise, other Express middleware may interfere with the functionality of `cors()`.

Verifying and publishing Swagger server

You can verify your Swagger server setup through the SwaggerUI, which will be located at `http://localhost:3000/docs`, or you can achieve a more integrated environment with the Preview Swagger extension in VS Code.

I will demonstrate how you can use this extension to test your API from within VS Code:

1. Select the YAML file in **Explorer**
2. Press *Shift + Alt + P* and execute the **Preview Swagger** command
3. You will see an interactive window to test your configuration, as illustrated:

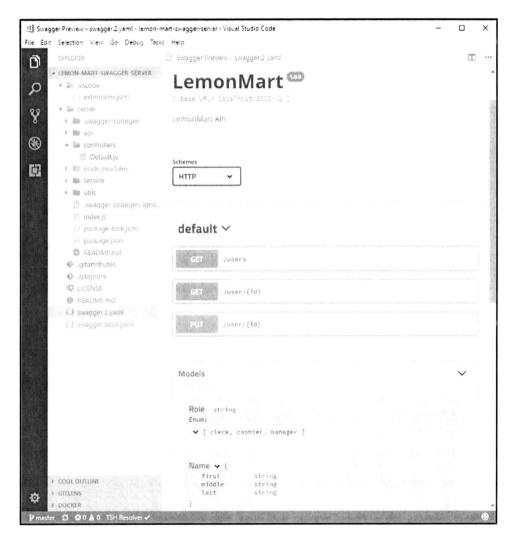

Preview Swagger Extension in Visual Studio Code

4. Click on the **Get** button for **/users**
5. Click on **Try it out** to see the results

In OpenAPI 3.0.0, instead of schemes, you will see a list of servers, including local and remote resources. This is a very convenient tool to explore various data sources as you code your frontend application.

Now that you have verified your Swagger server, you can publish your server to make it accessible to team members or **Automated Acceptance Test (AAT)** environments that require a predictable dataset to execute successfully.

Perform the following steps, as covered in Chapter 3, *Prepare Angular App for Production Release:*

6. Add **npm Scripts for Docker** to the root level `package.json` file
7. Add a `Dockerfile`:

```
Dockerfile
FROM duluca/minimal-node-build-env:8.11.2

RUN mkdir -p /usr/src
WORKDIR /usr/src

COPY server .

RUN npm ci

CMD ["node", "index"]
```

Once you build the container, you are ready to deploy it.

I have published a sample server on Docker Hub at `https://hub.docker.com/r/duluca/lemon-mart-swagger-server`.

Summary

In this chapter, you learned how to create a container-based Continuous Integration environment. We leveraged CircleCI as a cloud-based CI service and highlighted the fact that you can deploy the outcome of your builds to all major cloud hosting providers. If you enable such automated deployment, you will achieve **Continuous Deployment (CD)**. With a CI/CD pipeline, you can share every iteration of your app with clients and team members and quickly deliver bug fixes or new features to your end users.

We also discussed the importance of good API design and established Swagger as a tool that is beneficial to frontend and backend developers alike to define and develop against a live data-contract. If you create a Swagger mock server, you can enable team members to pull the mock server image and use it to develop their frontend applications before backend implementation is completed.

Both CircleCI and Swagger are highly sophisticated tools in their own ways. The techniques mentioned in this chapter are straightforward on purpose, but they are meant to enable sophisticated workflows, giving you a taste of the true power of such tools. You can improve upon the efficiency and the capability of this technique vastly, but the techniques will depend on your specific needs.

Armed with CI and mocked APIs that we can send real HTTP requests to, we are ready to iterate rapidly, while ensuring a high-quality deliverable. In the next chapter, we will dive deep into designing an authorization and authentication experience for your line-of-business app using token-based authentication and conditional navigation techniques to enable a smooth user experience, continuing the Router-first approach.

9
Design Authentication and Authorization

Designing a high-quality authentication and authorization system without frustrating the end user is a difficult problem to solve. Authentication is the act of verifying the identity of a user, and authorization specifies the privileges a user has to access a resource. Both processes, auth for short, must seamlessly work in tandem to address the needs of users with varying roles, needs, and job functions. In today's web, users have a high baseline level of expectations from any auth system they encounter through the browser, so this is a really important part of your application to get absolutely right the first time.

The user should always be aware of what they can and can't do in your app. If there are errors, failures, or mistakes, the user should be clearly informed as to why such an error occured. As your application grows, it is easy to miss all the ways an error condition could be triggered. Your implementation should be easy to extend or maintain, otherwise this basic backbone of your application will require a lot of maintenance. In this chapter, we will walk-through the various challenges of creating a great auth UX and implement a solid baseline experience.

We will be continuing the router-first approach to designing SPAs by implementing the authentication and authorization experience of LemonMart. In Chapter 7, *Create a Router-First Line-of-Business App*, we defined user roles, finished our build-out of all major routing and completed a rough walking-skeleton navigation experience of LemonMart, so we are well prepared to implement role-based routing and the nuances of pulling such an implementation.

In Chapter 8, *Continuous Integration and API Design*, we discussed the idea of designing around major data components, so you are already familiar with how a user entity looks like, which will come in handy in implementing a token-based login experience, including caching role information within the entity.

Before diving into auth, we will discuss the importance of completing high-level mock -ups for your application before starting to implement various conditional navigation elements, which may change significantly during the design phase.

In this chapter, you will learn about the following topics:

- Importance of high-level UX design
- Token-based authentication
- Conditional navigation
- Side Navigation bar
- Reusable UI Service for alerts
- Caching data
- JSON Web Tokens
- Angular HTTP interceptors
- Router guards

Wrapping up mock-ups

Mock-ups are important in determining what kind of components and user controls we will need throughout the app. Any user control or component that will be used across components will need to defined at the root level and others scoped with their own modules.

In Chapter 7, *Create a Router-First Line-of-Business App*, we have already identified the submodules and designed landing pages for them to complete the walking skeleton. Now that we have defined the major data components, we can complete mock-ups for the rest of the app. When designing screens at a high-level, keep several things in mind:

- Can a user complete common tasks required for their role with as little navigation as possible?
- Can users readily access all information and functionality of the app through visible elements on the screen?
- Can a user search for the data they need easily?
- Once a user finds a record of interest, can they drill-down into detail records or view related records with ease?
- Is that pop-up alert really necessary? You know users won't read it, right?

Keep in mind that there's no one right way to design any user experience, which is why when designing screens, always keep modularity and reusability in mind.

As you generate various design artifacts, such as mock-ups or design decisions, take care to post them on a wiki reachable by all team members:

1. On GitHub, switch over to the **Wiki** tab
2. You may check out my sample wiki at `Github.com/duluca/lemon-mart/wiki`, as shown:

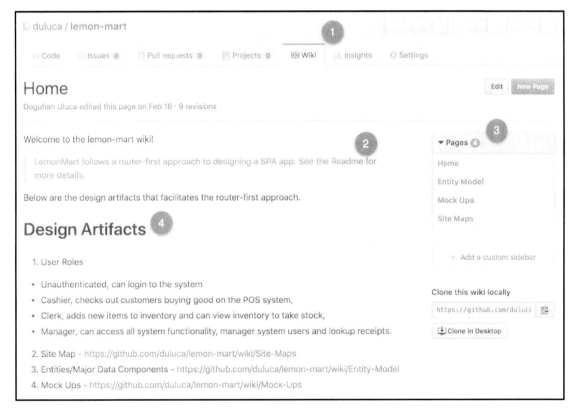

GitHub.com LemonMart Wiki

3. When creating a wiki page, ensure that you cross-link between any other documentation available, such as **Readme**

4. Note that GitHub shows subpages on the wiki under **Pages**
5. However, an additional summary is helpful, such as the **Design Artifacts** section, since some people may miss the navigational element on the right
6. As you complete mock-ups, post them on wiki

You can see a summary view of the wiki here:

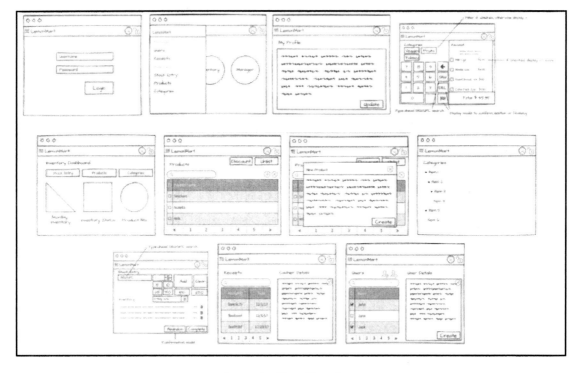

Summary view of Lemon Mart mock-ups

7. Optionally, place the mock-ups in the walking skeleton app so that testers can better envision the functionality that is yet to be developed

With the mock-ups completed, we can now continue the implementation of LemonMart with the Authentication and Authorization workflow.

Design authentication and authorization workflow

A well-designed authentication workflow is stateless so that there's no concept of an expiring session. User's are free to interact with your stateless REST APIs from as many devices and tabs as they wish, simultaneously or overtime. **JSON Web Token (JWT)** implements distributed claims-based authentication that can be digitally signed or integration protected and/or encrypted using a **Message Authentication Code (MAC)**. This means once a user's identity is authenticated through, let's say a password-challenge, they receive an encoded claim ticket or a token, which can then be used to make future requests to the system without having to reauthenticate the identity of a user. The server can independently verify the validity of this claim and process the requests without requiring any prior knowledge of having interacted with this user. Thus, we don't have to store session information regarding a user, making our solution stateless and easy to scale. Each token will expire after a predefined period and due to their distributed nature, they can't be remotely or individually revoked; however, we can bolster real-time security by interjecting custom account and user role status checks to ensure that the authenticated user is authorized to access server-side resources.

 JSON Web Tokens implement IETF industry standard RFC7519, found at `https://tools.ietf.org/html/rfc7519`.

A good authorization workflow enables conditional navigation based on a user's role so that users are automatically taken to the optimal landing screen; they are not shown routes or elements that are not suitable for their roles and if by mistake they try to access an authorized path, they're prevented from doing so. You must remember that any client-side role-based navigation is merely a convenience and is not meant for security. This means that every call made to the server should contain the necessary header information, with the secure token, so that the user can be reauthenticated by the server, their role independently verified and only then they are allowed to retrieve secured data. Client-side authentication can't be trusted, which is why password reset screens must be built with a server-side rendering technology so that both the user and the server can verify that the intended user is interacting with the system.

In the following sections, we will design a fully featured auth workflow around the **User** data entity, as follows:

User entity

Add auth service

We will start by creating an auth service with a real and a fake login provider:

1. Add an authentication and authorization service:

   ```
   $ npx ng g s auth -m app --flat false
   ```

2. Ensure that the service is provided in `app.module`:

   src/app/app.module.ts
   ```
   import { AuthService } from './auth/auth.service'
   ...
   providers: [AuthService],
   ```

   Creating a separate folder for the service will organize various related components to authentication and authorization, such as the `enum` definition for Role. Additionally, we will be able to add an `authService` fake to the same folder, essential for writing unit tests.

3. Define user roles as an `enum`:

   src/app/auth/role.enum.ts
   ```
   export enum Role {
     None = 'none',
     Clerk = 'clerk',
     Cashier = 'cashier',
     Manager = 'manager',
   }
   ```

Implement a basic authentication service

Now, let's build a local authentication service that will enable us to demonstrate a robust login form, caching, and conditional navigation concepts based on authentication status and a user's role:

1. Start by installing a JWT decoding library, and for faking authentication, a JWT encoding library:

   ```
   $ npm install jwt-decode fake-jwt-sign
   $ npm install -D @types/jwt-decode
   ```

2. Define your imports for `auth.service.ts`:

   src/app/auth/auth.service.ts
   ```
   import { HttpClient } from '@angular/common/http'
   import { Injectable } from '@angular/core'

   import { sign } from 'fake-jwt-sign' // For fakeAuthProvider only
   import * as decode from 'jwt-decode'

   import { BehaviorSubject, Observable, of, throwError as
   observableThrowError } from 'rxjs'
   import { catchError, map } from 'rxjs/operators'

   import { environment } from '../../environments/environment'
   import { Role } from './role.enum'
   ...
   ```

3. Implement an `IAuthStatus` interface to store decoded user information, a helper interface, and the secure by-default `defaultAuthStatus`:

   src/app/auth/auth.service.ts
   ```
   ...
   export interface IAuthStatus {
     isAuthenticated: boolean
     userRole: Role
     userId: string
   }

   interface IServerAuthResponse {
     accessToken: string
   }

   const defaultAuthStatus = { isAuthenticated: false, userRole:
   Role.None, userId: null }
   ...
   ```

`IAuthUser` is an interface that represents the shape of a typical JWT that you may receive from your authentication service. It contains minimal information about the user and its role, so it can be attached to the `header` of server calls and optionally cached in `localStorage` to remember the user's login state. In the preceding implementation, we're assuming the default role of a `Manager`.

4. Define the `AuthService` class with a `BehaviorSubject` to anchor the current `authStatus` of the user and configure an `authProvider` that can process an `email` and a `password` and return an `IServerAuthResponse` in the constructor:

src/app/auth/auth.service.ts

```
. . .
@Injectable({
  providedIn: 'root'
})
export class AuthService {
   private readonly authProvider: (
     email: string,
     password: string
   ) => Observable<IServerAuthResponse>

   authStatus = new BehaviorSubject<IAuthStatus>(defaultAuthStatus)

   constructor(private httpClient: HttpClient) {
      // Fake login function to simulate roles
     this.authProvider = this.fakeAuthProvider
      // Example of a real login call to server-side
      // this.authProvider = this.exampleAuthProvider
   }
. . .
```

Note that `fakeAuthProvider` is configured to be the `authProvider` for this service. A real auth provider may look like the following code, where users' email and password are sent to a POST endpoint, which verifies their information, creating and returning a JWT for our app to consume:

example

```
private exampleAuthProvider(
  email: string,
  password: string
): Observable<IServerAuthResponse> {
  return
this.httpClient.post<IServerAuthResponse>(`${environment.baseUrl}/v
1/login`, {
```

```
    email: email,
    password: password,
  })
}
```

It is pretty straightforward, since the hard work is done on the server side. This call can also be made to a third party.

Note that the API version, v1, in the URL path is defined at the service and not as part of the `baseUrl`. This is because each API can change versions independently from each other. Login may remain v1 for a long time, while other APIs may be upgraded to v2, v3, and such.

5. Implement a `fakeAuthProvider` that simulates the authentication process, including creating a fake JWT on the fly:

src/app/auth/auth.service.ts

```
...
private fakeAuthProvider(
  email: string,
  password: string
): Observable<IServerAuthResponse> {
  if (!email.toLowerCase().endsWith('@test.com')) {
    return observableThrowError('Failed to login! Email needs to
end with @test.com.')
  }

  const authStatus = {
    isAuthenticated: true,
    userId: 'e4d1bc2ab25c',
    userRole: email.toLowerCase().includes('cashier')
      ? Role.Cashier
      : email.toLowerCase().includes('clerk')
      ? Role.Clerk
      : email.toLowerCase().includes('manager') ? Role.Manager
: Role.None,
  } as IAuthStatus

  const authResponse = {
    accessToken: sign(authStatus, 'secret', {
      expiresIn: '1h',
      algorithm: 'none',
    }),
  } as IServerAuthResponse

  return of(authResponse)
```

```
}
...
```

The `fakeAuthProvider` implements what would otherwise be a server-side method right in the service, so you can conveniently experiment the code while fine-tuning your auth workflow. It creates and signs a JWT, with the temporary `fake-jwt-sign` library so that we can also demonstrate how to handle a properly-formed JWT.

 Do not ship your Angular app with the `fake-jwt-sign` dependency, since it is meant to be server-side code.

6. Before we move on, implement a `transformError` function to handle mixed `HttpErrorResponse` and string errors in an observable stream under `common/common.ts`:

src/app/common/common.ts
```
import { HttpErrorResponse } from '@angular/common/http'
import { throwError } from 'rxjs'

export function transformError(error: HttpErrorResponse | string) {
  let errorMessage = 'An unknown error has occurred'
  if (typeof error === 'string') {
    errorMessage = error
  } else if (error.error instanceof ErrorEvent) {
    errorMessage = `Error! ${error.error.message}`
  } else if (error.status) {
    errorMessage = `Request failed with ${error.status}
${error.statusText}`
  }
  return throwError(errorMessage)
}
```

7. Implement the `login` function that will be called from `LoginComponent`, shown in the next section

8. Add `import { transformError } from '../common/common'`

9. Also implement a corresponding `logout` function, which may be called by the **Logout** button in the top toolbar, a failed login attempt, or if an unauthorized access attempt is detected by a router auth guard as the user is navigating the app, which is a topic covered later in the chapter:

src/app/auth/auth.service.ts

```
. . .
login(email: string, password: string): Observable<IAuthStatus> {
  this.logout()

  const loginResponse = this.authProvider(email, password).pipe(
    map(value => {
      return decode(value.accessToken) as IAuthStatus
    }),
    catchError(transformError)
  )

  loginResponse.subscribe(
    res => {
      this.authStatus.next(res)
    },
    err => {
      this.logout()
      return observableThrowError(err)
    }
  )

  return loginResponse
}

logout() {
  this.authStatus.next(defaultAuthStatus)
}
}
```

The `login` method encapsulates the correct order of operations by calling the `logout` method, the `authProvider` with the `email` and `password` information, and throwing errors when necessary.

The `login` method adheres to the Open/Closed principle, from SOLID design, by being open to extension by our ability to externally supply different auth providers to it, but it remains closed to modification, since the variance in functionality is encapsulated with the auth provider.

In the next section, we will implement the `LoginComponent` so that users can enter their username and password information and attempt a login.

Implementing the login component

The `login` component leverages the `authService` that we just created and implements validation errors using reactive forms. The login component should be designed in a way to be rendered independently of any other component, because during a routing event, if we discover that the user is not properly authenticated or authorized, we will navigate them to this component. We can capture this origination URL as a `redirectUrl` so that once a user logs in successfully, we can navigate them back to it.

1. Let's start with implementing the routes to the `login` component:

   src/app/app-routing.modules.ts
   ```
   . . .
     { path: 'login', component: LoginComponent },
     { path: 'login/:redirectUrl', component: LoginComponent },
   . . .
   ```

2. Now implement the component itself:

   src/app/login/login.component.ts
   ```
   import { Component, OnInit } from '@angular/core'
   import { FormBuilder, FormGroup, Validators, NgForm } from
   '@angular/forms'
   import { AuthService } from '../auth/auth.service'
   import { Role } from '../auth/role.enum'

   @Component({
     selector: 'app-login',
     templateUrl: 'login.component.html',
     styles: [
       `
       .error {
          color: red
       }
       `,
       `
       div[fxLayout] {margin-top: 32px;}
       `,
     ],
   })
   export class LoginComponent implements OnInit {
     loginForm: FormGroup
   ```

```
loginError = ''
redirectUrl
constructor(
  private formBuilder: FormBuilder,
  private authService: AuthService,
  private router: Router,
  private route: ActivatedRoute
) {
  route.paramMap.subscribe(params => (this.redirectUrl =
params.get('redirectUrl')))
}

ngOnInit() {
  this.buildLoginForm()
}

buildLoginForm() {
  this.loginForm = this.formBuilder.group({
    email: ['', [Validators.required, Validators.email]],
    password: ['', [
      Validators.required,
      Validators.minLength(8),
      Validators.maxLength(50),
    ]],
  })
}

async login(submittedForm: FormGroup) {
  this.authService
    .login(submittedForm.value.email,
submittedForm.value.password)
    .subscribe(authStatus => {
      if (authStatus.isAuthenticated) {
        this.router.navigate([this.redirectUrl || '/manager'])
      }
    }, error => (this.loginError = error))
}
}
```

As the result of a successful login attempt, we leverage the router to navigate an authenticated user to their profile. In the case of an error sent from the server via the service, we assign that error to `loginError`.

3. Here's an implementation for a login form to capture and validate a user's `email` and `password`, and if there are any server errors, display them:

    src/app/login/login.component.html

```
<div fxLayout="row" fxLayoutAlign="center">
  <mat-card fxFlex="400px">
    <mat-card-header>
      <mat-card-title>
        <div class="mat-headline">Hello, Lemonite!</div>
      </mat-card-title>
    </mat-card-header>
    <mat-card-content>
      <form [formGroup]="loginForm" (ngSubmit)="login(loginForm)"
fxLayout="column">
        <div fxLayout="row" fxLayoutAlign="start center"
fxLayoutGap="10px">
          <mat-icon>email</mat-icon>
          <mat-form-field fxFlex>
            <input matInput placeholder="E-mail" aria-label="E-
mail" formControlName="email">
            <mat-error
*ngIf="loginForm.get('email').hasError('required')">
              E-mail is required
            </mat-error>
            <mat-error
*ngIf="loginForm.get('email').hasError('email')">
              E-mail is not valid
            </mat-error>
          </mat-form-field>
        </div>
        <div fxLayout="row" fxLayoutAlign="start center"
fxLayoutGap="10px">
          <mat-icon matPrefix>vpn_key</mat-icon>
          <mat-form-field fxFlex>
            <input matInput placeholder="Password" aria-
label="Password" type="password" formControlName="password">
            <mat-hint>Minimum 8 characters</mat-hint>
            <mat-error
*ngIf="loginForm.get('password').hasError('required')">
              Password is required
            </mat-error>
            <mat-error
*ngIf="loginForm.get('password').hasError('minlength')">
              Password is at least 8 characters long
            </mat-error>
            <mat-error
*ngIf="loginForm.get('password').hasError('maxlength')">
              Password cannot be longer than 50 characters
            </mat-error>
          </mat-form-field>
        </div>
        <div fxLayout="row" class="margin-top">
```

```
            <div *ngIf="loginError" class="mat-caption
error">{{loginError}}</div>
            <div class="flex-spacer"></div>
            <button mat-raised-button type="submit" color="primary"
[disabled]="loginForm.invalid">Login</button>
          </div>
        </form>
      </mat-card-content>
    </mat-card>
</div>
```

The **Login** button is disabled until email and password meets client site validation rules. Additionally, `<mat-form-field>` will only display one `mat-error` at a time, unless you create more space for more errors, so be sure place your error conditions in the correct order.

Once you're done implementing the `login` component, you can now update the home screen to conditionally display or hide the new component we created.

4. Update `home.component` to display login when a user opens up the app:

src/app/home/home.component.ts

```
  template: `
    <div *ngIf="displayLogin">
      <app-login></app-login>
    </div>
    <div *ngIf="!displayLogin">
      <span class="mat-display-3">You get a lemon, you get a lemon,
you get a lemon...</span>
    </div>
  `,

export class HomeComponent implements OnInit {
  displayLogin = true
  ...
```

Don't forget to import the requisite dependent modules for the code above in to your Angular application. It is intentionally left as an exercise for the reader to locate and import the missing modules.

Your app should look similar to this screenshot:

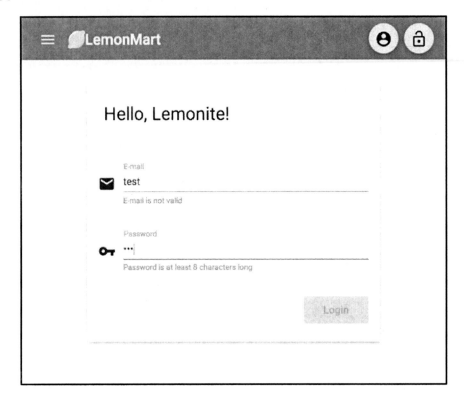

LemonMart with login

There's still some work to be done, in terms of implementing and showing/hiding the sidenav menu, profile and logout icons, given the user's authentication status.

Conditional navigation

Conditional navigation is necessary in creating a frustration-free user experience. By selectively showing the elements that the user has access to and hiding the ones they don't, we allow the user to confidently navigate through the app.

Let's start by hiding the login component after a user logs in to the app:

1. On the home component, import the `authService` in `home.component`
2. Set the `authStatus` to a local variable named `displayLogin`:

src/app/home/home.component

```
...
import { AuthService } from '../auth/auth.service'
...
export class HomeComponent implements OnInit {
  private _displayLogin = true
  constructor(private authService: AuthService) {}

  ngOnInit() {
    this.authService.authStatus.subscribe(
      authStatus => (this._displayLogin =
!authStatus.isAuthenticated)
    )
  }

  get displayLogin() {
    return this._displayLogin
  }
}
```

 A property getter for displayLogin here is necessary, otherwise you may receive a **Error: ExpressionChangedAfterItHasBeenCheckedError: Expression has changed after it was checked message**. This error is a side effect of how the Angular component life-cycle and change detection works. This behavior may very well change in future Angular versions.

3. On the app component, subscribe to the authentication status and store the current value in a local variable named displayAccountIcons:

src/app/app.component.ts

```
import { Component, OnInit } from '@angular/core'
import { AuthService } from './auth/auth.service'
...
export class AppComponent implements OnInit {
  displayAccountIcons = false
  constructor(..., private authService: AuthService) {
    ...
  ngOnInit() {
    this.authService.authStatus.subscribe(
      authStatus => (this.displayAccountIcons =
authStatus.isAuthenticated)
    )
  }
  ...
}
```

4. Use `*ngIf` to hide all buttons meant for logged in users:

src/app/app.component.ts
```
<button *ngIf="displayAccountIcons" ... >
```

Now, when a user is logged out, your toolbar should look all clean with no buttons, as shown:

LemonMart toolbar after log in

Common validations

Before we move on, we need to implement validations for `loginForm`. As we implement more forms in `Chapter 10`, *Angular App Design and Recipes*, you will realize that it gets tedious, fast, to repeatedly type out form validations in either template or reactive forms. Part of the allure of reactive forms is that it is driven by code, so we can easily extract out the validations to a shared class, unit test, and reuse them:

1. Create a `validations.ts` file under the `common` folder

2. Implement email and password validations:

src/app/common/validations.ts
```
import { Validators } from '@angular/forms'

export const EmailValidation = [Validators.required,
Validators.email]
export const PasswordValidation = [
  Validators.required,
  Validators.minLength(8),
  Validators.maxLength(50),
]
```

 Depending on your password validation needs, you can use a `RegEx` pattern with the `Validations.pattern()` function to enforce password complexity rules or leverage the OWASP npm package, `owasp-password-strength-test`, to enable pass-phrases as well as set more flexible password requirements.

3. Update the `login` component with the new validations:

src/app/login/login.component.ts
```
import { EmailValidation, PasswordValidation } from
'../common/validations'
  . . .
    this.loginForm = this.formBuilder.group({
      email: ['', EmailValidation],
      password: ['', PasswordValidation],
    })
```

UI service

As we start dealing with complicated workflows, such as the auth workflow, it is important to be able to programmatically display a toast notification for the user. In other cases, we may want to ask for a confirmation before executing a destructive action with a more intrusive pop-up notification.

No matter what component library you use, it gets tedious to recode the same boiler plate, just to display a quick notification. A UI service can neatly encapsulate a default implementation that can also be customized on a need basis:

1. Create a new `uiService` under `common`

2. Implement a `showToast` function:

src/app/common/ui.service.ts
```
import { Injectable, Component, Inject } from '@angular/core'
import {
  MatSnackBar,
  MatSnackBarConfig,
  MatDialog,
  MatDialogConfig,
} from '@angular/material'
import { Observable } from 'rxjs'

@Injectable()
export class UiService {
  constructor(private snackBar: MatSnackBar, private dialog:
MatDialog) {}

  showToast(message: string, action = 'Close', config?:
MatSnackBarConfig) {
    this.snackBar.open(
      message,
```

```
        action,
        config || {
          duration: 7000,
        }
      )
    }
    ...
}
```

For a showDialog function, we must implement a basic dialog component:

1. Add a new `simpleDialog` under the `common` folder provided in `app.module` with inline template and styling

    app/common/simple-dialog/simple-dialog.component.ts
    ```
    @Component({
      template: `
        <h2 mat-dialog-title>data.title</h2>
        <mat-dialog-content>
          <p>data.content</p>
        </mat-dialog-content>
        <mat-dialog-actions>
          <span class="flex-spacer"></span>
          <button mat-button mat-dialog-close
    *ngIf="data.cancelText">data.cancelText</button>
          <button mat-button mat-button-raised color="primary" [mat-
    dialog-close]="true"
            cdkFocusInitial>
            data.okText
          </button>
        </mat-dialog-actions>
      `,
    })
    export class SimpleDialogComponent {
      constructor(
        public dialogRef: MatDialogRef<SimpleDialogComponent, Boolean>,
        @Inject(MAT_DIALOG_DATA) public data: any
      ) {}
    }
    ```

Note that `SimpleDialogComponent` should not have app selector like `selector: 'app-simple-dialog'` since we only plan to use it with `UiService`. Remove this property from your component.

2. Then, implement a `showDialog` function to display the `SimpleDialogComponent`:

app/common/ui.service.ts
```
...
showDialog(
    title: string,
    content: string,
    okText = 'OK',
    cancelText?: string,
    customConfig?: MatDialogConfig
  ): Observable<Boolean> {
    const dialogRef = this.dialog.open(
      SimpleDialogComponent,
      customConfig || {
        width: '300px',
        data: { title: title, content: content, okText: okText,
cancelText: cancelText },
      }
    )

    return dialogRef.afterClosed()
  }
}
```

`ShowDialog` returns an `Observable<boolean>`, so you can implement a follow-on action, depending on what selection the user makes. Clicking on **OK** will return `true`, and **Cancel** will return `false`.

In `SimpleDialogComponent`, using `@Inject`, we're able to use all variables sent by `showDialog` to customize the content of the dialog.

 Don't forget to update `app.module.ts` and `material.module.ts` with the various dependencies that are being introduced.

3. Update the `login` component to display a toast message after login:

src/app/login/login.component.ts
```
import { UiService } from '../common/ui.service'
...
constructor(... ,
    private uiService: UiService)
...
    .subscribe(authStatus => {
```

```
    if (authStatus.isAuthenticated) {
        this.uiService.showToast(`Welcome! Role:
${authStatus.userRole}`)
        ...
```

A toast message will appear after a user logs in, as shown:

Material Snack bar

The `snackBar` will either take the full width of the screen or a portion depending on the size of the browser.

Caching with cookie and localStorage

We must be able to cache the authentication status of the logged in user. Otherwise, with every page refresh, the user will have go through the login routine. We need to update `AuthService` so that it persists the auth status.

There are three main ways to store data:

- `cookie`
- `localStorage`
- `sessionStorage`

Cookies should not be used to store secure data, because they can be sniffed or stolen by bad actors. In addition, cookies can store 4 KB of data and can be set to expire.

`localStorage` and `sessionStorage` are similar to each other. They are protected and isolated browser-side stores that allow for storing larger amounts of data for your application. You can't set an expiration date-time on either stores. `sessionStorage` values are removed, when the browser window is closed. The values survive page reloads and restores.

JSON Web Tokens are encrypted, and they include a timestamp for expiration, in essence, countering the weaknesses of `cookie` and `localStorage`. Either option should be secure to use with JWTs.

Let's start by implement a caching service that can abstract away our method of caching authentication information that the `AuthService` can consume:

1. Start by creating an abstract `cacheService` that encapsulates the method of caching:

   src/app/auth/cache.service.ts
   ```
   export abstract class CacheService {
     protected getItem<T>(key: string): T {
       const data = localStorage.getItem(key)
       if (data && data !== 'undefined') {
         return JSON.parse(data)
       }
       return null
     }

     protected setItem(key: string, data: object | string) {
       if (typeof data === 'string') {
         localStorage.setItem(key, data)
       }
       localStorage.setItem(key, JSON.stringify(data))
     }

     protected removeItem(key: string) {
       localStorage.removeItem(key)
     }

     protected clear() {
       localStorage.clear()
     }
   }
   ```

   This cache service base class can be used to give caching capabilities to any service. It is not the same as creating a centralized cache service that you inject into other service. By avoiding a centralized value store, we avoid inter-dependencies between various services.

2. Update `AuthService` to extend the `CacheService` and implement caching of the `authStatus`:

auth/auth.service

```
...
export class AuthService extends CacheService {
  authStatus = new BehaviorSubject<IAuthStatus>(
    this.getItem('authStatus') || defaultAuthStatus
  )

  constructor(private httpClient: HttpClient) {
    super()
    this.authStatus.subscribe(authStatus =>
this.setItem('authStatus', authStatus))
    ...
  }
  ...
}
```

The technique demonstrated here can be used to persist any kind of data and intentionally leverages RxJS events to update the cache. As you may note, we don't need to update the login function to call `setItem`, because it already calls `this.authStatus.next`, and we just tap in to the data stream. This helps with staying stateless and avoiding side effects, by decoupling functions from each other.

 When initializing the `BehaviorSubject`, take care to handle the `undefined/null` case, when loading data from the cache and still provide a default implementation.

 You can implement your own custom cache expiration scheme in `setItem` and `getItem` functions or leverage a service created by a third party.

If you are going after a high-security application, you may choose to only cache the JWT to ensure an additional layer security. In either case, the JWT should be cached separately, because the token must be sent to the server in the header with every request. It is important to understand how token-based authentication works well, to avoid revealing compromising secrets. In the next section, we will go over the JWT life cycle to improve your understanding.

JSON Web Token life cycle

JSON Web Tokens compliment a stateless REST API architecture with an encrypted token mechanism that allow for convenient, distributed, and high-performance authentication and authorization of requests sent by clients. There are three main components of a token-based authentication scheme:

- Client-side, captures login information and hides disallowed actions for a good UX
- Server-side, validates that every request is both authenticated and has the proper authorization
- Auth service, generates and validates encrypted tokens, independently verifies authentication and authorization status of user requests from a data store

A secure system presumes that data sent/received between the major components mentioned is encrypted in-transit. This means your REST API must be hosted with a properly configured SSL certificate, serving all API calls over HTTPS, so that user credentials are never exposed between the client and the server. Similarly, any database or third-party service call should happen over HTTPS. Furthermore, any data store storing passwords should utilize a secure one-way hashing algorithm with good salting practices. Any other sensitive user information should be encrypted at-rest with a secure two-way encryption algorithm. Following this layered approach to security is critical, because attackers will need to accomplish the unlikely feat of compromising all layers of security implemented at the same time to cause meaningful harm to your business.

The next sequence diagram highlights the life-cycle of JWT-based authentication:

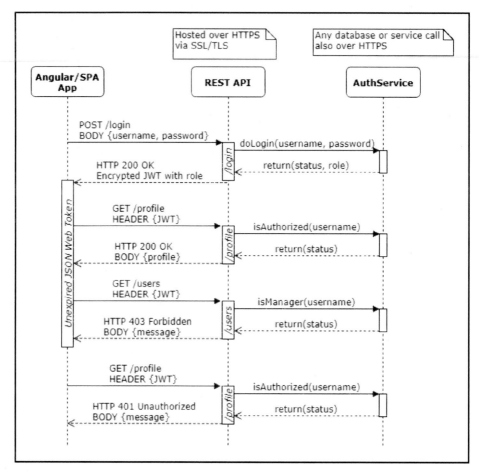

Life-Cycle of JWT-based authentication

Initially, a user logs in by providing their username and password. Once validated, the user's authentication status and role is encrypted to a JWT with an expiration date and time and is sent back to the browser.

Your Angular (or any other SPA) app can cache this token in local or session storage securely so that the user isn't forced to login with every request or worse yet, we don't store user credentials in the browser. Let's update the authentication service so that it can cache the token.

1. Update the service to be able to set, get, decode, and clear the token, as shown:

   src/app/auth/auth.service.ts

   ```
   . . .
     private setToken(jwt: string) {
       this.setItem('jwt', jwt)
     }

     private getDecodedToken(): IAuthStatus {
       return decode(this.getItem('jwt'))
     }

     getToken(): string {
       return this.getItem('jwt') || ''
     }

     private clearToken() {
       this.removeItem('jwt')
     }
   ```

2. Call setToken during login and clearToken during logout as highlight as follows:

   src/app/auth/auth.service.ts

   ```
   . . .
     login(email: string, password: string): Observable<IAuthStatus> {
       this.logout()

       const loginResponse = this.authProvider(email, password).pipe(
         map(value => {
           this.setToken(value.accessToken)
           return decode(value.accessToken) as IAuthStatus
         }),
         catchError(transformError)
       )
   . . .
     logout() {
       this.clearToken()
       this.authStatus.next(defaultAuthStatus)
     }
   ```

Every subsequent request will contain the JWT in the request header. You should secure every API to check for and validate the token received. For example, if a user wanted to access their profile, the `AuthService` would validate the token to check whether the user authenticated, but a further database call is required to check whether the user is also authorized to view the data. This ensures an independent confirmation of the users' access to the system and prevents any abuse of an unexpired token.

If an authenticated user makes a call to an API, where they don't have the proper authorization, say if a clerk wants to get access to a list of all the users, then the `AuthService` will return a falsy status and the client will receive a **403 Forbidden** response, which will be displayed as an error message to the user.

A user can make a request with an expired token; when this happens, a **401 Unauthorized** response is sent to the client. As a good UX practice, we should automatically prompt the user to login again and let them resume their workflow without any data loss.

In summary, real security is achieved by a robust server-side implementation and any client-side implementation is largely there to enable a good UX around good security practices.

HTTP interceptor

Implement an HTTP interceptor to inject the JWT into the header of every request sent to the user and also gracefully handle authentication failures by asking the user to log in:

1. Create `authHttpInterceptor` under auth:

    src/app/auth/auth-http-interceptor.ts
    ```
    import {
      HttpEvent,
      HttpHandler,
      HttpInterceptor,
      HttpRequest,
    } from '@angular/common/http'
    import { Injectable } from '@angular/core'
    import { Router } from '@angular/router'
    import { Observable, throwError as observableThrowError } from
    'rxjs'
    import { catchError } from 'rxjs/operators'
    import { AuthService } from './auth.service'

    @Injectable()
    export class AuthHttpInterceptor implements HttpInterceptor {
    ```

```
    constructor(private authService: AuthService, private router:
Router) {}
    intercept(req: HttpRequest<any>, next: HttpHandler):
Observable<HttpEvent<any>> {
        const jwt = this.authService.getToken()
        const authRequest = req.clone({ setHeaders: { authorization:
`Bearer ${jwt}` } })
        return next.handle(authRequest).pipe(
          catchError((err, caught) => {
            if (err.status === 401) {
              this.router.navigate(['/user/login'], {
                queryParams: { redirectUrl:
this.router.routerState.snapshot.url },
              })
            }

            return observableThrowError(err)
          })
        )
    }
}
```

Note that `AuthService` is leveraged to retrieve the token, and the `redirectUrl` is being set for the login component after a **401** error.

2. Update the `app` module to provide the interceptor:

src/app/app.module.ts
```
providers: [
  ...
  {
    provide: HTTP_INTERCEPTORS,
    useClass: AuthHttpInterceptor,
    multi: true,
  },
],
```

You can observe the interceptor in action, while the app is fetching the `lemon.svg` file, in the **Chrome Dev Tools** | **Network** tab, here:

Request header for lemon.svg

Side navigation

Enable mobile-first workflows and provide an easy navigation mechanism to quickly jump to desired functionality. Using the authentication service, given a user's current role, only display the links for features they can access. We will be implementing the side navigation mock-up, as follows:

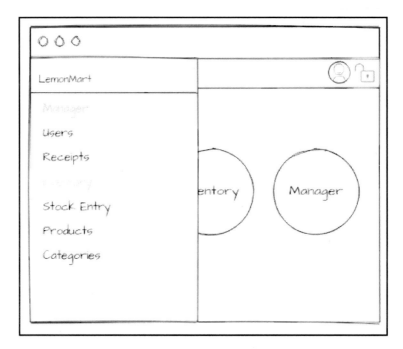

Side navigation mock-up

Let's implement the code for the side nav as a separate component, so that it is easier to maintain:

1. Create and declare a `NavigationMenuComponent` in `app.module`

   src/app/app.module.ts
   ```
   @NgModule({
     declarations: [
       ...
       NavigationMenuComponent,
     ],
   ```

The side navigation isn't technically required until after a user is logged in. However, in order to be able to launch the side navigation menu from the toolbar, we need to be able to trigger it from app.component. Since this component will be simple, we will eagerly load it. To do this lazily, Angular does have a Dynamic Component Loader pattern, which has a high implementation overhead that will only make sense if multi-hundred kilobyte savings will be made.

SideNav will be triggered from the toolbar, and it comes with a <mat-sidenav-container> parent container that hosts the SideNav itself and the content of the app. So we will need to render all app content by placing the <router-outlet> inside <mat-sidenav-content>.

2. Import MatSidenavModule and MatListModule to material.module

src/app/material.module.ts
```
@NgModule({
  imports: [
    ...
    MatSidenavModule,
    MatListModule,
  ],
  exports: [
    ...
    MatSidenavModule,
    MatListModule,
  ]
```

3. Define some styles that will ensure that the web app will expand to fill the entire page and remain properly scrollable on desktop and mobile scenarios:

src/app/app.component.ts
```
styles: [
    `.app-container {
      display: flex;
      flex-direction: column;
      position: absolute;
      top: 0;
      bottom: 0;
      left: 0;
      right: 0;
    }
    .app-is-mobile .app-toolbar {
      position: fixed;
      z-index: 2;
    }
```

```
        .app-sidenav-container {
          flex: 1;
        }
        .app-is-mobile .app-sidenav-container {
          flex: 1 0 auto;
        },
        mat-sidenav {
          width: 200px;
        }
        `
      ],
```

4. Import an `ObservableMedia` service in `AppComponent`:

   src/app/app.component.ts
   ```
   constructor(
       ...
       public media: ObservableMedia
   ) {
   ...
   }
   ```

5. Update the template with a responsive `SideNav` that will slide over the content in mobile or push the content aside in desktop scenarios:

   src/app/app.component.ts
   ```
   ...
   template: `
     <div class="app-container">
       <mat-toolbar color="primary" fxLayoutGap="8px" class="app-
   toolbar"
           [class.app-is-mobile]="media.isActive('xs')">
           <button *ngIf="displayAccountIcons" mat-icon-button
   (click)="sidenav.toggle()">
             <mat-icon>menu</mat-icon>
           </button>
           <a mat-icon-button routerLink="/home">
             <mat-icon svgIcon="lemon"></mat-icon><span class="mat-
   h2">LemonMart</span>
           </a>
           <span class="flex-spacer"></span>
           <button *ngIf="displayAccountIcons" mat-mini-fab
   routerLink="/user/profile"
             matTooltip="Profile" aria-label="User Profile"><mat-
   icon>account_circle</mat-icon>
           </button>
           <button *ngIf="displayAccountIcons" mat-mini-fab
   ```

```
routerLink="/user/logout"
        matTooltip="Logout" aria-label="Logout"><mat-
icon>lock_open</mat-icon>
    </button>
  </mat-toolbar>
  <mat-sidenav-container class="app-sidenav-container"
[style.marginTop.px]="media.isActive('xs') ? 56 : 0">
    <mat-sidenav #sidenav [mode]="media.isActive('xs') ? 'over' :
'side'"
                  [fixedInViewport]="media.isActive('xs')"
fixedTopGap="56">
      <app-navigation-menu></app-navigation-menu>
    </mat-sidenav>
    <mat-sidenav-content>
      <router-outlet class="app-container"></router-outlet>
    </mat-sidenav-content>
  </mat-sidenav-container>
</div>
`,
```

The preceding template leverages Angular Flex Layout media observable for a responsive implementation that was injected earlier.

Since the links that will be shown inside the `SiveNav` will be of variable length and subject various role-based business rules, it is a good practice to implement it in a separate component.

6. Implement a property getter for `displayAccountIcons` and a `setTimeout` so that you can avoid errors like `ExpressionChangedAfterItHasBeenCheckedError`

src/app/app.component.ts
```
export class AppComponent implements OnInit {
  _displayAccountIcons = false
  ...
  ngOnInit() {
    this.authService.authStatus.subscribe(authStatus => {
      setTimeout(() => {
        this._displayAccountIcons = authStatus.isAuthenticated
      }, 0)
    })
  }
```

```
      get displayAccountIcons() {
        return this._displayAccountIcons
      }
  }
```

7. Implement navigational links in `NavigationMenuComponent`:

   src/app/navigation-menu/navigation-menu.component.ts

```
...
  styles: [
    `
    .active-link {
      font-weight: bold;
      border-left: 3px solid green;
    }
    `,
  ],
  template: `
    <mat-nav-list>
      <h3 matSubheader>Manager</h3>
      <a mat-list-item routerLinkActive="active-link"
routerLink="/manager/users">Users</a>
      <a mat-list-item routerLinkActive="active-link"
routerLink="/manager/receipts">Receipts</a>
      <h3 matSubheader>Inventory</h3>
      <a mat-list-item routerLinkActive="active-link"
routerLink="/inventory/stockEntry">Stock Entry</a>
      <a mat-list-item routerLinkActive="active-link"
routerLink="/inventory/products">Products</a>
      <a mat-list-item routerLinkActive="active-link"
routerLink="/inventory/categories">Categories</a>
      <h3 matSubheader>Clerk</h3>
      <a mat-list-item routerLinkActive="active-link"
routerLink="/pos">POS</a>
    </mat-nav-list>
    `,
...
```

`<mat-nav-list>` is functionally equivalent to `<mat-list>`, so you can use the documentation for that component for layout purposes. Observe the subheaders for **Manager**, **Inventory**, and **Clerk** here:

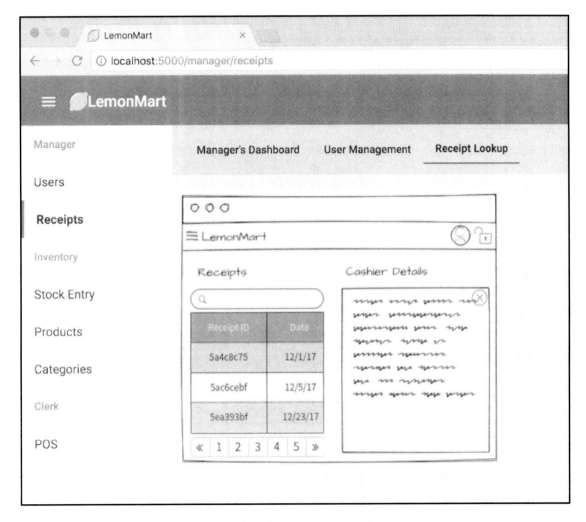

Manager dashboard showing receipt lookup on desktop

`routerLinkActive="active-link"` highlights the selected **Receipts** route, as shown in the preceding screenshot.

Additionally, you can see the difference in appearance and behavior on mobile devices as follows:

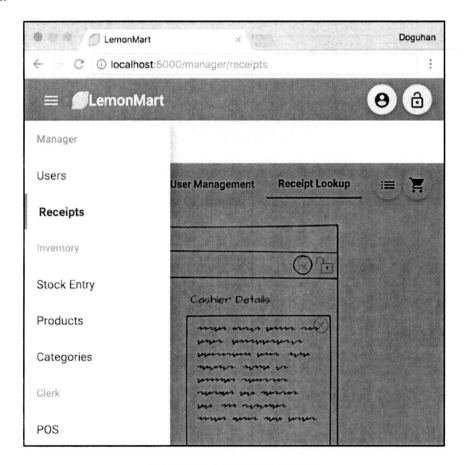

Manager dashboard showing receipt lookup on mobile

Log out

Now that we're caching the login status, we need to implement a log out experience:

1. In AuthService, implement a logout function:

   src/app/auth/auth.service.ts
   ```
   ...
     logout() {
   ```

```
        this.clearToken()
        this.authStatus.next(defaultAuthStatus)
      }
```

2. Implement the `logout` component:

   src/app/user/logout/logout.component.ts
   ```
   import { Component, OnInit } from '@angular/core'
   import { Router } from '@angular/router'
   import { AuthService } from '../../auth/auth.service'

   @Component({
     selector: 'app-logout',
     template: `
       <p>
         Logging out...
       </p>
     `,
     styles: [],
   })
   export class LogoutComponent implements OnInit {
     constructor(private router: Router, private authService:
   AuthService) {}

     ngOnInit() {
       this.authService.logout()
       this.router.navigate(['/'])
     }
   }
   ```

As you note, after a log out, user is navigated back to the home page.

Role-based routing after login

This is the most elemental and important part of your application. With lazy loading, we have ensured only the bare minimum amount of assets will be loaded to enable a user to login.

Once a user logs in, they should be routed to the appropriate landing screen as per their user role, so they're not guessing how they need to use the app. For example, a cashier needs to only access the POS to check out customers, so they can automatically be routed to that screen.

You find the mock up of the POS screen as illustrated:

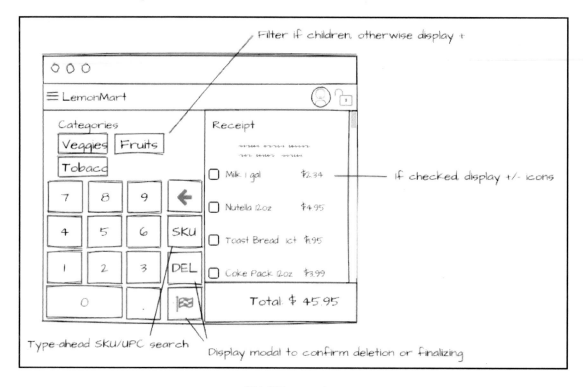

Point-of-Sale screen mock-up

Let's ensure that users get routed to the appropriate page after logging in by updating the `LoginComponent`:

1. Update the `login` logic to route per role:

   app/src/login/login.component.ts

   ```
   async login(submittedForm: FormGroup) {
       ...
       this.router.navigate([
         this.redirectUrl ||
   this.homeRoutePerRole(authStatus.userRole)
       ])
       ...
   }

     homeRoutePerRole(role: Role) {
       switch (role) {
   ```

```
      case Role.Cashier:
        return '/pos'
      case Role.Clerk:
        return '/inventory'
      case Role.Manager:
        return '/manager'
      default:
        return '/user/profile'
    }
  }
```

Similarly, clerks and manager are routed to their landing screens to access the features they need to accomplish their tasks, as shown earlier. Since we implemented a default manager role, the corresponding landing experience will be launched automatically. The other side of the coin is intentional and unintentional attempts to access routes that a user isn't meant to have access to. In the next section, we will learn about router guards that can help check authentication and even load requisite data before the form is rendered.

Router Guards

Router Guards enable further decoupling and reuse of logic and greater control over the component lifecycle.

Here are the four major guards you will most likely use:

1. CanActivate and CanActivateChild, used for checking auth access to a route
2. CanDeactivate, used to ask permission before navigating away from a route
3. Resolve, allows for pre-fetching of data from route parameters
4. CanLoad, allows for custom logic to execute before loading feature module assets

Refer to the following sections for how to leverage CanActivate and CanLoad. Resolve guard will be covered in Chapter 10, *Angular App Design and Recipes*.

Auth Guard

Auth Guards enable good UX by allowing or disallowing accidental navigation to a feature module or component before it is loaded and any data requests are made to the server.

For example, when a Manager logs in, they're automatically routed to the
/manager/home path. The browser will cache this URL, and it will be completely plausible
for a clerk to accidentally navigate to the same URL. Angular doesn't know whether a
particular route is accessible to a user or not and, without an AuthGuard, it will happily
render the Manager's home page and trigger server requests that will end up failing.

 Regardless of the robustness of your frontend implementation, every
REST API you implement should be properly secured server-side.

Let's update the router so that ProfileComponent can't be activated without an authenticated user and
the ManagerModule won't load unless a manager is logging in using an AuthGuard:

1. Implement an AuthGuard service:

    src/app/auth/auth-guard.service.ts
    ```
    import { Injectable } from '@angular/core'
    import {
      CanActivate,
      Router,
      ActivatedRouteSnapshot,
      RouterStateSnapshot,
      CanLoad,
      CanActivateChild,
    } from '@angular/router'
    import { AuthService, IAuthStatus } from './auth.service'
    import { Observable } from 'rxjs'
    import { Route } from '@angular/compiler/src/core'
    import { Role } from './role.enum'
    import { UiService } from '../common/ui.service'

    @Injectable({
      providedIn: 'root'
    })
    export class AuthGuard implements CanActivate, CanActivateChild,
    CanLoad {
      protected currentAuthStatus: IAuthStatus
      constructor(
        protected authService: AuthService,
        protected router: Router,
        private uiService: UiService
      ) {
        this.authService.authStatus.subscribe(
          authStatus => (this.currentAuthStatus = authStatus)
        )
    ```

```
    }

  canLoad(route: Route): boolean | Observable<boolean> |
Promise<boolean> {
    return this.checkLogin()
  }

  canActivate(
    route: ActivatedRouteSnapshot,
    state: RouterStateSnapshot
  ): boolean | Observable<boolean> | Promise<boolean> {
    return this.checkLogin(route)
  }

  canActivateChild(
    childRoute: ActivatedRouteSnapshot,
    state: RouterStateSnapshot
  ): boolean | Observable<boolean> | Promise<boolean> {
    return this.checkLogin(childRoute)
  }

  protected checkLogin(route?: ActivatedRouteSnapshot) {
    let roleMatch = true
    let params: any
    if (route) {
      const expectedRole = route.data.expectedRole

      if (expectedRole) {
        roleMatch = this.currentAuthStatus.userRole ===
expectedRole
      }

      if (roleMatch) {
        params = { redirectUrl: route.pathFromRoot.map(r =>
r.url).join('/') }
      }
    }

    if (!this.currentAuthStatus.isAuthenticated || !roleMatch) {
      this.showAlert(this.currentAuthStatus.isAuthenticated,
roleMatch)

      this.router.navigate(['login', params || {}])
      return false
    }

    return true
  }
```

```
    private showAlert(isAuth: boolean, roleMatch: boolean) {
      if (!isAuth) {
        this.uiService.showToast('You must login to continue')
      }

      if (!roleMatch) {
        this.uiService.showToast('You do not have the permissions to
view this resource')
      }
    }
  }
```

2. Use the `CanLoad` guard to prevent loading of lazily loaded module, such as Manager's module:

   src/app/app-routing.module.ts

```
. . .
  {
    path: 'manager',
    loadChildren: './manager/manager.module#ManagerModule',
    canLoad: [AuthGuard],
  },
. . .
```

   In this instance, when the `ManagerModule` is being loaded, `AuthGuard` will be activated during the `canLoad` event, and the `checkLogin` function will verify the authentication status of the user. If the guard returns `false`, the module will not be loaded. At this point, we don't have the metadata to check the role of the user.

3. Use the `CanActivate` guard to prevent activation of individual components, such as user's `profile`:

   user/user-routing.module.ts

```
. . .
{ path: 'profile', component: ProfileComponent, canActivate:
[AuthGuard] },
. . .
```

   In the case of `user-routing.module`, `AuthGuard` is activated during the `canActivate` event, and the `checkLogin` function controls where this route can be navigated to. Since the user is viewing their own profile, there's no need to check the user's role here.

4. Use `CanActivate` or `CanActivateChild` with an `expectedRole` property to prevent activation of components by other users, such as `ManagerHomeComponent`:

mananger/manager-routing.module.ts

```
...
  {
    path: 'home',
    component: ManagerHomeComponent,
    canActivate: [AuthGuard],
    data: {
      expectedRole: Role.Manager,
    },
  },
  {
    path: 'users',
    component: UserManagementComponent,
    canActivate: [AuthGuard],
    data: {
      expectedRole: Role.Manager,
    },
  },
  {
    path: 'receipts',
    component: ReceiptLookupComponent,
    canActivate: [AuthGuard],
    data: {
      expectedRole: Role.Manager,
    },
  },
...
```

Inside `ManagerModule`, we can verify whether the user is authorized to access a particular route. We can do this by defining some metadata in the route definition, like `expectedRole`, which will be passed into the `checkLogin` function by the `canActivate` event. If a user is authenticated but their role doesn't match `Role.Manager`, `AuthGuard` will return false and the navigation will be prevented.

5. Ensure that both `AuthService` and `AuthGuard` are provided in `app.module` and `manager.module` since they used in both contexts

As always, before moving on ensure that all your tests pass by executing `npm test` and `npm run e2e`.

Auth Service Fake and Common Testing Providers

We need to implement an `AuthServiceFake` so that our unit tests pass and use a pattern similar to `commonTestingModules` mentioned in `Chapter 7`, *Create a Router-First Line-of-Business App*, to conveniently provider this fake across our spec files.

To ensure that our fake will have the same public functions and properties as the actual `AuthService`, let's first start with creating an interface:

1. Add `IAuthService` to `auth.service.ts`

   src/app/auth/auth.service.ts

   ```
   export interface IAuthService {
     authStatus: BehaviorSubject<IAuthStatus>
     login(email: string, password: string): Observable<IAuthStatus>
     logout()
     getToken(): string
   }
   ```

2. Make sure `AuthService` implements the interface

3. Export `defaultAuthStatus` for reuse

   src/app/auth/auth.service.ts

   ```
   export const defaultAuthStatus = {
     isAuthenticated: false,
     userRole: Role.None,
     userId: null,
   }

   export class AuthService extends CacheService implements
   IAuthService
   ```

Now we can create a fake that implements the same interface, but provides functions that don't have any dependencies to any external authentication system.

1. Create a new file named `auth.service.fake.ts` under `auth`:

   src/app/auth/auth.service.fake.ts
   ```
   import { Injectable } from '@angular/core'
   import { BehaviorSubject, Observable, of } from 'rxjs'
   import { IAuthService, IAuthStatus, defaultAuthStatus } from
   ```

```
'./auth.service'

@Injectable()
export class AuthServiceFake implements IAuthService {
  authStatus = new BehaviorSubject<IAuthStatus>(defaultAuthStatus)
  constructor() {}

  login(email: string, password: string): Observable<IAuthStatus> {
    return of(defaultAuthStatus)
  }

  logout() {}

  getToken(): string {
    return ''
  }
}
```

2. Update `common.testing.ts` with `commonTestingProviders`:

src/app/common/common.testing.ts

```
export const commonTestingProviders: any[] = [
  { provide: AuthService, useClass: AuthServiceFake },
  UiService,
]
```

3. Observer the use of the fake in `app.component.spec.ts`:

src/app/app.component.spec.ts

```
...
  TestBed.configureTestingModule({
    imports: commonTestingModules,
    providers: commonTestingProviders.concat([
      { provide: ObservableMedia, useClass: ObservableMediaFake },
      ...
```

The empty `commonTestingProviders` array we created earlier is being concatenated with fakes that are specific to `app.component`, so our new `AuthServiceFake` should apply automatically.

4. Update the spec file for `AuthGuard` shown as follows:

src/app/auth/auth-guard.service.spec.ts

```
. . .
   TestBed.configureTestingModule({
      imports: commonTestingModules,
      providers: commonTestingProviders.concat(AuthGuard)
   })
```

5. Go ahead and apply this technique to all spec files that have a dependency on `AuthService` and `UiService`

6. The notable exception is in `auth.service.spec.ts` where you do *not* want to use the fake, since `AuthService` is the class under test, make sure it is configure shown as follows:

src/app/auth/auth.service.spec.ts

```
. . .
   TestBed.configureTestingModule({
      imports: [HttpClientTestingModule],
      providers: [AuthService, UiService],
   })
```

7. In addition `SimpleDialogComponent` tests require stubbing out some external dependencies like:

src/app/common/simple-dialog/simple-dialog.component.spec.ts

```
   . . .
     providers: [{
       provide: MatDialogRef,
       useValue: {}
     }, {
       provide: MAT_DIALOG_DATA,
       useValue: {} // Add any data you wish to test if it is
passed/used correctly
     }],
   . . .
```

Remember, don't move on until all your tests are passing!

Summary

You should now be familiar with how to create high-quality authentication and authorization experiences. We started by going over the importance of completing and documenting high-level UX design of our entire app so that we can properly design a great conditional navigation experience. We created a reusable UI service so that we can conveniently inject alerts into the flow-control logic of our app.

We covered the fundamentals of token-based authentication and JWTs so that you don't leak any critical user information. We learned that caching and HTTP interceptors are necessary so that users don't have to input their login information with every request. Finally, we covered router guards to prevent users from stumbling onto screens they are not authorized to use, and we reaffirmed the point that the real security of your application should be implemented on the server side.

In the next chapter, we will go over a comprehensive list of Angular recipes to complete the implementation of our line-of-business app—LemonMart.

10
Angular App Design and Recipes

In this chapter, we will complete the implementation of LemonMart. As part of the router-first approach, I will demonstrate the creation of reusable routable components that also support data binding - the ability to lay out components using auxiliary routes of the router, using resolve guards to reduce boilerplate code and leveraging class, interfaces, enums, validators, and pipes to maximize code reuse. In addition, we will create multi-step forms and implement data tables with pagination, and explore responsive design. Along the way, in this book, we will have touched upon most of the major functionality that Angular and Angular Material has to offer.

In this chapter, the training wheels are off. I will provide general guidance to get you started on an implementation; however, it will be up to you to try and complete the implementation on your own. If you need assistance, you may refer to the complete source code that is provided with the book or refer to up-to-date sample on GitHub at `Github.com/duluca/lemon-mart`.

In this chapter, you will learn about the following topics:

- Object-oriented class design
- Routable reusable components
- Caching service responses
- HTTP POST requests
- Multi-step responsive forms
- Resolve guards
- Master/detail views using auxiliary routes
- Data tables with pagination

User class and object-oriented programming

So far, we have only worked with interfaces to represent data, and we still want to continue using interfaces when passing data around various components and services. However, there's a need to create a default object to initialize a `BehaviorSubject`. In **Object-oriented Programming (OOP)**, it makes a lot of sense for the `User` object to own this functionality instead of a service. So, let's implement a `User` class to achieve this goal.

Inside the `user/user` folder, define an `IUser` interface and a `User` class provided in `UserModule`:

src/app/user/user/user.ts

```
import { Role } from '../../auth/role.enum'

export interface IUser {
  id: string
  email: string
  name: {
    first: string
    middle: string
    last: string
  }
  picture: string
  role: Role
  userStatus: boolean
  dateOfBirth: Date
  address: {
    line1: string
    line2: string
    city: string
    state: string
    zip: string
  }
  phones: IPhone[]
}

export interface IPhone {
  type: string
  number: string
  id: number
}
```

```
export class User implements IUser {
  constructor(
    public id = '',
    public email = '',
    public name = { first: '', middle: '', last: '' },
    public picture = '',
    public role = Role.None,
    public dateOfBirth = null,
    public userStatus = false,
    public address = {
      line1: '',
      line2: '',
      city: '',
      state: '',
      zip: '',
    },
    public phones = []
  ) {}

  static BuildUser(user: IUser) {
    return new User(
      user.id,
      user.email,
      user.name,
      user.picture,
      user.role,
      user.dateOfBirth,
      user.userStatus,
      user.address,
      user.phones
    )
  }
}
```

Note that by defining all properties with default values in the constructors as `public`
properties, we hit two birds with one stone; otherwise, we will need to define properties
and initialize them separately. This way, we achieve a concise implementation.

You can also implement calculated properties for use in templates, such as being able to conveniently display the `fullName` of a user:

src/app/user/user/user.ts
```
get fullName() {
  return `${this.name.first} ${this.name.middle} ${this.name.last}`
}
```

Using a `static BuildUser` function, you can quickly hydrate the object with data received from the server. You can also implement the `toJSON()` function to customize the serialization behavior of your object before sending the data up to the server.

Reusing components

We need a component that can display a given user's information. A natural place for this information to be presented is when the user navigates to `/user/profile`. You can see the mock-up `User` profile file:

User profile mock-up

User information is also displayed mocked up elsewhere in the app, at /manager/users:

Manager user management mock-up

To maximize code reuse, we need to ensure that you design a User component that can be used in both contexts.

As an example, let's complete the implementation of two user profile-related screens.

User service with caching, GET and POST

In order to implement a user profile, we must first implement a UserService that can perform CRUD operations on IUser. Before creating the service, you need to be running the lemon-mart-swagger-server, so you can pull fake data with it while developing:

1. Add a new script called mock:standalone to package.json

   package.json
   ```
   "mock:standalone": "docker run -p 3000:3000 -t duluca/lemon-mart-
   swagger-server",
   ```

Note that this script presumes that you have independently built your swagger server on your local machine and/or published from a repository you can pull from.

2. Execute the script

3. Create a `baseUrl` property in `environment.ts` and `environment.prod.ts` with the url to your mock server

src/environments/environment.ts
```
export const environment = {
  production: false,
  baseUrl: 'http://localhost:3000'
}
```

4. Create a `UserService` under `user/user`, as shown:

src/app/user/user/user.service.ts
```
@Injectable({
  providedIn: 'root'
})
export class UserService extends CacheService {
  currentUser = new BehaviorSubject<IUser>(this.getItem('user') ||
new User())
  private currentAuthStatus: IAuthStatus
  constructor(private httpClient: HttpClient, private authService:
AuthService) {
    super()
    this.currentUser.subscribe(user => this.setItem('user', user))
    this.authService.authStatus.subscribe(
      authStatus => (this.currentAuthStatus = authStatus)
    )
  }

  getCurrentUser(): Observable<IUser> {
    const userObservable =
this.getUser(this.currentAuthStatus.userId).pipe(
      catchError(transformError)
    )
    userObservable.subscribe(
      user => this.currentUser.next(user),
      err => Observable.throw(err)
    )
    return userObservable
  }
```

```
getUser(id): Observable<IUser> {
  return
this.httpClient.get<IUser>(`${environment.baseUrl}/v1/user/${id}`)
}

updateUser(user: IUser): Observable<IUser> {
  this.setItem('draft-user', user) // cache user data in case of
errors
  const updateResponse = this.httpClient
    .put<IUser>(`${environment.baseUrl}/v1/user/${user.id || 0}`,
user)
    .pipe(catchError(transformError))

  updateResponse.subscribe(
    res => {
      this.currentUser.next(res)
      this.removeItem('draft-user')
    },
    err => Observable.throw(err)
  )

  return updateResponse
}
}
```

In `UserService`, `currentUser` will serve as the anchor `BehaviorSubject`. For the sake of keeping our cache up to date, we subscribe to `currentUser` changes in the `constructor`. Additionally, we subscribe to `authStatus`, so when the user loads their own profile, `getProfile` can perform a GET call using the authenticated user's `userId`.

Additionally, we provide a `getUser` function separately and publicly so that the manager can load details of other user profiles, which will be needed when we implement a master/detail view later in the chapter. Finally, `updateUser` accepts an object that implements the `IUser` interface, so the data can be sent to a PUT endpoint. It is important to highlight that you should always stick to interface and not concrete implementations like `User`, when passing data around. This is the D in SOLID – the Dependency Inversion Principle. Depending on concrete implementations creates a lot of risk, because they change a lot, whereas an abstraction such as `IUser` will seldom change. After all, would you solder a lamp directly to the electrical wiring in the wall? No, you would first solder the lamp to a plug and then use the plug to get the electricity you need.

`UserService` can now be used for basic CRUD operations.

User profile with multi-step auth-enabled responsive forms

Now, let's implement a multi-step input form to capture user profile information. We will also make this multi-step form responsive for mobile devices using media queries.

1. Let's start with adding some helper data that will help us display an input form with options:

src/app/user/profile/data.ts
```
export interface IUSState {
  code: string
  name: string
}

export function USStateFilter(value: string): IUSState[] {
  return USStates.filter(state => {
    return (
      (state.code.length === 2 && state.code.toLowerCase() ===
value.toLowerCase()) ||
      state.name.toLowerCase().indexOf(value.toLowerCase()) === 0
    )
  })
}

export enum PhoneType {
  Mobile,
  Home,
  Work,
}

const USStates = [
  { code: 'AK', name: 'Alaska' },
  { code: 'AL', name: 'Alabama' },
  { code: 'AR', name: 'Arkansas' },
  { code: 'AS', name: 'American Samoa' },
  { code: 'AZ', name: 'Arizona' },
  { code: 'CA', name: 'California' },
  { code: 'CO', name: 'Colorado' },
  { code: 'CT', name: 'Connecticut' },
  { code: 'DC', name: 'District of Columbia' },
  { code: 'DE', name: 'Delaware' },
  { code: 'FL', name: 'Florida' },
  { code: 'GA', name: 'Georgia' },
  { code: 'GU', name: 'Guam' },
```

```
    { code: 'HI', name: 'Hawaii' },
    { code: 'IA', name: 'Iowa' },
    { code: 'ID', name: 'Idaho' },
    { code: 'IL', name: 'Illinois' },
    { code: 'IN', name: 'Indiana' },
    { code: 'KS', name: 'Kansas' },
    { code: 'KY', name: 'Kentucky' },
    { code: 'LA', name: 'Louisiana' },
    { code: 'MA', name: 'Massachusetts' },
    { code: 'MD', name: 'Maryland' },
    { code: 'ME', name: 'Maine' },
    { code: 'MI', name: 'Michigan' },
    { code: 'MN', name: 'Minnesota' },
    { code: 'MO', name: 'Missouri' },
    { code: 'MS', name: 'Mississippi' },
    { code: 'MT', name: 'Montana' },
    { code: 'NC', name: 'North Carolina' },
    { code: 'ND', name: 'North Dakota' },
    { code: 'NE', name: 'Nebraska' },
    { code: 'NH', name: 'New Hampshire' },
    { code: 'NJ', name: 'New Jersey' },
    { code: 'NM', name: 'New Mexico' },
    { code: 'NV', name: 'Nevada' },
    { code: 'NY', name: 'New York' },
    { code: 'OH', name: 'Ohio' },
    { code: 'OK', name: 'Oklahoma' },
    { code: 'OR', name: 'Oregon' },
    { code: 'PA', name: 'Pennsylvania' },
    { code: 'PR', name: 'Puerto Rico' },
    { code: 'RI', name: 'Rhode Island' },
    { code: 'SC', name: 'South Carolina' },
    { code: 'SD', name: 'South Dakota' },
    { code: 'TN', name: 'Tennessee' },
    { code: 'TX', name: 'Texas' },
    { code: 'UT', name: 'Utah' },
    { code: 'VA', name: 'Virginia' },
    { code: 'VI', name: 'Virgin Islands' },
    { code: 'VT', name: 'Vermont' },
    { code: 'WA', name: 'Washington' },
    { code: 'WI', name: 'Wisconsin' },
    { code: 'WV', name: 'West Virginia' },
    { code: 'WY', name: 'Wyoming' },
]
```

2. Install a helper library to programmatically access TypeScript enum values

```
$ npm i ts-enum-util
```

3. Add new validation rules to `common/validations.ts`

src/app/common/validations.ts

```
...

export const OptionalTextValidation = [Validators.minLength(2),
Validators.maxLength(50)]
export const RequiredTextValidation =
OptionalTextValidation.concat([Validators.required])
export const OneCharValidation = [Validators.minLength(1),
Validators.maxLength(1)]
export const BirthDateValidation = [
  Validators.required,
  Validators.min(new Date().getFullYear() - 100),
  Validators.max(new Date().getFullYear()),
]
export const USAZipCodeValidation = [
  Validators.required,
  Validators.pattern(/^\d{5}(?:[-\s]\d{4})?$/),
]
export const USAPhoneNumberValidation = [
  Validators.required,
  Validators.pattern(/^\D?(\d{3})\D?\D?(\d{3})\D?(\d{4})$/),
]
```

4. Now implement `profile.component.ts` as follows:

src/app/user/profile/profile.component.ts

```
import { Role as UserRole } from '../../auth/role.enum'
import { $enum } from 'ts-enum-util'
...
@Component({
  selector: 'app-profile',
  templateUrl: './profile.component.html',
  styleUrls: ['./profile.component.css'],
})
export class ProfileComponent implements OnInit {
  Role = UserRole
  PhoneTypes = $enum(PhoneType).getKeys()
  userForm: FormGroup
  states: Observable<IUSState[]>
  userError = ''
  currentUserRole = this.Role.None

  constructor(
    private formBuilder: FormBuilder,
    private router: Router,
```

```
      private userService: UserService,
      private authService: AuthService
    ) {}

    ngOnInit() {
      this.authService.authStatus.subscribe(
        authStatus => (this.currentUserRole = authStatus.userRole)
      )

      this.userService.getCurrentUser().subscribe(user => {
        this.buildUserForm(user)
      })
      this.buildUserForm()
    }
    ...
  }
```

Upon load, we request the current user from `userService`, but this will take a while, so we must first build an empty form with `this.buildUserForm()`. On this function, you can also implement a resolve guard, as discussed in a later section, to load a user based on their `userId` provided on a route, and pass that data into `buildUserForm(routeUser)` and skip loading `currentUser` to increase reusability of this component.

Form groups

Our form has many input fields, so we will use a `FormGroup`, created by `this.formBuilder.group` to house our various `FormControl` objects. Additionally, children `FormGroup` objects will allow us to maintain the correct shape of the data structure.

Start building the `buildUserForm` function, as follows:

src/app/user/profile/profile.component.ts

```
...
  buildUserForm(user?: IUser) {
    this.userForm = this.formBuilder.group({
      email: [
        {
          value: (user && user.email) || '',
          disabled: this.currentUserRole !== this.Role.Manager,
        },
        EmailValidation,
      ],
      name: this.formBuilder.group({
```

```
            first: [(user && user.name.first) || '', RequiredTextValidation],
            middle: [(user && user.name.middle) || '', OneCharValidation],
            last: [(user && user.name.last) || '', RequiredTextValidation],
          }),
          role: [
            {
              value: (user && user.role) || '',
              disabled: this.currentUserRole !== this.Role.Manager,
            },
            [Validators.required],
          ],
          dateOfBirth: [(user && user.dateOfBirth) || '', BirthDateValidation],
          address: this.formBuilder.group({
            line1: [
              (user && user.address && user.address.line1) || '',
              RequiredTextValidation,
            ],
            line2: [
              (user && user.address && user.address.line2) || '',
              OptionalTextValidation,
            ],
            city: [(user && user.address && user.address.city) || '',
  RequiredTextValidation],
            state: [
              (user && user.address && user.address.state) || '',
              RequiredTextValidation,
            ],
            zip: [(user && user.address && user.address.zip) || '',
  USAZipCodeValidation],
          }),
          ...
        })
        ...
    }
    ...
```

buildUserForm optionally accepts an IUser to prefill the form, otherwise all fields are set to their default values. The userForm itself is the top-level FormGroup. Various FormControls are added to it, such as email, with validators attached to them as needed. Note how name and address are their own FormGroup objects. This parent-child relationship ensures proper structure of the form data, when serialized to JSON, which fits the structure of IUser, in a manner that the rest of our application and server-side code can utilize.

You will completing the implementation of the userForm independently following the sample code provided for the chapter and I will be going over sections of the code piece by piece over the next few sections to explain certain key capabilities.

Stepper and responsive layout

Angular Material Stepper ships with the MatStepperModule. The stepper allows for form inputs to be broken up into multiple steps so that the user is not overwhelmed with processing dozens of input fields all at once. The user can still track their place in the process and as a side effect, as the developer we breakup our <form> implementation and enforce validation rules on a step-by-step basis or create optional workflows where certain steps can be skipped or required. As with all Material user controls, the stepper has been designed with a responsive UX in mind. In the next few sections, we will implement three steps covering different form-input techniques in the process:

1. Account Information
   - Input validation
   - Responsive layout with media queries
   - Calculated properties
   - DatePicker
2. Contact Information
   - Type ahead support
   - Dynamic form arrays
3. Review
   - Read-only views
   - Saving and clearing data

Let's prep the User module for some new Material modules:

1. Create a user-material.module containing the following Material modules:

```
MatAutocompleteModule,
MatDatepickerModule,
MatDividerModule,
MatLineModule,
MatNativeDateModule,
MatRadioModule,
MatSelectModule,
MatStepperModule,
```

2. Ensure `user.module` correctly imports:
    1. The new `user-material.module`
    2. The baseline `app-material.module`
    3. Required `FormsModule`, `ReactiveFormsModule` and `FlexLayoutModule`

As we start adding sub material modules, it makes sense to rename our root `material.module.ts` file to `app-material.modules.ts` inline with how `app-routing.module.ts` is named. Going forward, I will be using the latter convention.

3. Now, start implementing the first row of the Account Information step:

src/app/user/profile/profile.component.html

```html
<mat-toolbar color="accent">
  <h5>User Profile</h5>
</mat-toolbar>

<mat-horizontal-stepper #stepper="matHorizontalStepper">
  <mat-step [stepControl]="userForm">
    <form [formGroup]="userForm">
      <ng-template matStepLabel>Account Information</ng-template>
      <div class="stepContent">
        <div fxLayout="row" fxLayout.lt-sm="column"
[formGroup]="userForm.get('name')" fxLayoutGap="10px">
          <mat-form-field fxFlex="40%">
            <input matInput placeholder="First Name" aria-
label="First Name" formControlName="first">
            <mat-error
*ngIf="userForm.get('name').get('first').hasError('required')">
              First Name is required
            </mat-error>
            <mat-error
*ngIf="userForm.get('name').get('first').hasError('minLength')">
              Must be at least 2 characters
            </mat-error>
            <mat-error
*ngIf="userForm.get('name').get('first').hasError('maxLength')">
              Can't exceed 50 characters
            </mat-error>
          </mat-form-field>
          <mat-form-field fxFlex="20%">
            <input matInput placeholder="MI" aria-label="Middle
Initial" formControlName="middle">
            <mat-error
```

```
*ngIf="userForm.get('name').get('middle').invalid">
              Only inital
            </mat-error>
          </mat-form-field>
          <mat-form-field fxFlex="40%">
            <input matInput placeholder="Last Name" aria-
label="Last Name" formControlName="last">
            <mat-error
*ngIf="userForm.get('name').get('last').hasError('required')">
              Last Name is required
            </mat-error>
            <mat-error
*ngIf="userForm.get('name').get('last').hasError('minLength')">
              Must be at least 2 characters
            </mat-error>
            <mat-error
*ngIf="userForm.get('name').get('last').hasError('maxLength')">
              Can't exceed 50 characters
            </mat-error>
          </mat-form-field>
        </div>
        ...
      </div>
    </form>
  </mat-step>
  ...
</mat-horizontal-stepper>
```

4. Take care to understand how the stepper and the form configuration works so far, you should be seeing the first row render, pulling mock data:

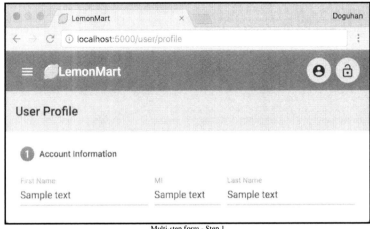

Multi-step form - Step 1

5. In order to complete the implementation of the form please refer to the sample code provided for this chapter or the reference implementation on `GitHub.com/duluca/lemon-mart`

During your implementation, you will notice that the **Review** step uses a directive named `<app-view-user>`. A minimal version of this component is implemented in the ViewUser component section below. However, feel free to implement the capability inline for now and refactor your code during the Reusable component with binding and route data section.

In the following screenshot, you can see what a completed implementation of the multi-step form looks like on a desktop:

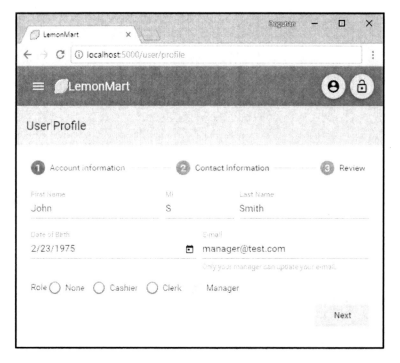

Multi-step form on desktop

Note that adding `fxLayout.lt-sm="column"` on a row with `fxLayout="row"` enables a responsive layout of the form, as shown:

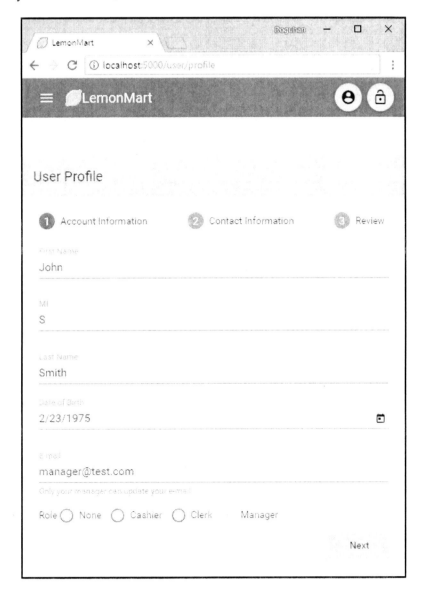

Multi-step form on mobile

Let's see how the **Date of Birth** field works in the next section.

Calculated properties and DatePicker

If you like to display calculated properties based on user input, you can follow the pattern shown here:

src/app/user/profile/profile.component.ts

```
. . .
get dateOfBirth() {
  return this.userForm.get('dateOfBirth').value || new Date()
}

get age() {
  return new Date().getFullYear() - this.dateOfBirth.getFullYear()
}
. . .
```

The usage of calculated properties in the template looks like this:

src/app/user/profile/profile.component

```
. . .
<mat-form-field fxFlex="50%">
  <input matInput placeholder="Date of Birth" aria-label="Date of Birth"
formControlName="dateOfBirth" [matDatepicker]="dateOfBirthPicker">
  <mat-hint *ngIf="userForm.get('dateOfBirth').touched">{{this.age}}
year(s) old</mat-hint>
  <mat-datepicker-toggle matSuffix [for]="dateOfBirthPicker"></mat-
datepicker-toggle>
  <mat-datepicker #dateOfBirthPicker></mat-datepicker>
  <mat-error *ngIf="userForm.get('dateOfBirth').invalid">
    Date must be with the last 100 years
  </mat-error>
</mat-form-field>
. . .
```

Here it is in action:

Selecting date with DatePicker

After the date is selected, the calculated age is displayed, as follows:

Calculated age property

Now, let's move on to the next step, **Contact Information** and see how we can enable a convenient way to display and input the state portion of the address field.

Type ahead support

In `buildUserForm`, we set a listener on `address.state` to support a type ahead filtering drop-down experience:

```
src/app/user/profile/profile.component.ts
...
this.states = this.userForm
  .get('address')
  .get('state')
  .valueChanges.pipe(startWith(''), map(value => USStateFilter(value)))
...
```

On the template, implement `mat-autocomplete` bound to the filtered states array with an `async` pipe:

src/app/user/profile/profile.component.html

```
...
<mat-form-field fxFlex="30%">
  <input type="text" placeholder="State" aria-label="State" matInput
formControlName="state" [matAutocomplete]="stateAuto">
  <mat-autocomplete #stateAuto="matAutocomplete">
    <mat-option *ngFor="let state of states | async" [value]="state.name">
      {{ state.name }}
    </mat-option>
  </mat-autocomplete>
  <mat-error
*ngIf="userForm.get('address').get('state').hasError('required')">
    State is required
  </mat-error>
</mat-form-field>
...
```

Here's how it looks when a user enters the V character:

Dropdown with Typeahead Support

In the next section, let's enable the input of multiple phone numbers.

Dynamic form arrays

Note that `phones` is an array, potentially allowing for many inputs. We can implement this by building a `FormArray` with `this.formBuilder.array` and with several helper functions:

src/app/user/profile/profile.component.ts

```
...
  phones: this.formBuilder.array(this.buildPhoneArray(user ? user.phones :
[])),
...
  private buildPhoneArray(phones: IPhone[]) {
    const groups = []

    if (!phones || (phones && phones.length === 0)) {
      groups.push(this.buildPhoneFormControl(1))
    } else {
      phones.forEach(p => {
        groups.push(this.buildPhoneFormControl(p.id, p.type, p.number))
      })
    }
    return groups
  }

  private buildPhoneFormControl(id, type?: string, number?: string) {
    return this.formBuilder.group({
      id: [id],
      type: [type || '', Validators.required],
      number: [number || '', USAPhoneNumberValidation],
    })
  }
...
```

BuildPhoneArray supports initializing a form with a single phone input or filling it with the existing data, working in tandem with BuildPhoneFormControl. The latter function comes in handy when a user clicks on an **Add** button to create a new row for entry:

src/app/user/profile/profile.component.ts

```
...
  addPhone() {
    this.phonesArray.push(
      this.buildPhoneFormControl(this.userForm.get('phones').value.length +
1)
    )
  }

  get phonesArray(): FormArray {
    return <FormArray>this.userForm.get('phones')
  }
...
```

The `phonesArray` property getter is a common pattern to make it easier to access certain form properties. However, in this case, it is also necessary, because `get('phones')` must be typecast to `FormArray` so that we can access the `length` property on it on the template:

src/app/user/profile/profile.component.html

```
...
<mat-list formArrayName="phones">
  <h2 mat-subheader>Phone Number(s)</h2>
  <button mat-button (click)="this.addPhone()">
    <mat-icon>add</mat-icon>
    Add Phone
  </button>
  <mat-list-item *ngFor="let position of this.phonesArray.controls let
i=index" [formGroupName]="i">
  <mat-form-field fxFlex="100px">
    <mat-select placeholder="Type" formControlName="type">
      <mat-option *ngFor="let type of this.PhoneTypes" [value]="type">
      {{ type }}
      </mat-option>
    </mat-select>
  </mat-form-field>
  <mat-form-field fxFlex fxFlexOffset="10px">
    <input matInput type="text" placeholder="Number"
formControlName="number">
    <mat-error *ngIf="this.phonesArray.controls[i].invalid">
      A valid phone number is required
    </mat-error>
  </mat-form-field>
  <button fxFlex="33px" mat-icon-button
(click)="this.phonesArray.removeAt(i)">
    <mat-icon>close</mat-icon>
  </button>
  </mat-list-item>
</mat-list>
...
```

The `remove` function is implemented inline.

Let's see how it should be working:

Multiple inputs using FormArray

Now that we're done with inputing data, we can move on to the last step of the stepper, **Review**. However, as it was mentioned earlier, the **Review** step uses the `app-view-user` directive to display its data. Let's build that view first.

ViewUser component

Here's a minimal implementation of the `<app-view-user>` directive that is a prerequisite for the **Review** step.

Create a new `viewUser` component under `user` as shown below:

src/app/user/view-user/view-user.component.ts
```
import { Component, OnInit, Input } from '@angular/core'
import { IUser, User } from '../user/user'

@Component({
  selector: 'app-view-user',
  template: `
    <mat-card>
      <mat-card-header>
        <div mat-card-avatar><mat-icon>account_circle</mat-icon></div>
        <mat-card-title>{{currentUser.fullName}}</mat-card-title>
```

```
              <mat-card-subtitle>{{currentUser.role}}</mat-card-subtitle>
          </mat-card-header>
          <mat-card-content>
            <p><span class="mat-input bold">E-mail</span></p>
            <p>{{currentUser.email}}</p>
            <p><span class="mat-input bold">Date of Birth</span></p>
            <p>{{currentUser.dateOfBirth | date:'mediumDate'}}</p>
          </mat-card-content>
          <mat-card-actions *ngIf="!this.user">
            <button mat-button mat-raised-button>Edit</button>
          </mat-card-actions>
        </mat-card>
      `,
    styles: [

      `
      .bold {
        font-weight: bold
      }
      `,
      ],
})
export class ViewUserComponent implements OnChanges {
    @Input() user: IUser
    currentUser = new User()

    constructor() {}

    ngOnChanges() {
      if (this.user) {
        this.currentUser = User.BuildUser(this.user)
      }
    }
}
```

The component above uses input binding with @Input to get user data, compliant with the IUser interface, from an outside component. We implement the ngOnChanges event, which fires whenever the bound data changes. In this event, we hydrate the simple JSON object stored in this.user as an instance of the class User with User.BuildUser and assign it to this.currentUser. The template uses this variable, because calculated properties like currentUser.fullName will only work if the data resides in an instance of the class User.

Now, we are ready to complete the multi-step form.

Review component and Save form

On the last step of the multistep form, users should be able to review and then save the form data. As a good practice, a successful POST request will return the data that was saved back to the browser. We can then reload the form with the information received back from the server:

src/app/user/profile/profile.component

```
...
async save(form: FormGroup) {
  this.userService
    .updateUser(form.value)
    .subscribe(res => this.buildUserForm(res), err => (this.userError =
err))
  }
...
```

If there are errors, they'll be set to userError to be displayed. Before saving, we will present the data in a compact form in a reusable component that we can bind the form data to:

src/app/user/profile/profile.component.html

```
...
<mat-step [stepControl]="userForm">
  <form [formGroup]="userForm" (ngSubmit)="save(userForm)">
  <ng-template matStepLabel>Review</ng-template>
  <div class="stepContent">
    Review and update your user profile.
    <app-view-user [user]="this.userForm.value"></app-view-user>
  </div>
  <div fxLayout="row" class="margin-top">
    <button mat-button matStepperPrevious color="accent">Back</button>
    <div class="flex-spacer"></div>
    <div *ngIf="userError" class="mat-caption error">{{userError}}</div>
    <button mat-button color="warn"
(click)="stepper.reset()">Reset</button>
    <button mat-raised-button matStepperNext color="primary" type="submit"
[disabled]="this.userForm.invalid">Update</button>
  </div>
  </form>
</mat-step>
...
```

This is how the final product should look:

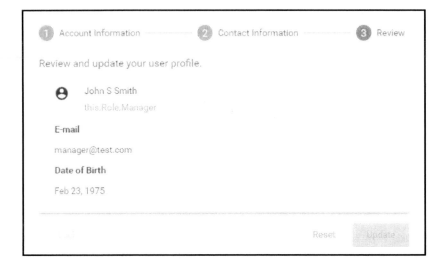

Review step

 Note the option to reset the form. Adding an alert dialog to confirm resetting of user input data would be good UX.

Now that the user profile input is done, we are about midway into our eventual goal of creating a master/detail view where a **Manager** can click on a user and view their profile details. We still have a lot more code to add, and along the way, we have fallen into a pattern of adding lots of boilerplate code to load the requisite data for a component. In the next section, we will learn about resolve guards so that we can simplify our code and reduce boilerplate.

Resolve guard

A resolve guard is a type of a router guard, as mentioned in Chapter 9, *Design Authentication and Authorization*. A resolve guard can load necessary data for a component by reading record IDs from route parameters, asynchronously load the data and have it ready by the time the component activates and initializes.

The major advantages for a resolve guard includes reusability of loading logic, reduction of boilerplate code, and also shedding dependencies, because the component can receive the data it needs without having to import any service:

1. Create a new `user.resolve.ts` class under `user/user`:

   src/app/user/user/user.resolve.ts
   ```
   import { Injectable } from '@angular/core'
   import { Resolve, ActivatedRouteSnapshot } from '@angular/router'
   import { UserService } from './user.service'
   import { IUser } from './user'

   @Injectable()
   export class UserResolve implements Resolve<IUser> {
     constructor(private userService: UserService) {}

     resolve(route: ActivatedRouteSnapshot) {
       return this.userService.getUser(route.paramMap.get('userId'))
     }
   }
   ```

2. You can use a resolve guard as shown:

   example
   ```
   {
     path: 'user',
     component: ViewUserComponent,
     resolve: {
       user: UserResolve,
     },
   },
   ```

3. The `routerLink` will look like this:

   example
   ```
   ['user', {userId: row.id}]
   ```

4. On the `ngOnInit` hook of the target component, you can read the resolved user like this:

   example
   ```
   this.route.snapshot.data['user']
   ```

You can observe this behavior in action in the next two sections, after we update `ViewUserComponent` and the router to leverage the resolve guard.

Reusable component with binding and route data

Now, let's refactor the `viewUser` component, so that we can reuse it in multiple contexts. One where it can load its own data using a resolve guard, suitable for a master/detail view and another, where we can bind the current user to it, as we have done in the Review step of the multi-step input form we built in the prior section:

1. Update `viewUser` component with the following changes:

   src/app/user/view-user/view-user.component.ts

   ```
   ...
   import { ActivatedRoute } from '@angular/router'

   export class ViewUserComponent implements OnChanges, OnInit {
     ...
     constructor(private route: ActivatedRoute) {}

     ngOnInit() {
       if (this.route.snapshot && this.route.snapshot.data['user']) {
         this.currentUser =
   User.BuildUser(this.route.snapshot.data['user'])
         this.currentUser.dateOfBirth = Date.now() // for data mocking
   purposes only
       }
     }
     ...
   ```

   We now have two independent events. One for ngOnChanges, which handles what value gets assigned to `this.currentUser`, if `this.user` has been bound to. `ngOnInit` will only fire once, when the component is first initialized or has been routed to. In this case, if any data for the route has been resolved then it'll be assigned to `this.currentUser`.

   To be able to use this component across multiple lazy loaded modules, we must wrap it in its own module.

2. Create a new `shared-components.module.ts` under app:

   src/app/shared-components.module.ts
   ```
   import { NgModule } from '@angular/core'
   import { ViewUserComponent } from './user/view-user/view-
   user.component'
   import { FormsModule, ReactiveFormsModule } from '@angular/forms'
   ```

```
import { FlexLayoutModule } from '@angular/flex-layout'
import { CommonModule } from '@angular/common'
import { MaterialModule } from './app-material.module'

@NgModule({
  imports: [
    CommonModule,
    FormsModule,
    ReactiveFormsModule,
    FlexLayoutModule,
    MaterialModule,
  ],
  declarations: [ViewUserComponent],
  exports: [ViewUserComponent],
})
export class SharedComponentsModule {}
```

3. Ensure that you import `SharedComponentsModule` module into each feature module you intended to use `ViewUserComponent` in. In our case, these will be `User` and `Manager` modules.

4. Remove `ViewUserComponent` from the `User` module declarations

We now have the key pieces in place to begin the implementation of master/detail view.

Master/detail view auxiliary routes

The true power of router-first architecture comes to fruition with the use of auxiliary routes, where we can influence the layout of components solely through router configuration, allowing for rich scenarios where we can remix the existing components into different layouts. Auxiliary routes are routes that are independent of each other where they can render content in named outlets that have been defined in the markup, such as `<router-outlet name="master">` or `<router-outlet name="detail">`. Furthermore, auxiliary routes can have their own parameters, browser history, children, and nested auxiliaries.

In the following example, we will implement a basic master/detail view using auxiliary routes:

1. Implement a simple component with two named outlets defined:

   src/app/manager/user-management/user-manager.component.ts
   ```
   template: `
       <div class="horizontal-padding">
         <router-outlet name="master"></router-outlet>
   ```

```
      <div style="min-height: 10px"></div>
      <router-outlet name="detail"></router-outlet>
    </div>
```

2. Create a `userTable` component under `manager`

3. Update `manager-routing.module` to define the auxiliary routes:

src/app/manager/manager-routing.module.ts
```
...
    {
      path: 'users',
      component: UserManagementComponent,
      children: [
        { path: '', component: UserTableComponent, outlet:
        'master' },
        {
          path: 'user',
          component: ViewUserComponent,
          outlet: 'detail',
          resolve: {
            user: UserResolve,
          },
        },
      ],
      canActivate: [AuthGuard],
      canActivateChild: [AuthGuard],
      data: {
        expectedRole: Role.Manager,
      },
    },
...
```

This means that when a user navigates to `/manager/users`, they'll see the `UserTableComponent`, because it is implemented with the `default` path.

4. Provide `UserResolve` in `manager.module` since `viewUser` depends on it

5. Implement a temporary button in `userTable`

src/app/manager/user-table/user-table.component.html
```
<a mat-button mat-icon-button [routerLink]="['/manager/users', {
outlets: { detail: ['user', {userId: 'fakeid'}] } }]"
skipLocationChange>
  <mat-icon>visibility</mat-icon>
</a>
```

Consider that a user clicks on a **View detail** button like the one defined above, then `ViewUserComponent` will be rendered for the user with the given `userId`. In the next screenshot, you can see what the **View Details** button will look like after we implement the data table in the next section:

Name	E-mail	Role	Status	View Details
Sample text Sample text	Sample text	clerk		

Items per page: 5 ▾   1 - 1 of 1   〈 〉

View Details button

You can have as many combinations and alternative components defined for master and detail, allowing for an infinite possibilities of dynamic layouts. However, setting up the `routerLink` can be a frustrating experience. Depending on the exact condition, you have to either supply or not supply all or some outlets in the link. For example, for the preceding scenario, if the link was `['/manager/users', { outlets: { master: [''], detail: ['user', {userId: row.id}] } }]`, the route will silently fail to load. Expect these quirks to be ironed out in future Angular releases.

Now that, we've completed the implementation of the resolve guard for `ViewUserComponent`, you can use Chrome Dev Tools to see the data being loaded correctly. Before debugging, ensure that the mock server we created in `Chapter 8`, *Continuous Integration and API Design*, is running.

6. Ensure that mock server is running by executing either `docker run -p 3000:3000 -t duluca/lemon-mart-swagger-server` or `npm run mock:standalone`.

7. In Chrome Dev Tools, set a break point right after `this.currentUser` is assigned to, as shown:

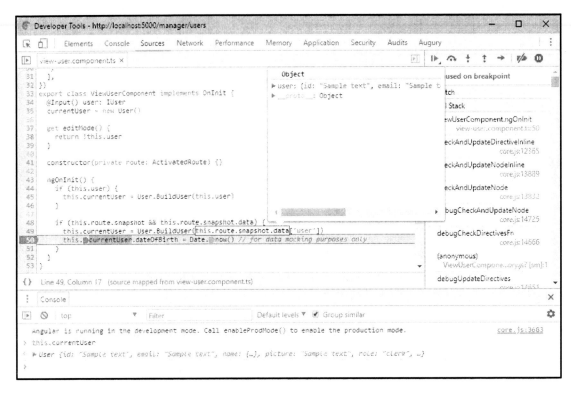

Dev Tools Debugging ViewUserComponent

You will observe that `this.currentUser` is correctly set without any boilerplate code for loading data inside the `ngOnInit` function, showing the true benefit of a resolve guard. `ViewUserComponent` is the detail view; now let's implement the master view as a data table with pagination.

Data table with pagination

We have created the scaffolding to lay out our master/detail view. In the master outlet, we will have a paginated data table of users, so let's implement `UserTableComponent`, which will contain a `MatTableDataSource` property named `dataSource`. We will need to be able to fetch user data in bulk using standard pagination controls like `pageSize` and `pagesToSkip` and be able to further narrow down the selection with user provided `searchText`.

Let's start by adding the necessary functionality to the `UserService`.

1. Implement a new interface `IUsers` to describe the data structure of paginated data

   src/app/user/user/user.service.ts
   ```
   ...
   export interface IUsers {
     items: IUser[]
     total: number
   }
   ```

2. Add `getUsers` to `UserService`

   src/app/user/user/user.service.ts
   ```
   ...
   getUsers(pageSize: number, searchText = '', pagesToSkip = 0):
   Observable<IUsers> {
     return
   this.httpClient.get<IUsers>(`${environment.baseUrl}/v1/users`, {
       params: {
         search: searchText,
         offset: pagesToSkip.toString(),
         limit: pageSize.toString(),
       },
     })
   }
   ...
   ```

3. Set up `UserTable` with pagination, sorting, and filtering:

   src/app/manager/user-table/user-table.component
   ```
   import { AfterViewInit, Component, OnInit, ViewChild } from
   '@angular/core'
   import { FormControl } from '@angular/forms'
   import { MatPaginator, MatSort, MatTableDataSource } from
   '@angular/material'
   ```

```
import { merge, of } from 'rxjs'
import { catchError, debounceTime, map, startWith, switchMap } from
'rxjs/operators'
import { OptionalTextValidation } from '../../common/validations'
import { IUser } from '../../user/user/user'
import { UserService } from '../../user/user/user.service'

@Component({
  selector: 'app-user-table',
  templateUrl: './user-table.component.html',
  styleUrls: ['./user-table.component.css'],
})
export class UserTableComponent implements OnInit, AfterViewInit {
  displayedColumns = ['name', 'email', 'role', 'status', 'id']
  dataSource = new MatTableDataSource()
  resultsLength = 0
  _isLoadingResults = true
  _hasError = false
  errorText = ''
  _skipLoading = false

  search = new FormControl('', OptionalTextValidation)

  @ViewChild(MatPaginator) paginator: MatPaginator
  @ViewChild(MatSort) sort: MatSort

  constructor(private userService: UserService) {}

  ngOnInit() {}

  ngAfterViewInit() {
    this.dataSource.paginator = this.paginator
    this.dataSource.sort = this.sort

    this.sort.sortChange.subscribe(() => (this.paginator.pageIndex
= 0))

    if (this._skipLoading) {
      return
    }

    merge(
      this.sort.sortChange,
      this.paginator.page,
      this.search.valueChanges.pipe(debounceTime(1000))
    )
      .pipe(
        startWith({}),
```

```
    switchMap(() => {
      this._isLoadingResults = true
      return this.userService.getUsers(
        this.paginator.pageSize,
        this.search.value,
        this.paginator.pageIndex
      )
    }),
    map((data: { total: number; items: IUser[] }) => {
      this._isLoadingResults = false
      this._hasError = false
      this.resultsLength = data.total

      return data.items
    }),
    catchError(err => {
      this._isLoadingResults = false
      this._hasError = true
      this.errorText = err
      return of([])
    })
  )
  .subscribe(data => (this.dataSource.data = data))
}

get isLoadingResults() {
  return this._isLoadingResults
}

get hasError() {
  return this._hasError
}
}
```

After initializing the pagination, sorting, and the filter properties, we use the merge method to listen for changes in all three data streams. If one changes, the whole pipe is triggered, which contains a call to this.userService.getUsers. Results are then mapped to the table's datasource property, otherwise errors are caught and handled.

4. Create a `manager-material.module` containing the following Material modules:

```
MatTableModule,
MatSortModule,
MatPaginatorModule,
MatProgressSpinnerModule
```

5. Ensure `manager.module` correctly imports:
   1. The new `manager-material.module`
   2. The baseline `app-material.module`
   3. Required `FormsModule`, `ReactiveFormsModule` and `FlexLayoutModule`

6. Finally, implement the `userTable` template:

src/app/manager/user-table/user-table.component.html
```html
<div class="filter-row">
  <form style="margin-bottom: 32px">
    <div fxLayout="row">
      <mat-form-field class="full-width">
        <mat-icon matPrefix>search</mat-icon>
        <input matInput placeholder="Search" aria-label="Search"
[formControl]="search">
        <mat-hint>Search by e-mail or name</mat-hint>
        <mat-error *ngIf="search.invalid">
          Type more than one character to search
        </mat-error>
      </mat-form-field>
    </div>
  </form>
</div>
<div class="mat-elevation-z8">
  <div class="loading-shade" *ngIf="isLoadingResults">
    <mat-spinner *ngIf="isLoadingResults"></mat-spinner>
    <div class="error" *ngIf="hasError">
      {{errorText}}
    </div>
  </div>
  <mat-table [dataSource]="dataSource" matSort>
    <ng-container matColumnDef="name">
      <mat-header-cell *matHeaderCellDef mat-sort-header> Name
</mat-header-cell>
      <mat-cell *matCellDef="let row"> {{row.name.first}}
{{row.name.last}} </mat-cell>
    </ng-container>
```

```
    <ng-container matColumnDef="email">
      <mat-header-cell *matHeaderCellDef mat-sort-header> E-mail
</mat-header-cell>
      <mat-cell *matCellDef="let row"> {{row.email}} </mat-cell>
    </ng-container>
    <ng-container matColumnDef="role">
      <mat-header-cell *matHeaderCellDef mat-sort-header> Role
</mat-header-cell>
      <mat-cell *matCellDef="let row"> {{row.role}} </mat-cell>
    </ng-container>
    <ng-container matColumnDef="status">
      <mat-header-cell *matHeaderCellDef mat-sort-header> Status
</mat-header-cell>
      <mat-cell *matCellDef="let row"> {{row.status}} </mat-cell>
    </ng-container>
    <ng-container matColumnDef="id">
      <mat-header-cell *matHeaderCellDef fxLayoutAlign="end
center">View Details</mat-header-cell>
      <mat-cell *matCellDef="let row" fxLayoutAlign="end center"
style="margin-right: 8px">
        <a mat-button mat-icon-button
[routerLink]="['/manager/users', { outlets: { detail: ['user',
{userId: row.id}] } }]" skipLocationChange>
          <mat-icon>visibility</mat-icon>
        </a>
      </mat-cell>
    </ng-container>
    <mat-header-row *matHeaderRowDef="displayedColumns"></mat-
header-row>
    <mat-row *matRowDef="let row; columns: displayedColumns;">
    </mat-row>
  </mat-table>

  <mat-paginator [pageSizeOptions]="[5, 10, 25, 100]"></mat-
paginator>
</div>
```

With just the master view, the table looks like this screenshot:

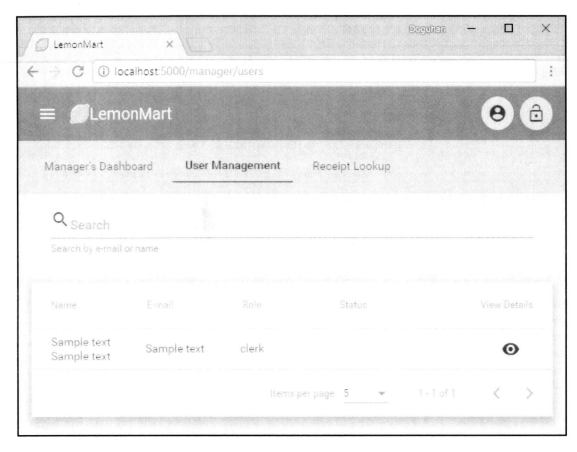

UserTable

If you click on the **View** icon, `ViewUserComponent` will get rendered in the detail outlet, as shown:

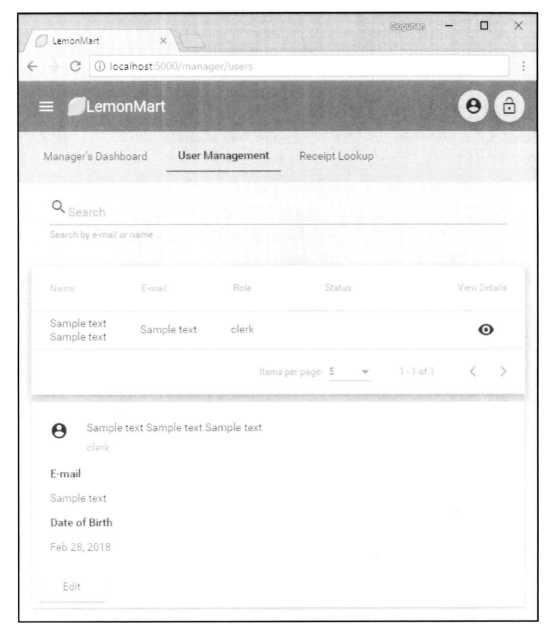

Master/Detail view

You can then wire up the **Edit** button and pass the `userId` to the `UserProfile` so that the data can be edited and updated. Alternatively, you can render the `UserProfile` in place in the detail outlet.

Data table with pagination completes the implementation of LemonMart for the purpose of this book. Now let's make sure all our tests our passing, before we move on.

Updating Unit Tests

Since we introduced a new `userService`, create a fake implementation for it, using the same pattern from `authService` and `commonTestingProviders` with it.

1. Implement `IUserService` interface for `UserService`

   src/app/user/user/user.service.ts
   ```
   export interface IUserService {
     currentUser: BehaviorSubject<IUser>
     getCurrentUser(): Observable<IUser>
     getUser(id): Observable<IUser>
     updateUser(user: IUser): Observable<IUser>
     getUsers(pageSize: number, searchText: string, pagesToSkip:
   number): Observable<IUsers>
   }
   . . .
   export class UserService extends CacheService implements
   IUserService {
   ```

2. Implement the fake user service

   src/app/user/user/user.service.fake.ts
   ```
   import { Injectable } from '@angular/core'
   import { BehaviorSubject, Observable, of } from 'rxjs'

   import { IUser, User } from './user'
   import { IUsers, IUserService } from './user.service'

   @Injectable()
   export class UserServiceFake implements IUserService {
     currentUser = new BehaviorSubject<IUser>(new User())

     constructor() {}
   ```

```
  getCurrentUser(): Observable<IUser> {
    return of(new User())
  }

  getUser(id): Observable<IUser> {
    return of(new User((id = id)))
  }

  updateUser(user: IUser): Observable<IUser> {
    return of(user)
  }

  getUsers(pageSize: number, searchText = '', pagesToSkip = 0):
Observable<IUsers> {
    return of({
      total: 1,
      items: [new User()],
    } as IUsers)
  }
}
```

3. Add the user service fake to `commonTestingProviders`

   src/app/common/common.testing.ts
   ```
   export const commonTestingProviders: any[] = [
     ...
     { provide: UserService, useClass: UserServiceFake },
   ]
   ```

4. Add `SharedComponentsModule` to `commonTestingModules`

   src/app/common/common.testing.ts
   ```
   export const commonTestingModules: any[] = [
     ...
     SharedComponentsModule
   ]
   ```

5. Instantiate default data for `UserTableComponent`

After fixing up its providers and imports, you will notice `UserTableComponent` is still failing to create. This is because, the component initialization logic requires `dataSource` to be defined. If undefined, the component can't be created. However, we can easily modify component properties in the second `beforeEach` method, which executes after the `TestBed` has injected real, mocked or fake dependencies to the component class. See the changes bolded below for test data setup:

src/app/manager/user-table/user-table.component.spec.ts

```
. . .
  beforeEach(() => {
    fixture = TestBed.createComponent(UserTableComponent)
    component = fixture.componentInstance
    component.dataSource = new MatTableDataSource()
    component.dataSource.data = [new User()]
    component._skipLoading = true
    fixture.detectChanges()
  })
. . .
```

By now, you may have noticed that just by updating some of our central configuration some tests are passing and the rest of tests can be resolved by applying the various patterns we have been using throughout the book. For example `user-management.component.spec.ts` uses the common testing modules and providers we have created:

src/app/manager/user-management/user-management.component.spec.ts
```
providers: commonTestingProviders,
imports: commonTestingModules.concat([ManagerMaterialModule]),
```

When you are working with providers and fakes, keep in mind what module, component, service or class is under test and take care to only provide fakes of dependencies.

 `ViewUserComponent` is a special case, where we can't use our common testing modules and providers, otherwise we would end up creating a circular dependency. In this case, manually specify the modules that need to be imported.

6. Continue fixing unit test configurations until all of them are passing!

In this book, we didn't cover any functional unit testing, where we would test some business logic to test its correctness. Instead, we focused on keeping the auto-generated tests in working order. I highly recommend implementing unit tests to cover key business logic using the excellent framework provided by Angular out-of-the-box.

You always have the option to write even further elemental unit tests, testing classes and functions in isolation using Jasmine. Jasmine has rich test double functionality, able to mock and spy on dependencies. It is easier and cheaper to write and maintain these kinds of elemental unit tests. However, this topic is a deep one in its own right and is beyond the scope of this book.

Summary

In this chapter, we completed going over all major Angular app design considerations, along with recipes, to be able to implement a line-of-business app with ease. We talked about applying object-oriented class design to make hydrating or serializing data easier. We created reusable components that can be activated by the router or embedded within another component with data binding. We showed that you can POST data to the server and cache responses. We also created a rich multistep input forms that is responsive to changing screen sizes. We removed boilerplate code from components by leveraging a resolve guard to load user data. We then implemented a master/detail view using auxiliary routes and demonstrated how to build data tables with pagination.

Overall, by using the router-first design, architecture, and implementation approach, we approached our application's design with a good high-level understanding of what we wanted to achieve. Also, by identifying reuse opportunities early on, we were able to optimize our implementation strategy to implement reusable components ahead of time without running the risk of grossly over-engineering our solution.

In the next chapter, we will set up a highly-available infrastructure on AWS to host LemonMart. We will update the project with new scripts to enable no-downtime Blue-Green deployments.

11
Highly-Available Cloud Infrastructure on AWS

The web is a hostile environment. There are good and bad actors. Bad actors can try to poke holes in your security or try to bring down your website with a **Distributed Denial of Service (DDoS)** attack. Good actors, if you're lucky, will love your website and won't stop using it. They'll shower you with recommendations to improve your site, but also, they may run into bugs and they may be so enthusiastic that your site may slow down to a crawl due to high traffic. Real-world deployments on the web require a lot of expertise to get it right. As a full-stack developer, you can only know about so many nuances of hardware, software, and networking. Luckily, with the advent of cloud service providers, a lot of this expertise has been translated into software configurations, with the difficult hardware and networking concerns taken care of by the provider.

One of the best features of a cloud service provider is cloud scalability, which refers to your server automatically scaling out to respond to high volumes of unexpected traffic and scaling down to save costs when the traffic returns back to normal levels. **Amazon Web Services (AWS)** goes beyond basic cloud scalability and introduces high-availability and fault tolerant concepts, allowing for resilient local and global deployments. I have chosen to introduce you to AWS, because of its vast capabilities that go way beyond what I will touch in this book. With Route 53, you can get free DDoS protection; with API Gateway, you create API keys, with AWS Lambda you can handle millions of transactions for only a few dollars a month and with CloudFront you can cache your content at secret edge-locations that are scattered around major cities of the world. In addition, Blue-Green deployments will allow you to achieve no-downtime deployments of your software.

Overall, the tools and techniques you will be learning in this chapter are adaptable to any cloud provider and is fast becoming critical knowledge for any full-stack developer. We will be going over the following topics:

- Creating and protecting AWS accounts
- Right-sizing infrastructure

- Simple load testing to optimize instance
- Configuring and deploying to AWS ECS Fargate
- Scripted Blue-Green deployments
- Billing

Creating a secure AWS account

Account access and control is of paramount importance in any cloud service, and this includes AWS as well. After initial account creation, you will have your root credentials, which is your email and password combination.

Let's start by creating an AWS account:

1. Start by navigating to `https://console.aws.amazon.com`
2. If you don't have one, create a new account
3. If you are new to AWS, you can get 12 months of free tier access to various services, as shown on the sign-up screen here:

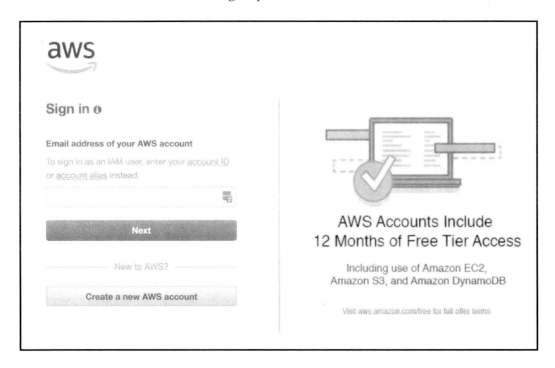

AWS Account Sign Up

Your AWS billing is tied to your root credentials. If compromised, a lot of damage can be done on your account before you can gain back access.

4. Ensure that you enable 2FA on your root credentials:

   To add another layer of security, going forward, you need to stop logging in to your AWS account using your root credentials. You can create user accounts using the AWS **Identity and Access Management (IAM)** module. If these accounts get compromised, unlike your root account, you can easily and quickly delete or replace them.

5. Navigate to the `IAM` module
6. Create a new user account with global admin rights
7. Log in to the AWS console using these credentials
8. You should enable 2FA for these credentials as well
9. A secure account setup looks as follows, with every status reported as green:

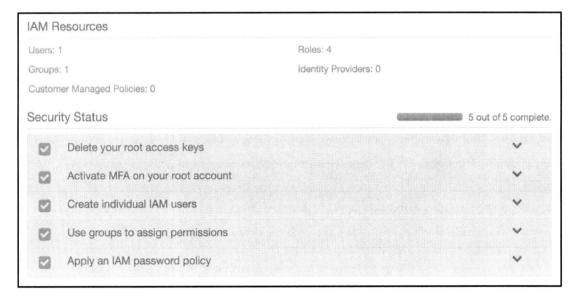

AWS IAM Module After Secure Setup

The major benefit of working with user accounts is programmatic access. For each user account, you can create a public access ID and private access key pair. When you're working with third parties, such as hosted continuous integration services, your own application code or CLI tools, you use your programmatic access keys to connect to your AWS resources. When, inevitably, the access keys leak, it is quick and convenient to disable access to the old keys and create new ones.

Furthermore, user account access can be tightly controlled by very granular permissions. You can also create roles with a group of permissions and further control communication between AWS services and some external services.

When creating user accounts and roles, always err on the side of minimal permissions. This can be an exercise in frustration, when working with clients, contractors, or colleagues who are unfamiliar with AWS; however, it is a worthwhile exercise.

You're only as secure and reliable as your weakest link, so you must plan for failures and, most importantly, practice recovery plans on a regular basis.

Securing secrets

Password and private key leaks occur more commonly than you may think. Your keys may be compromised in unsecured public Wi-Fi networks; you may accidentally check them in to your code repository or use the superbly insecure communication methods like email. Accidental code check-ins, however, are the biggest issue, since most junior developers don't realize that deletion isn't an option in source control systems.

As a developer, there are a few noteworthy best practices to follow to safeguard your secrets:

1. Always use a VPN service on public Wi-Fi, such as `tunnelbear.com`
2. Leverage the `.aws/credentials` file located under your user's home folder, to create profiles and store access keys
3. Create a `.env` file in the root of your project that is in `.gitignore` to store any secrets that your CI server may later inject as a team norm
4. Always review commits before pushing them

Following these conventions every single time will get you in the good habit of never checking in your secrets to a code repository. In the next section, we will delve into resource considerations for your cloud environment.

Right-sizing infrastructure

The point of optimizing your infrastructure is to protect your companies revenue, while minimizing the cost of operating your infrastructure. Your goal should be to ensure that users don't encounter high-latency, otherwise known as bad performance or worse, unfulfilled or dropped requests, all the while making your venture remains a sustainable endeavor.

The three pillars of web application performance are as follows:

1. CPU utilization
2. Memory usage
3. Network bandwidth

I have intentionally left disk access out of the key consideration metrics, since only particular workloads executed on an application server or data store are affected by it. Disk access would rarely ever impact the performance of serving a web application as long as application assets are delivered by a **Content Delivery Network (CDN)**. That said, still keep an eye on any unexpected runaway disk access, such as high frequency creation of temp and log files. Docker, for example, can spit out logs that can easily fill up a drive.

In an ideal scenario, CPU, memory, and network bandwidth use should be utilized evenly around 60-80% of available capacity. If you encounter performance issues due to various other factors such as disk I/O, a slow third-party service, or inefficient code, most likely one of your metrics will peek at or near maximum capacity, while the other two are idling or severely underutilized. This is an opportunity to use more CPU, memory, or bandwidth to compensate for the performance issue and also evenly utilize available resources.

The reason behind targeting 60-80% utilization is to allow for some time for a new instance (server or container) to be provisioned and ready to serve users. After your predefined threshold has been crossed, while a new instance is provisioned, you can continue serving the increasing number of users, thus minimizing unfulfilled requests.

Throughout this book, I have discouraged over-engineering or perfect solutions. In today's complicated IT landscape, it is nearly impossible to predict where you will encounter performance bottlenecks. Your engineering may, very easily, spend $100,000+ worth of engineering hours, where the solution to your problem may be a few hundred dollars of new hardware, whether it be a network switch, solid state drive, CPU, and more memory.

If your CPU is too busy, you may want to introduce more bookkeeping logic to your code, via index, hash tables, or dictionaries, that you can cache in memory to speed up subsequent or intermediary steps of your logic. For example, if you are constantly running array lookup operations to locate particular properties of a record, you can perform an operation on that record, saving the ID and/or the property of the record in a hash table that you keep in memory will reduce your runtime cost from $O(n)$ down to $O(1)$.

Following the preceding example, you may end up using too much memory with hash tables. In this case, you may want to more aggressively offload or transfer caches to slower, but more plentiful data stores using your spare network bandwidth, such as a Redis instance.

If your network utilization is too high, you may want to investigate usage of CDNs with expiring links, client-side caching, throttling requests, API access limits for customers abusing their quotas, or optimize your instances to have disproportionately more network capacity compared to its CPU or Memory capacity.

Optimizing instance

In an earlier example, I demonstrated the use of my `duluca/minimal-node-web-server` Docker image to host our Angular apps. Even though Node.js is a very lightweight server, it is simply not optimized to just be a web server. In addition, Node.js has single-threaded execution environment, making it a poor choice for serving static content to many concurrent users at once.

You can observe the resource that a Docker image is utilizing by executing `docker stats`:

```
$ docker stats
CONTAINER ID   CPU %   MEM USAGE / LIMIT     MEM %   NET I/O         BLOCK I/O
PIDS
27d431e289c9   0.00%   1.797MiB / 1.952GiB   0.09%   13.7kB / 285kB  0B / 0B
2
```

Here are comparative results of the system resources that a Node and NGINX-based servers utilize at rest:

Server	Image Size	Memory Usage
duluca/minimal-nginx-web-server	16.8 MB	1.8 MB
duluca/minimal-node-web-server	71.8 MB	37.0 MB

However, at rest values only tell a portion of the story. To get a better understanding, we must perform a simple load test to see memory and CPU utilization under load.

Simple load testing

To get a better understanding of the performance characteristics of our server, let's put them under some load and stress them:

1. Start your container using `docker run`:

   ```
   $ docker run --name <imageName> -d -p 8080:<internal_port>
   <imageRepo>
   ```

   If you're using `npm Scripts for Docker`, execute the following command to start your container:

   ```
   $ npm run docker:debug
   ```

2. Execute the following bash script to start the load test:

   ```
   $ curl -L http://bit.ly/load-test-bash | bash -s 100
   "http://localhost:8080"
   ```

   This script will send 100 requests/second to the server until you terminate it.

3. Execute `docker stats` to observe the performance characteristics.

Here are high-level observations of CPU and memory utilization:

CPU Utilization Statistics	Low	Mid	High	Max Memory
`duluca/minimal-nginx-web-server`	2%	15%	60%	2.4 MB
`duluca/minimal-node-web-server`	20%	45%	130%	75 MB

As you can see, there's a significant performance difference between the two servers serving the exact same content. Note that this kind of testing based on requests/second is good for a comparative analysis and does not necessarily reflect real-world usage.

It is clear that our NGINX server will give us the best bang for our buck. Armed with an optimal solution, let's deploy the application on AWS.

Deploy to AWS ECS Fargate

AWS **Elastic Container Service (ECS)** Fargate is a cost effective and an easy-to-configure way to deploy your container in the cloud.

ECS consists of four major parts:

1. Container Repository, **Elastic Container Registry (ECR)**, where you publish your Docker images
2. Services, Tasks and Task Definitions, where you define runtime parameters and port mappings for your container as a task definition that a service runs as tasks
3. Cluster, a collection of EC2 instances, where tasks can be provisioned and scaled out or in
4. Fargate, a managed cluster service, that abstracts away EC2 instances, load balancer, and security group concerns

 At the time of publishing, Fargate is only available in the AWS `us-east-1` region.

Our goal is to create a highly-available blue-green deployment, meaning that at least one instance of our application will be up and running in the event of a server failure or even during a deployment. These concepts are explored in detail in `Chapter 12`, *Google Analytics and Advanced Cloud Ops*, in the *Cost Per User in a Scalable Environment* section.

Configuring ECS Fargate

You can access ECS functions under the AWS **Services** menu, selecting the **Elastic Container Service** link.

If this is your first time logging in, you must go through a tutorial, where you will be forced to create a sample app. I would recommend going through the tutorial and deleting your sample app afterward. In order to delete a service, you'll need to update your service's number of tasks to 0. In addition, delete the default cluster to avoid any unforeseen charges.

Creating a Fargate Cluster

Let's start by configuring the Fargate Cluster, which act as a point of anchor when configuring other AWS services. Our cluster will eventually run a cluster service, which we will gradually build up in the following sections.

At the time of publishing, AWS Fargate is only available in AWS US East region, with support for more regions and Amazon Elastic Container Service for Kubernetes (Amazon EKS) coming soon. Kubernetes is a widely preferred open source alternative to AWS ECS with richer capabilities for container orchestration with on-premises, cloud, and cloud-hybrid deployments.

Let's create the cluster:

1. Navigate to **Elastic Container Service**
2. Click on **Clusters | Create Cluster**
3. Select the **Networking only... powered by AWS Fargate** template

4. Click on the **Next** step and you see the **Create Cluster** step, as shown:

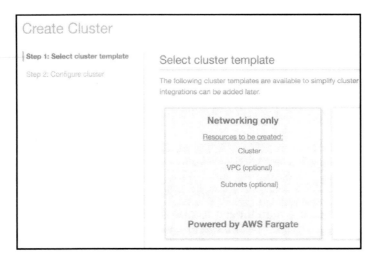

AWS ECS Create Cluster

5. Enter **Cluster name** as `fargate-cluster`
6. Create a **VPC** to isolate your resources from other AWS resources
7. Click on **Create Cluster** to finish the setup

You will see the summary of your actions, as follows:

AWS ECS Fargate Cluster

Now that you have created a cluster within it's own **Virtual Private Cloud (VPC)**, you can view it under **Elastic Container Service | Clusters**.

Creating container repository

Next, we need to set up a repository where we can publish the container images we build in our local or CI environment:

1. Navigate to **Elastic Container Service**
2. Click on **Repositories | Create Repository**
3. Enter repository name as `lemon-mart`
4. Copy the **Repository URI** generated on the screen
5. Paste the URI in `package.json` of your application as the new `imageRepo` variable:

   package.json
   ```
   . . .
   "config": {
     "imageRepo": "000000000000.dkr.ecr.us-east-1.amazonaws.com/lemon-
   mart",
       . . .
   }
   ```

6. Click on **Create Repository**
7. Click on **Next step** and then on **Done** to finish setup

In the summary screen, you will get further instructions on how to use your repository with Docker. Later in the chapter, we will go over scripts that will take care of this for us.

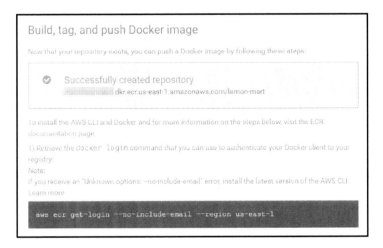

AWS ECS Repository

You can view your new repository under **Elastic Container Service | Repositories**. We will go over how to publish your image in the upcoming `npm Scripts for AWS` section.

Creating task definition

With a container target defined in our repository, we can define a task definition, which contains the necessary metadata to run our container, such as port mappings, reserved CPU, and memory allocations:

1. Navigate to **Elastic Container Service**
2. Click on **Task Definitions | Create new Task Definition**
3. Select **Fargate** launch type compatibility
4. Enter **Task Definition Name** as `lemon-mart-task`
5. Select **Task role** `none` (you can add one later to enable access other AWS services)
6. Enter **Task Size** `0.5` GB
7. Enter **Task CPU** `0.25` CPU
8. Click on **Add Container**:
    1. Enter **Container name** as `lemon-mart`
    2. For **Image**, paste the image repo URI from earlier, but append the `:latest` tag to it so that it always pulls the latest image in the repository, such as `000000000000.dkr.ecr.us-east-1.amazonaws.com/lemon-mart:latest`
    3. Set a **Soft limit** of `128` MB for NGINX and `256` MB for Node.js
    4. Under **Port mappings**, specify **Container port** as `80` for NGINX and `3000` for Node.js
9. Accept the remaining defaults

10. Click on **Add**; this is how your task definition will look before creating it:

AWS ECS Task Definition

11. Click on **Create** to finish setup

View your new **Task Definition** under **Elastic Container Service | Task Definitions**.

Note that the default settings will enable AWS CloudWatch logging, which is a way you can retroactively access console logs of your container instance. In this example, a CloudWatch Log Group named `/ecs/lemon-mart-task` will be created.

View your new Log Group under **Cloud Watch | Logs**.

If you're adding a container that needs to persist data, the task definition allows you to define a volume and mount a folder to your Docker container. I've published a guide a for configuring AWS **Elastic File System (EFS)** with your ECS Container at `bit.ly/mount-aws-efs-ecs-container`.

Creating elastic load balancer

In a highly-available deployment, we will want to be running two instances of your container, as defined by the task definition we just created, across two different **Availability Zones (AZs)**. For this kind of dynamically scaling out and scaling in, we need to configure an **Application Load Balancer (ALB)** to handle request routing and draining:

1. On a seperate tab, navigate to **EC2 | Load Balancers | Create Load Balancer**
2. Create an **Application Load Balancer**
3. Enter **Name** `lemon-mart-alb`:

   In order to support SSL traffic under listeners, you can add a new listener for HTTPS on port 443. An SSL setup can be achieved conveniently via AWS services and wizards. During the ALB configuration process, AWS offers links to these wizards to create your certificates. However, it is an involved process and one that can vary depending on your existing domain hosting and SSL certification setup. I will be skipping over SSL-related configuration in this book. You can find SSL related steps, published on the guide I've published at `bit.ly/setupAWSECSCluster`.

4. Under **Availability Zones**, select the **VPC** that was created for your **fargate-cluster**
5. Select all AZs listed
6. Expand **Tags** and add a key/value pair to be able to identify the ALB, like `"App": " LemonMart"`

7. Click on **Next**
8. Select **Default ELB security policy**
9. Click on **Next**
10. Create a new cluster specific security group, lemon-mart-sg, only allowing port 80 inbound or 443 if using HTTPS

> When creating your Cluster Service in the next section, ensure that the security group created here is the one selected during service creation. Otherwise, your ALB won't be able to connect to your instances.

11. Click on **Next**
12. Name a new **Target group** as lemon-mart-target-group
13. Change protocol type from instance to ip
14. Under **Health check**, keep the default route /, if serving a website on HTTP

Health checks are critical for scaling and deployment operations to work. This is the mechanism that AWS can use to check whether an instance has been created successfully or not.

> If deploying an API and/or redirecting all HTTP calls to HTTPS, ensure that your app defines a custom route that is not redirected to HTTPS. On HTTP server GET /healthCheck return simple 200 message saying I'm healthy and verify that this does not redirect to HTTPS. Otherwise, you will go through a lot of pain and suffering trying to figure out what's wrong, as all health checks fail and deployments inexplicably fail. duluca/minimal-node-web-server provides HTTPS redirection, along with an HTTP-only /healthCheck endpoint out of the box. With duluca/minimal-nginx-web-server, you will need to provide your own configuration.

15. Click on **Next**
16. Do *not* register any **Targets** or **IP Ranges**. ECS Fargate will magically manage this for you, if you do so yourself, you will provision a semi broken infrastructure

17. Click on **Next:Review**; your ALB settings should look similar to the one shown:

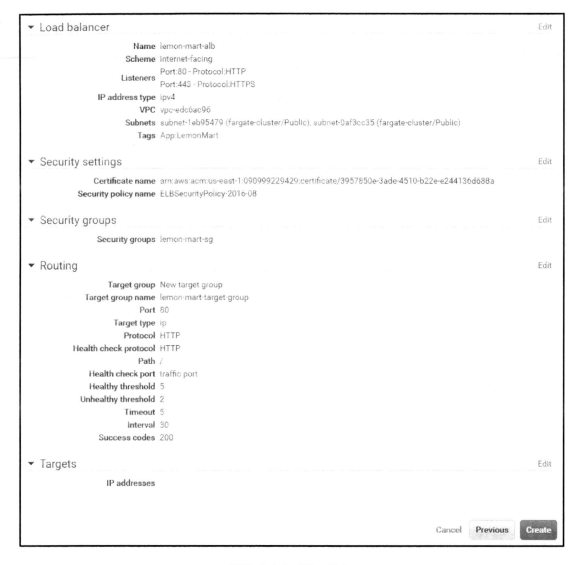

AWS Application Load Balancer Settings

18. Click on **Create** to finish setup

You will be using the **lemon-mart-alb** when creating your Cluster Service in the next section.

Creating cluster service

Now, we will bring it all together by creating a service in our cluster using the task definition and the ALB we created:

1. Navigate to **Elastic Container Service**
2. Click on **Clusters | fargate-cluster**
3. Under **Services** tab, click on **Create**
4. Select **Launch type** Fargate
5. Select the task definition you created earlier

   Note that task definitions are versioned, such as lemon-mart-task:1. If you were to make a change to the task definition, AWS will create lemon-mart-task:2. You will need to update the service with this new version for your changes to take effect.

6. Enter **Service name** lemon-mart-service
7. **Number of tasks** 2
8. **Minimum healthy percent** 50
9. **Maximum percent** 200
10. Click on **Next**

> Set minimum health percent to 100 for high-availability even during deployment. Fargate pricing is based on usage per second, so while deploying your application, you will be charged extra for the additional instances, while the old ones are being deprovisioned.

11. Under **Configure network**, select the same **VPC** as your cluster from earlier
12. Select all subnets that are available; there should be at least two for high-availability
13. Select the security group you created in the previous section—lemon-mart-sg
14. Select **Load Balancer** type as **Application Load Balancer**
15. Select the **lemon-mart-alb** option
16. Add **Container port** to the ALB, such as 80 or 3000, by clicking on the **Add to Load Balancer** button
17. Select the **Listener port** that you had already defined
18. Select the **Target group** you had already defined
19. Uncheck **Enable service discovery integration**
20. Click on **Next**

21. If you'd like your instances to scale out and in automatically, when their capacities are reach a certain limit, then set **Auto Scaling**

I would recommend skipping the set up of auto scaling during the initial setup of your service to make it easier to troubleshoot any potential configuration issues. You can come back and set it up later. Automatic task scaling policies rely on alarms, such as CPU Utilization. In Chapter 12, *Google Analytics and Advanced Cloud Ops,* in the *Cost Per User in Scalable Environment* section, you can read about calculating your optimum target server utilization and set your alarms based on this number.

22. Click on **Next** and review your changes, as illustrated:

AWS Fargate cluster service settings

23. Finally, click on **Save** to finish setup

Observe your new service under **Elastic Container Service** | **Clusters** | **fargate-cluster** | **lemon-mart-service**. Until you publish an image to your container repository, your AWS service won't be able to provision an instance, since the health check will continually fail. After you publish an image, you will want to ensure that there are no errors present in the **Events** tab for your service.

AWS is a complicated beast and with Fargate, you can avoid a lot of complexity. However, if you're interested in setting up your own ECS cluster using your own Ec2 instances, you can get significant discounts with 1-3 year reserved instances. I have a 75+ setup guide available at `bit.ly/setupAWSECSCluster`.

We have executed a lot of steps manually to create our Cluster. AWS CloudFormation resolves this issue by offering configuration templates that you can customize to your needs or script your own templates from scratch. If you would like to get serious about AWS, this kind of code-as-infrastructure setup is definitely the way to go.

For production deployments, ensure that your configuration is defined by a CloudFormation template, so it can be easily reprovisioned, not if, but when a deployment related faux pas occurs.

Configuring the DNS

If you use AWS Route 53 to manage your domain, it is easy to assign a domain or a subdomain to an ALB:

1. Navigate to **Route 53** | **Hosted Zones**
2. Select your domain, like `thejavascriptpromise.com`
3. Click on **Create record set**
4. Enter **Name** as `lemonmart`
5. Set **Alias** to `yes`
6. Select the **lemon-mart-alb** from the load balancer list

7. Click on **Create** to finish setup

Create Record Set

Name: | lemonmart | .excellalabs.com.

Type: A – IPv4 address ▼

Alias: ● Yes ○ No

Alias Target: dualstack.lemon-mart-alb-1859482442

Alias Hosted Zone ID: Z35SXDOTRQ7X7K

You can also type the domain name for the resource. Examples:
- CloudFront distribution domain name: d111111abcdef8.cloudfront.net
- Elastic Beanstalk environment CNAME: example.elasticbeanstalk.com
- ELB load balancer DNS name: example-1.us-east-1.elb.amazonaws.com
- S3 website endpoint: s3-website.us-east-2.amazonaws.com
- Resource record set in this hosted zone: www.example.com

Learn More

Routing Policy: Simple ▼

Route 53 responds to queries based only on the values in this record. Learn More

Evaluate Target Health: ○ Yes ● No

Route 53 - Create record set

Now, your site will be reachable on the subdomain you just defined, for example `http://lemonmart.thejavascriptpromise.com`.

If don't use Route 53, don't panic. On your domain provider's website, edit the `Zone` file to create an `A` record to the ELB's DNS address and you're done.

Getting the DNS Name

In order to get your load balancers' DNS address, perform these steps:

1. Navigate to **EC2 | Load Balancers**
2. Select the **lemon-mart-alb**

3. In the **Description** tab note the DNS name; consider this example:

DNS name:
```
lemon-mart-alb-1871778644.us-east-1.elb.amazonaws.com (A Record)
```

Prep Angular app

This section presumes that you have set up Docker and `npm Scripts for Docker` as detailed in `Chapter 3`, *Prepare Angular App for Production Release*. You can get the latest version of these scripts at `bit.ly/npmScriptsForDocker`.

Implement an optimized `Dockerfile`:

```
Dockerfile
FROM duluca/minimal-nginx-web-server:1.13.8-alpine
COPY dist /var/www
CMD 'nginx'
```

Note that if you're using `npm Scripts for Docker`, **update the internal image port from** `3000` **to** `80`, **as shown**:

```
"docker:runHelper": "cross-conf-env docker run -e NODE_ENV=local --name
$npm_package_config_imageName -d -p $npm_package_config_imagePort:80
$npm_package_config_imageRepo",
```

Adding npm Scripts for AWS

Just like `npm Scripts for Docker`, I have developed a set of scripts, called `npm Scripts for AWS`, that work on Windows 10 and macOS. These scripts will allow you to upload and release your Docker images in spectacular, no-downtime, blue-green fashion. You can get the latest version of these scripts at `bit.ly/npmScriptsForAWS`:

1. Ensure that `bit.ly/npmScriptsForDocker` are set up on your project
2. Create a `.env` file and set `AWS_ACCESS_KEY_ID` and `AWS_SECRET_ACCESS_KEY`:

   .env
   ```
   AWS_ACCESS_KEY_ID=your_own_key_id
   AWS_SECRET_ACCESS_KEY=your_own_secret_key
   ```

3. Ensure that your `.env` file is in your `.gitignore` file to protect your secrets

4. Install or upgrade to latest AWS CLI:
   - On macOS `brew install awscli`
   - On Windows `choco install awscli`

5. Log in to AWS CLI with your credentials:
   1. Run `aws configure`
   2. You'll need your **Access Key ID** and **Secret Access Key** from when you configured your IAM account
   3. Set **Default region name** like `us-east-1`

6. Update `package.json` to add a new `config` property with the following configuration properties:

   package.json
   ```
   . . .
   "config": {
     . . .
     "awsRegion": "us-east-1",
     "awsEcsCluster": "fargate-cluster",
     "awsService": "lemon-mart-service"
   },
   . . .
   ```

 Ensure that you update `package.json` from when you configured npm `Scripts for Docker` so that the `imageRepo` property has the address of your new ECS repository.

7. Add AWS `scripts` to `package.json`, as illustrated:

   package.json
   ```
   . . .
   "scripts": {
     . . .
     "aws:login": "run-p -cs aws:login:win aws:login:mac",
     "aws:login:win": "cross-conf-env aws ecr get-login --no-include-
   email --region $npm_package_config_awsRegion > dockerLogin.cmd &&
   call dockerLogin.cmd && del dockerLogin.cmd",
     "aws:login:mac": "eval $(aws ecr get-login --no-include-email --
   region $npm_package_config_awsRegion)"
   }
   ```

`npm run aws:login` calls platform-specific commands that automate an otherwise multi-step action to get a Docker login command from the AWS CLI tool, as shown:

example
```
$ aws ecr get-login --no-include-email --region us-east-1
docker login -u AWS -p eyJwYXl...3ODk1fQ==
https://073020584345.dkr.ecr.us-east-1.amazonaws.com
```

You would first execute `aws ecr get-login` and then copy-paste the resulting `docker login` command and execute it so that your local Docker instance is pointed to AWS ECR:

package.json
```
...
"scripts": {
  ...
  "aws:deploy": "cross-conf-env docker run --env-file ./.env duluca/ecs-
deploy-fargate -c $npm_package_config_awsEcsCluster -n
$npm_package_config_awsService -i $npm_package_config_imageRepo:latest -r
$npm_package_config_awsRegion --timeout 1000"
  }
...
```

`npm run aws:deploy` pulls a Docker container that itself executes blue-green deployment, using the parameters you have provided using the `aws ecr` commands. The details of how this works are beyond the scope of this book. To see more examples using native `aws ecr` commands, refer to the `aws-samples` repository at `github.com/aws-samples/ecs-blue-green-deployment`.

Note that the `duluca/ecs-deploy-fargate` blue-green deployment script is a fork of the original `silintl/ecs-deploy` image modified to support AWS ECS Fargate using PR `https://github.com/silinternational/ecs-deploy/pull/129`. Once `silintl/ecs-deploy` merges this change, I recommend using `silintl/ecs-deploy` for your blue-green deployments:

package.json
```
...
"scripts": {
  ...
  "aws:release": "run-s -cs aws:login docker:publish aws:deploy"
}
...
```

Finally, `npm run aws:release` **simply runs** `aws:login, docker:publish` from `npm Scripts for Docker` and `aws:deploy` commands in the right order.

Publish

Your project is configured to be deployed on AWS. You mostly need to use two of the commands we created to build and publish an image:

1. Execute `docker:debug` to test, build, tag, run, tail, and launch your app in a browser to test the image:

   ```
   $ npm run docker:debug
   ```

2. Execute `aws:release` to configure Docker login with AWS, publish your latest image build, and release it on ECS:

   ```
   $ npm run aws:release
   ```

3. Verify that your tasks are up and running at the **Service** level:

Clusters > fargate-cluster > Service: lemon-mart-service

Service : lemon-mart-service

Cluster	fargate-cluster	**Desired count**	2
Status	ACTIVE	**Pending count**	0
Task definition	lemon-mart-task:1	**Running count**	2
Launch type	FARGATE		
Platform version	LATEST		
Service role	aws-service-role/ecs.amazonaws.com/AWSServiceRoleForECS		

AWS ECS Service

Ensure that running count and desired count are the same.

4. Verify that your instances are running at the **Task** level:

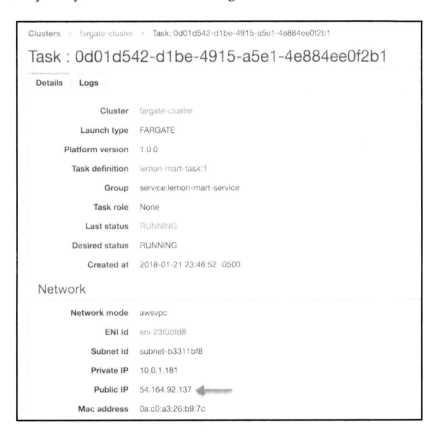

Clusters › fargate-cluster › Task: 0d01d542-d1be-4915-a5e1-4e884ee0f2b1

Task : 0d01d542-d1be-4915-a5e1-4e884ee0f2b1

Details Logs

Cluster	fargate-cluster
Launch type	FARGATE
Platform version	1.0.0
Task definition	lemon-mart-task:1
Group	service:lemon-mart-service
Task role	None
Last status	RUNNING
Desired status	RUNNING
Created at	2018-01-21 23:46:52 -0500

Network

Network mode	awsvpc
ENI Id	eni-23f0bfd8
Subnet Id	subnet-b3311bf8
Private IP	10.0.1.181
Public IP	54.164.92.137
Mac address	0a:c0:a3:26:b9:7c

AWS ECS task instance

Note the **Public IP** address and navigate to it; for example, `http://54.164.92.137` and you should see your application or LemonMart running.

5. Verify that the **Load Balancer** setup is correct at the DNS level.

6. Navigate to the **ALB DNS address**, for
   example `http://lemon-mart-alb-1871778644.us-east-1.elb.amazonaws`
   `.com`, and confirm that the app renders, as follows:

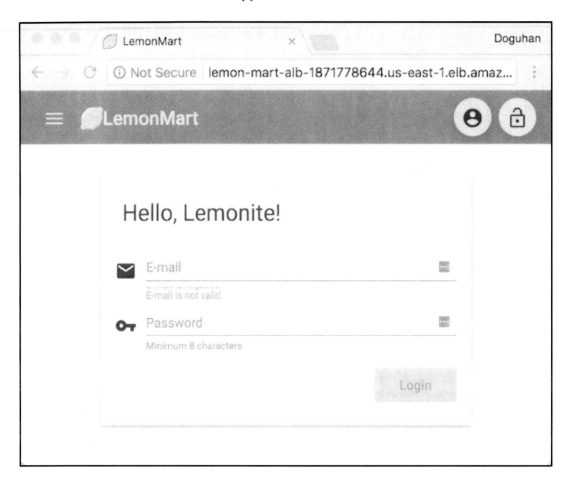

LemonMart running on AWS Fargate

Et voilà! Your site should be up and running.

In subsequent releases, following your first, you will be able to observe blue-green deployment in action, as shown:

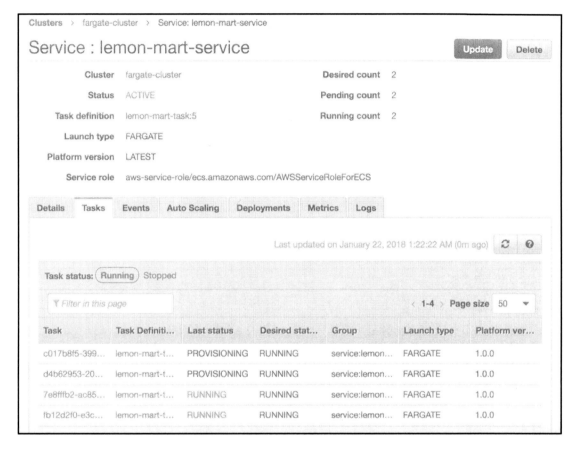

AWS Service during Blue-Green Deployment

There are two tasks running, with two new ones being provisioned. While the new tasks are being verified, running count will rise up to four tasks. After the new tasks are verified and the connections from old ones drained, the running count will return to two.

You can automate your deployments by configuring CircleCI with your AWS credentials, using a container that has the `awscli` tool installed and running `npm Scripts for AWS`. With this technique, you can achieve Continuous Deployment to a staging environment or Continuous Delivery to a production environment.

This is all great, but how much does a basic highly-available configuration cost? Let's examine that in the next section.

AWS Billing

My highly-available deployment of LemonMart on AWS Fargate cost roughly $45 a month. Here's the breakdown:

Description	Cost
Amazon Simple Storage Service (S3)	$0.01
AWS Data Transfer	$0.02
Amazon CloudWatch	$0.00
Amazon EC2 Container Service (ECS Fargate)	$27.35
Amazon Elastic Compute Cloud (EC2 Load Balancer instances)	$16.21
Amazon EC2 Container Registry (ECR)	$0.01
Amazon Route 53	$0.50
Total	**$44.10**

Note that the bill is very detailed, but it does accurate all the AWS services we end up using. The major costs are running two instances of our web server on **EC2 Container Service (ECS)** and running load balances on **Elastic Compute Cloud (EC2)**. Objectively speaking, $45/month may seem like a lot of money to host one web application. It is possible to get a lot more for your money if you're willing to set up your own cluster with dedicated EC2 servers where you can pay in 1 or 3-year increments and get cost savings of up to 50%. A similar, highly available deployment with two-instances on Heroku starts at $50/month with other rich features you can get access to. Similarly, two-instances on Zeit Now will cost $30/month. Note that both Heroku and Zeit Now don't give you access to physically diverse availability zones. Digital Ocean, on the other hands, allows you to provision servers in different data centers; however, you must code your own infrastructure. For $15/month, you can set up your own highly-available cluster across three servers and be able to host multiple sites on it.

Summary

In this chapter, you learned about the nuances and various security considerations in properly protecting your AWS account. We went over the concepts of right-sizing your infrastructure. You conducted simple load testing in an isolated manner to find out relative differences in performance between two web servers. Armed with an optimized web server, you configured an AWS ECS Fargate cluster to achieve a highly-available cloud infrastructure. Using npm Scripts for AWS, you learned how to script repeatable and reliable no-downtime Blue-Green deployments. Finally, you became aware of the basic costs of running your infrastructure on AWS and other cloud providers such as Heroku, Zeit Now, and Digital Ocean.

In the next and final chapter, we will complete our coverage of the breadth of topics that a full-stack web developer should know about when deploying applications on the web. We will add Google Analytics to LemonMart to measure user behavior, leverage advanced load testing to understand the financial impact of deploying a well-configured scalable infrastructure, and measure actual use of important application features with custom analytics events.

Google Analytics and Advanced Cloud Ops

12

You have designed, developed, and deployed a word-class web application; however, that is only the beginning of the story of your app. The web is an ever-evolving, living, breathing environment that demands attention to continue to succeed as a business. In `Chapter 11`, *Highly-Available Cloud Infrastructure on AWS*, we went over the basic concepts and costs of ownership of a cloud infrastructure. In this chapter, we will dig deeper in truly understanding how users actually use our application with Google Analytics. We will then use that information to create realistic load tests to simulate actual user behavior to understand the true capacity of a single instance of our server. Knowing the capacity of a single server, we can fine-tune how our infrastructure scales out to reduce waste and discuss the implications of various scaling strategies. Finally, we will go over advanced analytics concepts such as custom events to gain more granular understanding and tracking of user behavior.

In this chapter, you will learn about the following topics:

- Google Analytics
- Google Tag Manager
- Budgeting and Scaling
- Advanced Load Testing to Predict Capacity
- Custom Analytics Events

Throughout the chapter, you will be setting up these:

- A Google Analytics Account
- A Google Tag Manager Account
- An OctoPerf Account

Collecting Analytics

Now that our site is up and running, we need to start collecting metrics to understand how it is being used. Metrics are key to operating a web application.

Google Analytics has many facets; the main three are as follows:

1. Acquisition, which measures how visitors arrive at your website
2. Behavior, which measures how visitors interact with your website
3. Conversions, which measures how visitors completed various goals on your website

Here's a look at the **Behavior** | **Overview** from my website `TheJavaScriptPromise.com`:

Google Analytics Behavior Overview

`TheJavaScriptPromise.com` is a simple one page HTML site, so the metrics are quite simple. Let's go over the various metrics on the screen:

1. **Pageviews** show the number of visitors
2. **Unique Pageviews** show the number of unique visitors
3. **Avg. Time on Page** shows the amount of time each user spent on the site
4. **Bounce Rate** shows that users left the site without navigating to a subpage or interacting with the site in any manner, such as clicking on a link or button with a custom event
5. **% Exit** indicates how often users leave the site after viewing a particular or set of pages

At high-level, in 2017, the site had about 1,090 unique visitors and on an average, each visitor spent about 2.5 minutes or 157 seconds on the site. Given that this is just a one page site, bounce rate and % exit metrics do not apply in any meaningful manner. Later, we will use these numbers to calculate the Cost Per User.

In addition to page views, Google Analytics can also capture specific events, such as clicking on a button that triggers a server request. These events can then be viewed on the **Events | Overview** page, as shown:

Google Analytics Events Overview

It is possible to capture metrics on the server side as well, but this will give requests-over-time statistics. You will need additional code and state management to track the behavior of a particular user, so you can calculate users-over-time statistics. By implementing such tracking on the client side with Google Analytics, you gain a far more detailed understanding where the user came from, what they did, if they succeeded or not and when they left your app without adding unnecessary code complexity and infrastructure load to your backend.

Adding Google Tag Manager to Angular App

Let's start capturing analytics in your Angular app. Google is in the process of phasing out the legacy `ga.js` and `analytics.js` products that ships with Google Analytics, with its new, more flexible Global Site Tag `gtag.js` that ships with Google Tag Manager. This is by no means an end to Google Analytics; instead, it's a shift in toward an easier-to-configure and manage analytics tool. Global Site Tag can be configured and managed remotely via Google Tag Manager. Tags are snippets of JavaScript tracking code that is delivered to the client, and they can enable tracking of new metrics and integration with multiple analytics tools without having to change already deployed code. You can still continue to use Google Analytics to analyze and view your analytics data. Another major advantage of Google Tag Manager is that its version controlled, so you can experiment with different kinds of tags that are triggered under various kinds of conditions without fear of doing any irreversible damage to your analytics configuration.

Set up Google Tag Manager

Let's start off with setting up a Google Tag Manager account for your application:

1. Sign in to Google Tag Manager at `GoogleTagManager.com`

2. Add a new account with a **Web** container, as follows:

Google Tag Manager

3. Paste the generated scripts at or near the top `<head>` and `<body>` sections of your `index.html` as instructed:

src/index.html

```
<head>
<!-- Google Tag Manager -->
<script>(function(w,d,s,l,i){w[l]=w[l]||[];w[l].push({'gtm.start':
new Date().getTime(),event:'gtm.js'});var
f=d.getElementsByTagName(s)[0],
j=d.createElement(s),dl=l!='dataLayer'?'&l='+l:'';j.async=true;j.sr
c=
'https://www.googletagmanager.com/gtm.js?id='+i+dl;f.parentNode.ins
ertBefore(j,f);
})(window,document,'script','dataLayer','GTM-56D4F6K');</script>
```

```
<!-- End Google Tag Manager -->
...
</head>
<body>
<!-- Google Tag Manager (noscript) -->
<noscript><iframe
src="https://www.googletagmanager.com/ns.html?id=GTM-56D4F6K"
height="0" width="0"
style="display:none;visibility:hidden"></iframe></noscript>
<!-- End Google Tag Manager (noscript) -->
<app-root></app-root>
</body>
```

Note that the `<noscript>` tag will only execute if the user has disabled JavaScript execution in their browser. This way, we can collect metrics from such users, rather than being blind to their presence.

4. Submit and publish your tag manager container
5. You should see the initial setup of your tag manager completed, as shown:

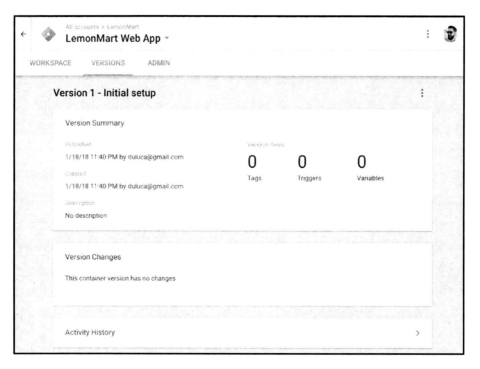

Published Tag

6. Verify that your Angular app runs without any errors.

Note that if you don't publish your tag manager container, you will see a **404** error in loading `gtm.js` in the `dev` console or the **Network** tab.

Setting up Google Analytics

Now, let's generate a Tracking ID through Google Analytics:

1. Log in to Google Analytics at `analytics.google.com`
2. Open the **Admin console**, pointed out as the *gear* icon in the following screenshot:

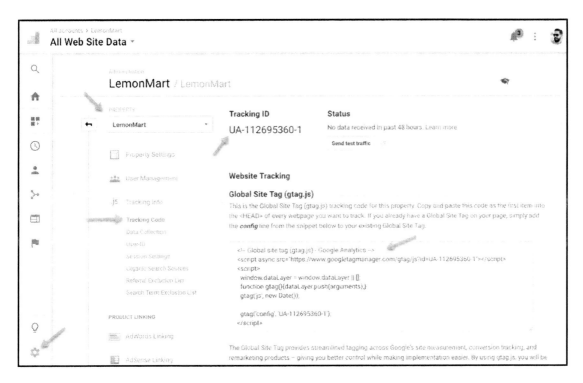

Google Analytics admin console

3. Create a new analytics account
4. Using the arrows from the image as a guide:
     1. Add a new **Property** LemonMart
     2. Configure the property to your preferences
     3. Click on **Tracking Code**
     4. Copy the **Tracking ID** that starts with UA-xxxxxxxxxx-1
     5. Ignore the gtag.js code provided

Configuring Google Analytics Tag in Tag Manager

Now, let's connect our Google Analytics ID to Google Tag Manager:

1. At tagmanager.google.com, open the **Workspace** tab
2. Click on **Add a new tag**
3. Name it Google Analytics
4. Click on **Tag configuration** and select **Universal Analytics**
5. Under **Google Analytics settings**, add a new variable
6. Paste the **Tracking ID** you copied in the previous section
7. Click on **Triggers** and add the **All pages** trigger

8. Click on **Save**, as shown on the following screenshot:

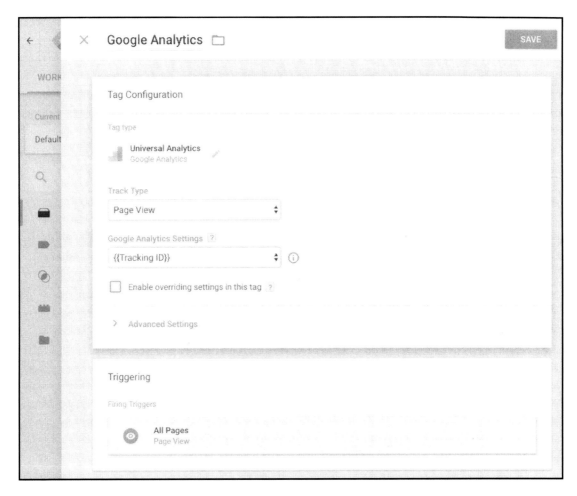

Creating Google Analytics Tag

9. Submit and publish your changes, and observe the version summary with 1 tag, as shown:

Version Summary Showing one Tag

10. Now refresh your Angular app, where you'll be on the `/home` route

11. In a private window, open a new instance of your Angular app and navigate to the `/manager/home` route

12. At `analytics.google.com`, open the **Real-time | Overview** pane, as shown:

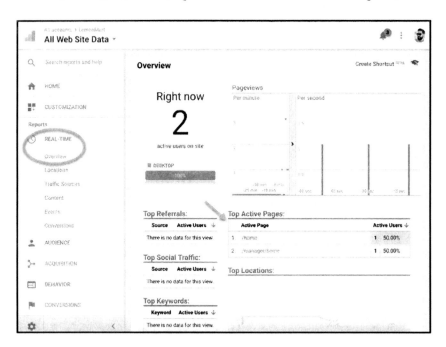

Google Analytics Real-time Overview

13. Note that the two active users are being tracked
14. Under **Top Active Pages**, you should see the pages that the users are on

By leveraging Google Tag Manager and Google Analytics together, we have been able to accomplish page tracking without changing any code inside of our Angular app.

 Search Engine Optimization (SEO) is an important part of Analytics. To gain a better understanding of how crawlers perceive your Angular site, use the Google Search Console, found at `https://www.google.com/webmasters/tools`, to identify optimizations. Further, consider using Angular Universal to render certain dynamic content server side, so crawlers can index your dynamic data sources and drive more traffic to your site.

Budgeting and scaling

In the AWS Billing section of `Chapter 11`, *Highly-Available Cloud Infrastructure on AWS*, we covered the monthly costs of operating a web server, ranging from $5/month to $45/month, from a single-server instance scenario to a highly-available infrastructure. For most needs, budgeting discussions will begin and end with this monthly number. You can execute load tests, as suggested in the Advanced Load Testing section, to predict your per server user capacity and get a general idea of how many servers you may need. In a dynamically scaling cloud environment with dozens of servers running 24/7, this is an overly simplistic way to calculate a budget.

If you operate a web property of any significant scale, things get invariably complicated. You will be operating multiple servers on different tech stacks, serving different purposes. It can be difficult to gauge or justify how much of a budget to spare for seemingly excess capacity or unnecessarily high-performance servers. Somehow, you need to be able to communicate the efficiency of your infrastructure given the number of users you serve and ensure that your infrastructure is fine-tuned so that you don't lose users due to an unresponsive application or overpay because you're using more capacity than you need. For this reason, we will take a user-centered approach and translate our IT infrastructure costs to a per user cost metric that the business and the marketing side of your organization can make sense of.

In the next section, we will investigate what it means to calculate the per user cost of your infrastructure and how these calculations change when cloud scaling comes in to play using one of my websites as an example.

Calculating per user cost

We will be leveraging behavior metrics from Google Analytics with the goal of calculating per user cost over a given period of time:

Per User Cost

$$perUserCost/time = \frac{infrastructureCost/time}{users/time}$$

Using the `TheJavaScriptPromise.com` data from earlier, let's plug in the data to the formula to calculate *perUserCost/month*.

This website is deployed on an Ubuntu server on DigitalOcean, so the monthly infrastructure cost, including weekly backups, is $6 a month. From Google Analytics, we know there were 1,090 unique visitors in 2017:

$$\frac{\$6/mo}{1,090users/year \div 12/mo} = \$0.07/user$$

In 2017, I have paid 7 cents per user. Money well spent? At $6/month, I don't mind it. In 2017, `TheJavaScriptPromise.com` was deployed on a traditional server setup, as a static site that doesn't scale out or in. These conditions make it very straightforward to use the unique visitor metric and find the per user cost. The very same simplicity that allows for an easy calculation also leads to a suboptimal infrastructure. If I were to serve 1,000,000 users on the same infrastructure, my costs would add up to $70,000 a year. If I were to earn $100 per every 1,000 user through Google Ads, my site would make a $100,000 per year. After taxes, development expenses, and our unreasonable hosting expense, the operation would likely lose money.

If you took advantage of cloud scaling, where instances can scale out or in dynamically based on current user demand, the preceding formula becomes useless pretty quickly, because you must take provisioning time and target server utilization into account. Provisioning time is the amount of time it takes your cloud provider to start a new server from scratch. Target server utilization is the maximum usage metric of a given server, where a scale-out alert must be sent out so that a new server is ready before your current servers max out their capacity. In order to calculate these variables, we must execute a series of load tests against our servers.

Page views are an overly simplistic way to determine user behavior in SPAs such as Angular, where page views do not necessarily correlate to a request or vice versa. If we execute load tests simply based on page views, we won't get a realistic simulation of how your platform may perform under load.

User behavior, or how users actually use your app, can drastically impact your performance forecasts and wildly fluctuate budget numbers. You can use Google Analytics custom events to capture complicated sets of actions that result in various types of requests served by your platform. Later in this chapter, we will explore how you can measure actual use in the *Measuring actual use* section.

Initially, you won't have any of the aforementioned metrics, and any metrics you may have will be invalidated any time you make a meaningful change to your software or hardware stack. Therefore, it is imperative to execute load tests on a regular basis to simulate realistic user loads.

Advanced load testing

In order to be able to predict capacity, we need to run load tests. In `Chapter 11`, *Highly-Available Cloud Infrastructure on AWS*, I discussed a simple load testing technique of just sending a bunch of web requests to a server. In a relative comparison scenario, this works fine to test raw power. However, actual users generate dozens of requests at varying intervals, while they navigate your website resulting in a wide-variety of API calls to your backend server.

We must be able to model virtual users and unleash a whole bunch of them on our servers to find the breaking point of our server. OctoPerf is an easy-to-use service to execute such load tests, and it's located at `https://octoperf.com`. OctoPerf offers a free-tier that allows for 50 concurrent users/test over unlimited test runs with two load generators:

1. Create an OctoPerf account

2. Login and add a new project for LemonMart, as shown:

OctoPerf Add Project

OctoPerf allows you to create multiple virtual users with different usage characteristics. Since it is a URL-based setup, any click-based user action can also be simulated by directly calling the application server URL with test parameters.

3. Create two virtual users: one as a `Manager` who navigates to Manager-based pages and second a `POS` user who would only stick to POS functions

4. Click on **Create scenario**:

POS User Scenario

5. Name the scenario `Evening Rush`

6. You can add a mixture of **Managers** and **POS Users**, as shown:

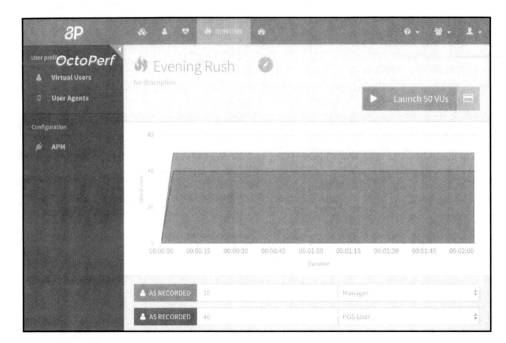

Evening Rush Scenario

7. Click on the **Launch 50 VUs** button to start the load test

You can observe the number of **users** and **hits/sec** being achieved in real time, as shown in the following screenshot:

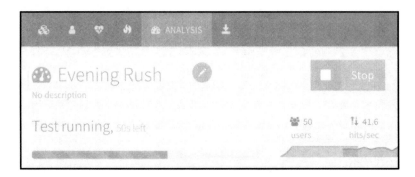

Evening Rush Load Test Underway

8. ECS service metrics also give us a high-level idea of real-time utilization, as shown in the following screenshot:

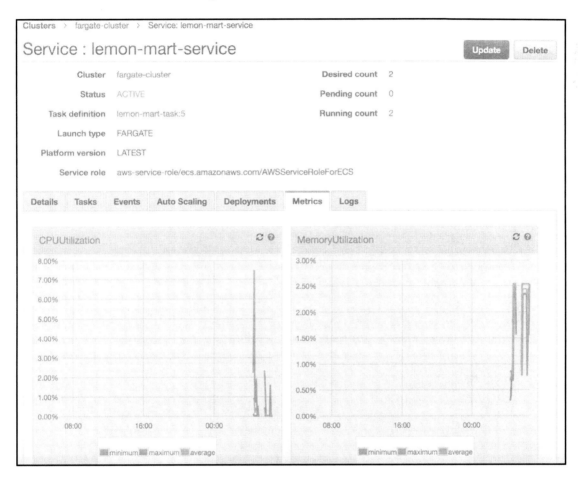

ECS Real-time Metrics

9. Analyze load test results.

You can get more accurate results from ECS by clicking on the **CPUUtilization** link from **ECS Service Metrics** or by navigating to **CloudWatch | Metrics** section, as follows:

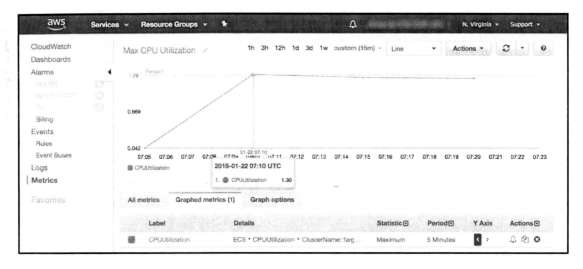

AWS CloudWatch Metrics

As you can see in the preceding graph, CPU utilization was fairly consistent around 1.3%, given a sustained 50 user load over 10 minutes. During this period, there were no request errors, as shown in the statistics summary from OctoPerf:

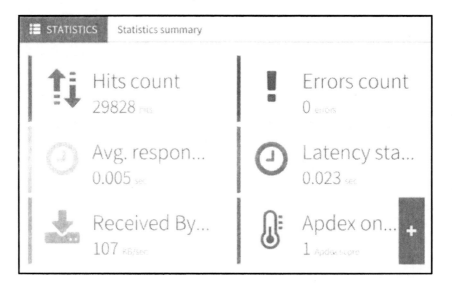

OctoPerf Statistics Summary

Ideally, we would measure maximum users/second until the moment errors were being generated. However, given only 50 virtuals users and the information we already have, we can predict how many users could be handled at 100% utilization:

$$\frac{100 percent}{1.3 percent} \times 50 users/sec = 3,846 users/sec$$

Our load test results reveal that our infrastructure can handle 3,846 users/second. Given this information, we can calculate cost per user in a Scalable Environment in the next section. However, performance and reliability go hand in hand. How you choose to architect your infrastructure will also provide important information of budgeting, because the level of reliability you need will dictate the minimum number of instances you must keep around at all times.

Reliable Cloud Scaling

Reliability can be expressed in terms of your organization's Recovery Point Objective (RPO) and **Recovery Time Objective (RTO)** defined. RPO represents how much data you're willing to lose, and RTO represents how fast you can rebuild your infrastructure in the event of a failure.

Let's suppose that you run an e-commerce site. Around noon every weekday, you reach peak sales. Every time a user adds an item to their shopping cart, you store the items on a server-side cache so that users can resume their shopping spree later at home. In addition, you process hundreds of transactions per minute. Business is good, your infrastructure is scale-out beautifully, and everything is going smoothly. Meanwhile, a hungry rat or an overly charged lightning cloud decides to strike your data center. Initially, a seemingly harmless power unit goes down, but it's fine, because nearby power units can pick up the slack. However, this is the lunch rush; other websites on the data center are also facing a high traffic volume. As a result, several power units overheat and fail. There aren't enough power units to pick up the slack, so in quick succession, power units overheat one by one and start failing, triggering a cascade of failures that end up taking down the entire data center. Meanwhile, some of your users just clicked on add to cart, others on the pay button, and some others are just about to arrive on your site. If your RPO is one hour, meaning you persisted your shopping cart cache every one hour, then you can say goodbye to valuable data and potential sales by those night time shoppers. If your RTO is one hour, it will take you up to one hour to get your site back up and running again, and you can be assured that most of those customers, who just clicked on the buy button or arrived to an unresponsive site won't be making a purchase on your site that day.

A well thought out RPO and RTO is a critical business need, but they must also be paired with the right infrastructure that makes it possible to implement your objectives in a cost-effective manner. AWS is made up of more than two dozen regions around the world, each region containing at least their **Availability Zones (AZs)**. Each AZ is a physically separated infrastructure that is not affected by a failure in another AZ.

A highly-available configuration on AWS means that your application is up and running on at least two AZs, so if a server instance fails, nay even if the entire data center fails, you have another instance already live in a physically separate data center that is able to pick up incoming requests seamlessly.

A fault-tolerant architecture means that your application is deployed across multiple regions. Even if an entire region comes down due to a natural disaster, **Distributed Denial of Service (DDoS)** attack, or a bad software update, your infrastructure remains standing and able to respond to user request. Your data is protected via layers upon layers of security and via staggered back ups of back ups.

AWS has great services such as Shield to protect against DDoS attacks targeted against your website, Pilot Light service to keep a minimal infrastructure waiting dormant in another region that can scale to full capacity if needed, while keeping operational costs down, and Glacier service to store large amounts for data for long periods of time in an affordable manner.

A highly-available configuration will require two instances at a minimum in a multi-AZ setup at all times. For a fault-tolerant setup, you need two highly-available configuration in at least two regions. Most AWS cloud services such as DynamoDB for data-storage or Redis for caching are highly available by default, including serverless technologies such as Lambda. Lambda charges on a per use basis and can scale to match any need you can throw at it in a cost effective manner. If you can move heavy compute tasks to Lambda, you can reduce your server utilization and your scaling needs dramatically in the process. When planning your infrastructure, you should consider all these variables to set up the right scalable environment for your needs.

Cost per user in a scalable environment

In a scalable environment, you can't plan on 100% utilization. It takes time to provision a new server. A server that is at 100% utilization can't process additional incoming requests in a timely manner, which results in dropped or erroneous requests from the users' perspective. So the server in question must send a trigger well before it reaches 100% utilization so that no requests are dropped. Earlier in the chapter, I suggested a 60-80% target utilization before scaling. The exact number will highly depend on your specific choice software and hardware stack. Given your custom utilization target, we can calculate the number of users your infrastructure is expected to serve on average per instance. Using this information, you can calculate a more accurate cost per user, which should allow the right-sizing of your IT budget, given your specific needs. It is equally as bad to underspend as it is to overspend. You may be foregoing growth, security, data, reliability, and resilience than it may be acceptable.

In the next section, we will walk through the calculation of an optimal target server utilization metric so that you can calculate a more accurate per user cost; then, we will explore scaling that can occur during preplanned time frames and software deployments.

Calculating target server utilization

First, calculate your custom server utilization target, which is the point where your server is under increasing load and triggers a new server to provision with enough time so that the original server does not reach 100% utilization and drop requests. Consider this formula:

Target Utilization

$$targetUtilization = 1 - \frac{provisioningSpeed \times requests/time}{maxRequestCapacity/time}$$

Let's demonstrate how the formula works with a concrete example:

1. Load test your instances to find out user capacity per instance: *Load test results:* 3,846 users/second

Requests/sec and users/sec are not equivalents, since a user makes multiple requests to complete an action and may execute multiple requests/sec. Advanced load testing tools such as OctoPerf are necessary to execute realistic and varied workloads and measure user capacity over request capacity.

2. Measure instance provisioning speed, from creation/cold boot to first fulfilled request: *Measured instance provisioning speed:* 60 seconds

   In order to measure this speed, you can put the stopwatch away. Depending on your exact setup, AWS provides event and application logs in ECS Service Events tab, CloudWatch, and CloudTrail to correlate enough information to figure out when a new instance was requested and how long it took for the instance to be ready to fulfill requests. For example, in the **ECS Service Events** tab, take the target registration event as the beginning time. Once the task has been started, click on the task ID to see the creation time. Using the task ID, check the task's logs in CloudWatch to see the time the task served its first web request as the end time and then calculate the duration.

3. Measure 95th-percentile user growth rate, excluding known capacity increases: *95th-percentile user growth rate:* 10 users/second

 If you don't have prior metrics, initially defining user growth rate will be an educated guess at best. However, once you start collecting data, you can update your assumptions. In addition, it is impossible to operate an infrastructure that can respond to any imaginable outlier without dropping a request in a cost-effective manner. Given your metrics, a business decision should be consciously made to what percentile of outliers should be ignored as an acceptable business risk.

4. Let's plug in the numbers to the formula:

$$1 - \frac{60s \times 10users/s}{3,846/s} = 0.8439$$

The custom target utilization rate, rounded down, would be 84%. Setting your scale out trigger at 84% will avoid instances from being over provisioned, while avoiding dropping users requests.

With this custom target utilization in mind, let's update the Per User Cost formula with scaling in mind:

Per User Cost with Scaling

$$perUserCost/time = \frac{infrastructureCost/time}{users/time \times targetUtilization}$$

So if our infrastructure cost was $100 per month serving 150 users, at a 100% utilization, you calculate the Per User Cost to be $0.67/user/month. If you were to take scaling in to account, the cost would be as follows:

$$\frac{\$100/mo}{150users/mo \times 0.84utilization} = \$0.79/user/mo$$

Scaling without dropping requests would cost 16% more of the original $0.67 at $0.79 per user per month. However, it is important to keep in mind that your infrastructure won't always be so efficient, at lower utilization targets, or misconfigured with scaling triggers costs can easily double, triple, or quadruple the original cost. The ultimate goal here is to find the sweet spot, so you will be paying the right amount per user.

There's no prescriptive per user cost you should be targeting for. However, if you are running a service where you charge users $5 per month after all other operational costs and profit margins are accounted for, you're still left over with an additional budget *and* your users complaining about poor performance, then you're underspending. However, if you're eating into your profits margins, or worse breaking even, then you may be overspending or you may need to reconsider your business model.

There are several other factors that can impact your per user cost such as Blue-Green deployments. You can also increase the efficiency of your scaling by leveraging pre-scheduled provisioning.

Pre-scheduled provisioning

Dynamic scaling out and then back in is what defines cloud computing. However, the algorithms currently available still require some planning if you know certain days, weeks, or months of a year will require uncharacteristically higher capacity of resources. Given a sudden deluge of new traffic, your infrastructure will attempt to dynamically scale out, but if the rate of increase in traffic is logarithmic, even an optimized server utilization target won't help. Servers will frequently reach and operate at 100% utilization, resulting in dropped or erroneous requests. To prevent this from happening, you should proactively provision additional capacity during such predictable periods of high demand.

Blue-Green deployments

In `Chapter 11`, *Highly-Available Cloud Infrastructure on AWS*, you configured no-downtime Blue-Green deployments. Blue-Green deployments are reliable code deployments that ensure continuous up-time of your site, while minimizing the risk of bad deployments.

Let's presume that you have a highly-available deployment, meaning you have two instances active at any given time. During a blue-green deployment, two additional instances would be provisioned. Once these additional instances are ready to fulfill requests, their health is determined using your predefined health metric.

If your new instances are found to be healthy, it means they're in working order. There will be a period of time, like 5 minutes, while connections in the original instance are drained and rerouted to the new instances. At this time, the original instances are deprovisioned.

If the new instances are found to be unhealthy, then these new instances will be deprovisioned, resulting in a failed deployment. However, a service will remain available without interruption, because the original instance will remain intact and keep serving users during the entire process.

Revising estimates with metrics

Load testing and predicting user growth rates give you an idea of how your system may behave in production. Collecting more granular metrics and data is critical in revising your estimates and nailing down a more accurate IT budget.

Measuring actual use

As we discussed earlier, keeping track of page views alone isn't reflective of the amount of requests that a user sends to the server. With Google Tag Manager and Google Analytics, you can keep track of more than just page views with ease.

As of publishing time, here are some of the default events you can configure across various categories. This list will grow over time:

- Page View: Used to track whether a user is sticking around as page resources load and the page is fully rendered:
    - Page View, fired at first opportunity
    - DOM Ready, when DOM structure is loaded
    - Window Loaded, when all elements are finished loading
- Click: Used to track user's click interactions with the page:
    - All Elements
    - Just Links
- User Engagement: Tracks user behavior:
    - Element Visibility, whether elements have been shown
    - Form Submission, whether a form was submitted
    - Scroll Depth, how far they scrolled down the page
    - YouTube Video, if they played an embedded YouTube Video
- Other events track:
    - Custom Event: Defined by programmer to track a single or multistep event, such as a user going through the steps of a checkout process
    - History Change: Whether the user navigates back in browser's history
    - JavaScript Error: Whether JavaScript errors have been generated
    - Timer: To trigger or delay time-based analytics events

Most of these events don't require any extra coding to implement, so we will implement a custom event to demonstrate how you can capture any single or series of events you want with custom coding. Capturing workflows with a series of events can reveal where you should be focusing your development efforts.

For more information on Google Tag Manager events, triggers, or tips and tricks, I recommend that you check out the blog by Simo Ahava at `www.simoahava.com`.

Creating a custom event

For this example, we will capture the event for when a customer is successfully checked out and a sale is completed. We will implement two events, one for checkout initiation and the other for when the transaction has been successfully completed:

1. Log on to your Google Tag Manager Workspace at `tagmanager.google.com`
2. Under the **Triggers** menu, click on **New**, as pointed out:

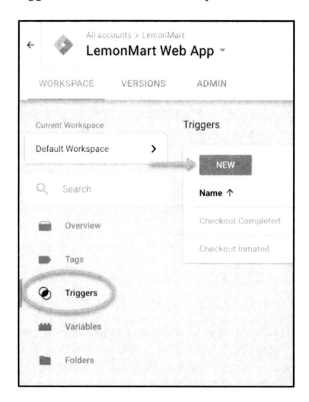

Tag Manager Workspace

3. Name your trigger
4. Click on the empty trigger card to select the event type
5. Select **Custom Event**
6. Create a custom event named `checkoutCompleted`, as illustrated:

Custom Checkout Event

By selecting the **Some Custom Events** option, you can limit or control the collection of a particular event, that is, only when on a particular page or a domain such as on `lemonmart.com`. In the following screenshot, you can see a custom rule that would filter out any checkout event that didn't happen on `lemonmart.com` to weed out development or test data:

Some Custom Events

7. **Save** your new event
8. Repeat the process for an event named `checkoutInitiated`
9. Add two new Google Analytics event tags, as highlighted here:

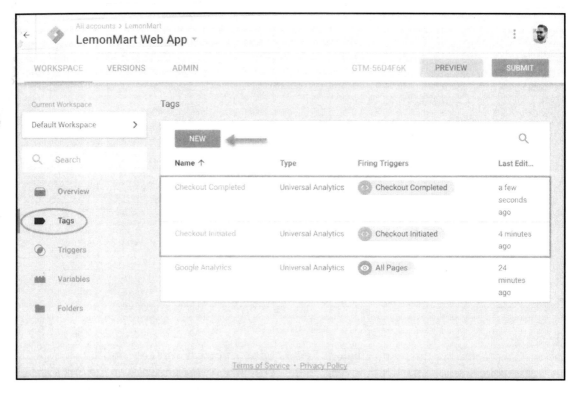

New Custom Event Tags

10. Configure the event and attach the relevant trigger you created to it, as shown:

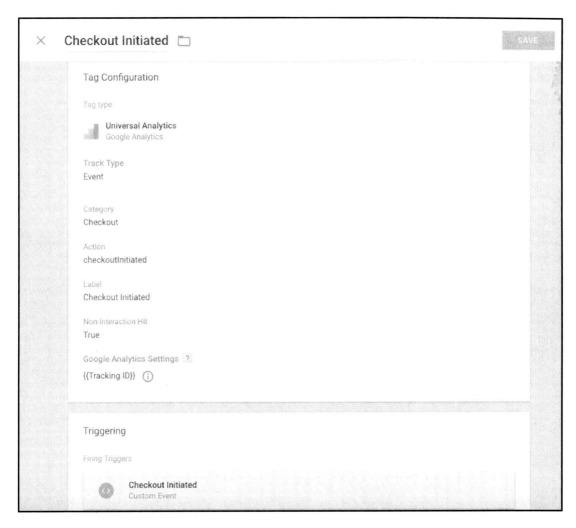

Trigger Setup

11. Submit and publish your workspace

We are now ready to receive custom events in our analytics environment.

Adding custom events in Angular

Now, let's edit the Angular code to trigger the events:

1. Observe the POS template with a **Checkout** button:

   `src/app/pos/pos/pos.component.html`

   ```
   . . .
     <button mat-icon-button (click)="checkout({amount: 12.25})">
       <mat-icon>check_circle</mat-icon>
     </button>
   . . .
   ```

   The circular checkout button is pointed out at the bottom-left corner of the following diagram:

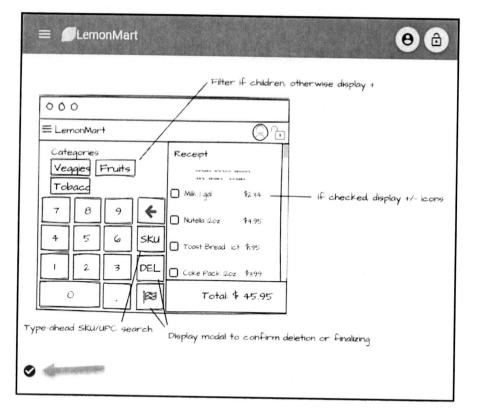

POS Page with Checkout Button

Optionally, you can add an `onclick` event handler directly in the template, like `onclick="dataLayer.push({'event': 'checkoutInitiated'})"` on the checkout button. This pushes the `checkoutInitiated` event to the `dataLayer` object, made available by `gtm.js`.

2. In the POS compoment, declare an interface for `dataLayer` events you intend to push:

src/app/pos/pos/pos.component.ts

```
. . .
interface IEvent {
   event: 'checkoutCompleted' | 'checkoutInitiated'
}
declare let dataLayer: IEvent[]
. . .
export class PosComponent implements OnInit {
   . . .
```

3. Create the `checkout` function to call `checkoutInitiated` before a service call is made

4. Simulate a fake transaction using `setTimeout` and call the `checkoutCompleted` event, when the timeout ends:

src/app/pos/pos/pos.component.ts

```
export class PosComponent implements OnInit {
. . .
checkout(transaction) {
    dataLayer.push({
      event: 'checkoutInitiated',
    })

    setTimeout(() => {
      dataLayer.push({
        event: 'checkoutCompleted',
      })
    }, 500)
   }
}
```

In a real implementation, you would only call `checkoutCompleted` if your service call succeeds. To not to miss any data during your analytics collection, consider covering failure cases as well, such as adding multiple `checkoutFailed` events that cover various failure cases.

Now, we are ready to see the analytics in action.

5. On the POS page, click on the **Checkout** button
6. In Google Analytics, observe the **Real-Time** | **Events** tab to see events as they occur
7. After 5-10 minutes, the events will also show up under the **Behavior** | **Events** tab, as shown:

Google Analytics Top Events

Using custom events, you can keep track of various nuanced user behavior happening on your site. By collecting `checkoutInitiated` and `checkoutCompleted` events, you can calculate a conversion rate of how many initiated checkouts are taken to completion. In the case of a point-of-sale system, that rate should be very high; otherwise, it means you may have systematic issues in place.

Advanced Analytics events

It is possible to collect additional metadata along with each event, such as payment amount or type when checkout is initiated or the `transactionId`, when checkout is completed.

To work with these more advanced features, I would recommend that you check out `angulartics2`, which can be found at `https://www.npmjs.com/package/angulartics2`. `angulartics2` is a vendor-agnostic analytics library for Angular that can enable unique and granular event tracking needs using popular vendors, such as Google Tag Manager, Google Analytics, Adobe, Facebook, Baidu and more, as highlighted on the tool's homepage, shown here:

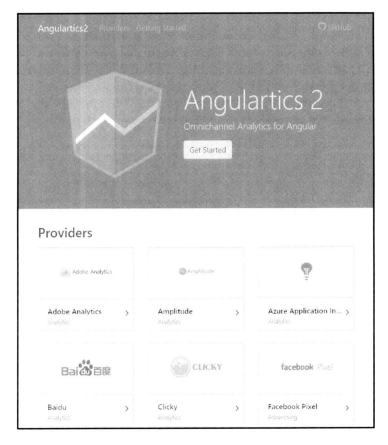

Angulartics2

`angulartics2` integrates with the Angular router and the UI-Router with the ability to implement custom rules and exceptions on route-per-route basis. The library makes it easy to implement custom events and enables metadata tracking with data binding. Check out the following example:

```
example
<div angulartics2On="click" angularticsEvent="DownloadClick"
angularticsCategory="{{ song.name }}" [angularticsProperties]="{label:
'Fall Campaign'}"></div>
```

We can keep track of a click event named `DownloadClick`, which would have a `category` and a `label` attached to it for rich events tracking within Google Analytics.

With advanced analytics under your belt, you can use actual usage data to inform how you improve or host your app. This topic concludes a journey that started by creating pencil drawn mock ups at the beginning of this book, covering a wide-variety of tools, techniques, and technologies a full-stack web developer must be familiar with in today's web to succeed. We dove deep into Angular, Angular Material, Docker, and automation in general to make you the most productive developer you can be, delivering the highest quality web app, while juggling a lot of complexity along the way. Good luck out there!

Summary

In this chapter, you have rounded out your knowledge of developing web apps. You learned how to work with Google Tag Manager and Google Analytics to capture page views of your Angular application. Using high-level metrics, we went over how you can calculate the cost of your infrastructure per user. We then investigated the nuances of the effect high-availability and scaling can have on your budget. We covered load testing complex user workflows to estimate how many users any given server can host concurrently. Using this information, we calculated a target server utilization to fine-tune your scaling settings.

All of our pre-release calculations were mostly estimates and educated guesses. We went over the kinds of metrics and custom events you can use to measure the actual use of your application. When your application goes live and you start gathering these metrics, you can update your calculations to gain a better understanding of the viability and the affordability of your infrastructure.

Over the course of this book, I've shown that web development is so much more than just coding a website. In the first half of the book, we went over a variety of topics from process, design, approach, architecture to your development environment, the libraries and tools you use, including going over the basics of the Angular platform and Angular Material, finally deploying your application on the web using Zeit Now.

In the second half of the book, we followed the Router-first approach to designing, architecting, and implementing a large line-of-business application going over most major design patterns you may encounter in real life. Along the way, we covered unit testing, Docker, Continuous Integration with CircleCI, designing APIs with Swagger, gathering analytics using Google Tag Manager, and deploying a highly-available application on AWS. As you master these wide variety of skills and techniques, you will become a true full-stack web developer capable of delivering small and large web apps leveraging Angular.

Other Books You May Enjoy

If you enjoyed this book, you may be interested in these other books by Packt:

Hands-on Full Stack Development with Angular 5
Uttam Agarwal

ISBN: 978-1-78829-873-5

- Understand the core concepts of Angular framework
- Create web pages with Angular as front end and Firebase as back end
- Develop a real-time social networking application
- Make your application live with Firebase hosting
- Engage your user using Firebase cloud messaging
- Grow your application with Google analytics
- Learn about Progressive Web App

Architecting Angular Applications with Redux, RxJS, and NgRx
Christoffer Noring

ISBN: 978-1-78712-240-6

- Understand the one-way data flow and Flux pattern
- Work with functional programming and asynchronous data streams
- Figure out how RxJS can help us address the flaws in promises
- Set up different versions of cascading calls
- Explore advanced operators
- Get familiar with the Redux pattern and its principles
- Test and debug different features of your application
- Build your own lightweight app using Flux, Redux, and NgRx

Leave a review - let other readers know what you think

Please share your thoughts on this book with others by leaving a review on the site that you bought it from. If you purchased the book from Amazon, please leave us an honest review on this book's Amazon page. This is vital so that other potential readers can see and use your unbiased opinion to make purchasing decisions, we can understand what our customers think about our products, and our authors can see your feedback on the title that they have worked with Packt to create. It will only take a few minutes of your time, but is valuable to other potential customers, our authors, and Packt. Thank you!

Index

CPSIA information can be obtained
at www.ICGtesting.com
Printed in the USA
FFOW01n2305310518
47007270-49286FF

9 781786 462909